STYLE

Also by F. L. LUCAS

THE WORKS OF JOHN WEBSTER

AUTHORS DEAD AND LIVING
TRAGEDY
TEN VICTORIAN POETS
THE DECLINE AND FALL OF THE ROMANTIC IDEAL
STUDIES FRENCH AND ENGLISH
LITERATURE AND PSYCHOLOGY
THE SEARCH FOR GOOD SENSE
THE ART OF LIVING
THE GREATEST PROBLEM
   and other essays

IBSEN AND STRINDBERG
THE DRAMA OF CHEKHOV, SYNGE, YEATS, AND PIRANDELLO
BEDDOES
CRABBE
D. G. ROSSETTI
TENNYSON

FROM OLYMPUS TO THE STYX

JOURNAL UNDER THE TERROR, 1938

CÉCILE
DOCTOR DIDO
THE WOMAN CLOTHED WITH THE SUN

THE BEAR DANCES
FOUR PLAYS

POEMS 1935
ARIADNE
GILGAMESH
HERO AND LEANDER
APHRODITE
A GREEK GARLAND
GREEK POETRY FOR EVERYMAN
GREEK DRAMA FOR EVERYMAN
FROM MANY TIMES AND LANDS
THE ENGLISH AGENT

STYLE

F. L. LUCAS

With a Foreword by
SIR BRUCE FRASER

CASSELL · LONDON

CASSELL & COMPANY LTD
35 Red Lion Square, London WC1R 4SG
Sydney, Auckland
Toronto, Johannesburg

First published July 1955
Second impression November 1955
Third impression April 1956
Fourth impression November 1958
Fifth impression June 1960
Sixth impression February 1962
Seventh impression May 1964
Second edition August 1974
I.S.B.N. 0 304 29365 2

Printed in Great Britain by
The Camelot Press Ltd, London and Southampton

FOREWORD

THIS book was first published nearly twenty years ago. It is as fresh, as friendly and as entertaining today as it was then. It is also, unfortunately, every bit as necessary, and this new edition seems eminently well timed. When writers (and speakers) of English are no longer wordy, obscure, dull or pompous, then let this book go out of print; but not before.

I would advise new readers to start with the last couple of pages (from 'Here are a great many words . . .'). There they will find clearly revealed the author's characteristic sanity, modesty and sincerity; and they will surely be eager to get to know him better.

The next step might be to look at the chapter headings, so as to savour the book's freshness of approach. Not every writer, setting out to examine 'the qualities that endow language, written or spoken, with persuasiveness or power', would begin on a moral note by pronouncing that the foundation of style is character. But the reader need not be alarmed. Lucas is no prig; and his thesis, as he develops it, is completely convincing. Who will deny that 'if [a writer's] mood in writing is mean or peevish or petty or vain or false, no cleverness and no technique are likely in the end to save him'? It is perhaps unlikely that any man will say to himself 'I'm rather a stinker, so I won't write anything',—though it might be a good thing if he did. But it is not too much to hope that some writers may say 'I'm in a bad mood today, so I won't write anything until tomorrow'.

Then we have *Courtesy to Readers*—(1) *Clarity*, (2) *Brevity and Variety*, (3) *Urbanity and Simplicity*. Well, other writers on style might well have chosen these (though some might forget to include Urbanity). But how many would devote their next three chapters to *Good Humour and Gaiety*, *Good Sense and Sincerity* and *Good Health and Vitality*? Here, surely, is a man who must be nice to know. And his own writing certainly has all these engaging qualities.

To flick over the pages of the book is to get an impression of immense erudition. Erudite it certainly is. But Lucas wears his learning lightly. He has a nice feeling for the apt anecdote and the witty analogy; and from the storehouse of his vast knowledge come many fascinating tit-bits thrown out quite casually. For instance, we learn from a footnote that Housman achieved his *coloured counties* only after he had tried *sunny*, *pleasant*, *checkered*, *patterned* and *painted*. Above all, Lucas is never dogmatic or superior. He can be scathing about half-baked thinking and muddled or turgid phraseology. But he never says, in effect, 'You must accept what I say because I am much better read than you are'. Rather, his tone is 'I may be wrong, but here are my reasons and here is my evidence—what do *you* think?'

Most readers will find something—though not much—to disagree with. This is only to be expected in the work of a literary critic with individuality and gusto who is no slave to established reputations. He clearly thinks better of Landor, and less well of Bernard Shaw, than I do. And for my part I could do with fewer quotations from the French. When Lucas says that 'some ability to read French prose does seem to me most desirable for anyone who would write well in English', I find myself reflecting that many good writers seem to have got on without it. It seems odd, too, to find no mention of either Lamb or Jane Austen. True, they were highly individual stylists; but so were Tacitus, Sir Thomas Browne, Sterne and Sam Johnson, who all appear frequently. Mrs. Gaskell, the Brontës and George Eliot share Jane's fate, and there is more about Hardy than about Dickens and Thackeray put together. This is not, of course, a literary judgement on Lucas's part, just an indication that he found some authors more apt to his purpose than others; but it is a little odd all the same.

Lucas can be delightfully disrespectful to famous writers like Coleridge and Swinburne when they are below form. The passage in which he dissects a great hunk of Swinburne's prose, reduces it by more than half, recognizes that it could be made shorter still, and ends by suggesting that it need not have been written at all, is in itself worth the whole price of the book.

It would be quite wrong to think that this is a book only for students of 'Eng. Lit.' It is for all writers who would please or persuade their readers, for all readers who would enjoy good writing more (and also enjoy more good writing). Just what readership Lucas himself had in mind may be doubtful. A few passages seem to be addressed to undergraduates who serve up silly essays (for the book is founded on a course of lectures); some to his fellow-teachers; some (such as the last two chapters) to seriously aspiring authors; a great deal to a more general readership.

But my own firm conclusion is that Lucas wrote it specially for me (he even remembered to include an apology for quoting so much French); and I am only sorry that he did not get round to it till 1955, when I was already in my forties. Many new readers, I am sure, will likewise find that he wrote it specially for them; and I particularly envy those who discover this book for the first time in their twenties or thirties, and who will therefore have longer than I to study it, to enjoy it and to profit from it.

BRUCE D. FRASER

To
Sir Charles Tennyson

ACKNOWLEDGEMENTS

G RATEFUL acknowledgement is due to the following authors (or their executors) and publishers for permission to reprint in this volume extracts from works in which they hold the copyright:

Hilaire Belloc: 'The Normans' from *Hills and the Sea* (Methuen & Co. Ltd.); G. K. Chesterton: 'The Battle of the Marne' from *The Crimes of England* (Miss D. E. Collins); S. T. Coleridge: *Unpublished Letters* (Constable & Co. Ltd.); Thomas Hardy: *The Woodlanders* (Macmillan & Co. Ltd. and the Trustees of the Hardy Estate); Geoffrey Keynes and Brian Hill (Ed.): *Samuel Butler's Notebooks* (Jonathan Cape Ltd.); D. H. Lawrence: 'Galsworthy' from *Scrutinies* (Lawrence & Wishart Ltd.); George Saintsbury: *History of English Prose Rhythm* (Macmillan & Co. Ltd.); Lytton Strachey: *Queen Victoria* (Chatto & Windus Ltd.); A. C. Swinburne: *Miscellanies* (William Heinemann Ltd.); J. M. Synge: *The Playboy of the Western World* (George Allen & Unwin Ltd.); Virginia Woolf: *The Waves* (Mr. Leonard Woolf and The Hogarth Press Ltd.).

I am also indebted to J. M. Dent & Sons Ltd. for leave to reprint here some translations from my *Greek Poetry for Everyman*.

PREFACE

THIS book consists of lectures given at Cambridge. Though they have been largely rewritten, I have kept a good deal of their original lecture-form, as being (I hope) rather less formal and less dogmatic. For to dogmatism those who write on language seem, for some reason, particularly prone; and I should like to make it clear at once that, if at times I have put my views strongly, I do not forget that such matters of taste must remain mere matters of opinion.

On the other hand I have here added a good many more specimen passages from various authors. Perhaps I have quoted too much. But a book on style without abundant examples seems to me as ineffectual as a book on art, or biology, without abundant illustrations. Many of these passages are in French. That may be gallomania on my part; and I must apologize if they trouble some readers. But some ability to read French prose does seem to me most desirable for anyone who would write well in English. I have tried to choose pieces not too difficult in syntax or vocabulary. And in these days less than ever can we afford to be insular.

I should perhaps also make it clear from the outset that this book is not concerned, except incidentally, with linguistic or grammatical details such as are dealt with in H. W. Fowler's admirable *Modern English Usage* or its many successors. It is not that I undervalue these—on the contrary. They may be at times too purist, or too conservative; but they were never more needed. 'Correctness', however, is not my real concern; a style, like a person, may be perfectly correct, yet perfectly boring or unbearable. I have merely tried, successfully or not, to pursue the more general, more positive, but more elusive question—what are the qualities that endow language, spoken or written, with persuasiveness or power?

CONTENTS

I

THE VALUE OF STYLE

'IN this day's silly *Sunday Times*,' says Samuel Butler,[1] 'there is an article on Mrs. Browning's letters which begins with some remarks about style. "It is recorded," says the writer, "of Plato, that in a rough draft of one of his Dialogues, found after his death, the first paragraph was written in seventy different forms.[2] Wordsworth spared no pains to sharpen and polish to the utmost the gifts with which nature had endowed him; and Cardinal Newman, one of the greatest masters of English style, has related in an amusing essay the pains he took to acquire his style."[3]

'I never knew a writer yet who took the smallest pains with his style and was at the same time readable. Plato's having had seventy shies at one sentence is quite enough to explain to me why I hate him.'

[1] *S. Butler's Notebooks*, ed. G. Keynes and B. Hill, 1951, p. 290.

[2] This story has not lost in the telling. Actually Plato is said to have left 'a number' of versions, not *seventy*, of the beginning (according to Quintilian, VIII, 6, 64, only of the first four words), not of the whole 'first *paragraph*', of his *Republic*.

There is a similar story of Ariosto composing fifty-six variants of the first line of his *Orlando Furioso* (E. E. Kellett, *Fashion in Literature* (1931), p. 172; G. Murray, *The Classical Tradition in Poetry* (1927), p. 46). But I cannot trace the source of this. According to A. Panizzi's edition of the poem (1834; I, cxx), the poet composed *three* versions—'Di donne e cavalier gli antiqui amori', 'Di donne e cavalier l'arme e gli amori', 'Le donne, i cavalier, l'arme, gli amori'. In any case Ariosto's elaborate revisions in general are sufficiently illustrated in the facsimile pages of S. Debenedetti's *Frammenti Autografi dell'Orlando Furioso*, 1937.

[3] See *The Idea of a University*, 1935 ed., p. 322.

Few of us are as bold and blunt as Butler (who took an impish delight in pulling the legs or noses of the conventional); and yet when I read examination answers, or Ph.D. dissertations, or some things that are published in books and periodicals even by professional critics of literature, I sometimes wonder if a good many of us, although we give years of our lives to English, do not practise what Butler preached, a good deal more thoroughly than Butler himself. For, in practice, Butler took pains to write well, vividly, amusingly; and even in theory, as we shall see,[1] Butler proceeded to eat a good deal of what he had said in disparagement of style. For he was really rebelling, not against style, but against what he considered preciousness in style. And in art it seems to me true enough that the 'precious' is worthless.

In fact, Butler's quarrel, like so many quarrels, remains largely verbal. He is here using 'style' to mean a deliberately cultivated, individual, peculiar style of one's own—something that he associated with pretentious aesthetes. In this sense, Hazlitt too denied having a style.[2] And, again, Southey wrote, 'Of what is called *style*, not a thought enters my head at any time'—his only endeavour was, he said, 'to write plain English, and to put my thoughts in language which every one can understand'. Yet this has not prevented critics from praising both Hazlitt and Southey for their 'style'. And rightly. Why should we thus narrow a useful word to mean merely a special manner of writing that approaches mannerism—as in Lamb or De Quincey, Pater or Doughty? It robs us of a general term we need.

[1] P. 64.
[2] But I do not believe him. It would be very hard for anyone with as much individuality as Hazlitt, or Butler, to keep it out of his writing. And thank Heaven! How much duller life would be if they could! Indeed, the essential in writing, as in living, is not to seem 'somebody', but to be one's true self.

Often, indeed, I suspect that those who decry 'style'
are impelled by that humble-seeming pride which is too
proud to make pretensions, and therefore belittles what
it disdains to pretend to. Sometimes, too, men have been
influenced by an odd belief in the virtue of generality and
impersonality. 'A marked *manner*,' says Horace Walpole,
denouncing the style of the hated Johnson, 'when it runs
through all the compositions of any master, is a defect in
itself, and indicates a deviation from nature. ... It is
true that the greatest masters of composition are so far
imperfect, as that they always leave some marks by which
we may discover their *hand*. He approaches the nearest
to universality whose works make it difficult for our
quickness and sagacity to observe certain characteristic
touches which ascertain the specific author.'[1]

Fortunately no one practised this less than Walpole
himself, in his letters. But we are not at the moment
concerned whether this bleak Act of Uniformity is wise
or not (though it seems to me no wiser than its opposite
extreme, the rage at all costs for originality). The point
is that those who dislike any personal mannerism would
do better to call it that; and not to confuse matters by
calling it, without qualification, 'style'.

What, in fact, is 'style'? A dead metaphor. It meant
originally 'a writing-implement'[2]—a pointed object, of

---

[1] *Works* (1798), IV, p. 361. It is curious how much less well
Horace Walpole writes when, as here, he writes formally. Montesquieu, on the other hand (like Buffon), did not share this neo-
classic prejudice: 'Un homme qui écrit bien, n'écrit pas comme on
écrit, mais comme il écrit.' This seems to me much truer; though,
of course, there are also some bad writers who write like no one
else. Some may think *Euphues* an example of this; some, Meredith.

[2] Also, adds the Oxford Dictionary (with unintended irony),
'used as a weapon of offence, for stabbing, etc.' For the Latin
stilus comes from the root STIG—cf. Greek στίζω, stigma, stimulus,
instigate, stick, German *stechen*, *stecken*. We should, were English
a logical language, write 'stile' (cf. German *Stil*, Italian *stile*,

bone or metal, for inscribing wax. But already in Classical Latin the word *stĭlus* was extended to mean, first, a man's '*way* of writing'; then, more generally, his 'way of expressing himself', in speech as well as in writing. In modern English, 'style' has acquired further senses. As in French, it has been narrowed to signify 'a *good* way of expressing oneself'—'his writing lacked style'; and it has been extended to other arts than literature, even to the art of living—'her behaviour showed always a certain style'.[1] But the two main meanings which concern us here, are (1) 'a way of writing'; (2) 'a *good* way of writing'.

Our subject, then, is simply the effective use of language, especially in prose, whether to make statements or to rouse emotions. It involves, first of all, the power to put facts with clarity and brevity; but facts are usually none the worse for being put also with as much grace and interest as the subject permits. For grace or interest, indeed, if the subject is purely practical, like conics or conchology, there may not be much room; though even cookery books have been salted with occasional irony; and even mathematicians have indulged in jests, as of going to Heaven in a perpendicular straight line.[2] But, further,

Spanish *estilo*). But the Latin *stĭlus* became corrupted to *stylus* by confusion with the Greek στῦλος, 'a pillar'; and this spurious 'y' does at least save us now from confusing the 'styles' of writers with the 'stiles' of field-paths.

[1] Compare some of the diverse meanings of 'poetry', which have similarly provoked futile controversy: (1) verse writing; (2) *good* verse writing; (3) writing, not in metre, which excites similar feelings to those aroused by good verse; (4) qualities in things outside literature (*e.g.* painting, spring, moonlight) which also excite similar feelings.

[2] It is superbly ironical to find Voltaire, of all people, objecting to this: 'Point de plaisanterie en mathématiques. . . . La plaisanterie n'est jamais bonne dans le genre sérieux.' (*Dictionnaire Philosophique*, 'Style'.) Fontenelle and Gibbon knew better; and so, indeed, did Voltaire.

men need also to express and convey their emotions (even animals do); and to kindle emotions in others. Without emotion, no art of literature; nor any other art.

You may of course answer, like Butler: 'But this is all affectation—fiddling with phrases and trifling with cadences! Give me simple English and common sense.' And yet, just as 'common sense' is far from common, simple English can prove in practice far from simple to attain. Further, this difficulty has more serious consequences, both public and private, than is sometimes realized. Our verbal communications remain often badly ambiguous; and, in another sense than the Apostle intended, 'evil communications corrupt good manners'.

For two thousand years Christendom has been rent with controversy because men could not agree about the meaning of passages in Holy Writ; both Old and New Testaments have been more disputed than any human will. The gardens and porticoes of philosophy are hung with philosophers entangled in their own verbal cobwebs. Statesmen meet at Yalta or Potsdam to make agreements, about the meaning of which they then proceed to disagree. Employers and workers reach settlements that lead only to fresh unsettlement, because they misunderstand the understandings they themselves have made. Sharp legal minds spend their lives drafting documents in a verbose jargon of their own which shall be knave-proof and fool-proof; but it is seldom that other legal minds as sharp cannot find in those documents, if they try, some fruitful points for litigation. Even in war, where clarity may be a matter of life or death for thousands, disasters occur through orders misunderstood. Some adore ambiguities in poetry; in prose they can be a constant curse.

For example it seems that, within a few hours in the Crimea, first of all, Lord Cardigan's misinterpreting of Lord Lucan's orders wasted the victory of the Heavy Brigade, and then Lord Lucan's misinterpreting of Lord

[17]

Raglan's orders[1] caused the suicide of the Light Brigade.
It is said that Sir Roger Casement was hanged on a comma
in a statute of Edward III. And Professor Ifor Evans has
adduced the strange case of Caleb Diplock who bequeathed
half a million for 'charitable *or* benevolent objects'.
Clear enough, one would have thought—though needlessly verbose. But the law regularly sacrifices brevity
to make sure of clarity—and too often loses both. In this
case legal lynxes discerned that 'benevolent' objects are
not necessarily 'charitable'. The suit was carried from
the Court of First Instance to the Court of Appeal, from
the Court of Appeal to the Lords; judges uttered seventy
thousand words of collective wisdom; and poor Mr.
Diplock's will was pronounced invalid. Much virtue in
an 'or'. Well did the Chinese say that when a piece of
paper blows into a law-court, it may take a yoke of oxen
to drag it out again.

But men not only underestimate the difficulty of
language; they often underestimate also its appalling
power. True, the literary (for very human reasons) are
sometimes tempted, on the contrary, to exaggerate it.
We may well smile at writers who too confidently claim
that the pen is mightier than the sword. Fletcher of
Saltoun's exaltation of the songs of a people as more
important than its laws, Shelley's glorification of poets
as the unacknowledged legislators of mankind, Tennyson's poet whose word shakes the world, O'Shaughnessy's
three men who trample down empires with the lilt of a
new song—these, I feel, are somewhat too complacent
half-truths. With all his powers of speech, Demosthenes
could not save Greece; nor Cicero the Roman Republic;
nor Milton the English Commonwealth. Yet it does seem

[1] Lord Lucan in his turn maintained that the fatal charge was
due to a further misunderstanding of his own orders to Lord
Cardigan, commanding the Light Brigade. (Kinglake, *Invasion of
the Crimea*, IV, p. 248.)

rational to say that Voltaire and Burke became, in a sense, European powers; that Rousseau's *Contrat Social* left a permanent mark on the history of Europe, and Paine's *Common Sense* on that of America. This, if we brush away the blur of familiarity, remains astonishing enough. And these men, I think, won their triumphs not more (if so much) by force of thought than by force of style. Nor let us forget the influence of the English Bible.

How different, too, might have been the history of our own time if the written and spoken style of Adolf Hitler, detestable in itself, had been less potent to intoxicate the German people; or if the German people had had enough sense of style to reject that repellent claptrap; or again if Winston Churchill had not possessed a gift of phrase to voice and fortify the feelings of his countrymen in their darkest and their finest hour! Even the curious mind of Communism does not reject style as a bauble of the bourgeoisie. 'It is the business', we have been told, 'of the linguist and the critic to study the style of Stalin.' 'Learn to write as Stalin writes.' In such fulsome hyperboles there is at least a sense of the importance of style; if little sense of any other kind.

Some years ago, indeed, a distinguished scientist, enraged by the airs of the literary, protested impatiently that in this, 'the hydro-electric age', men's worship of mere verbiage was out of date—for 'the spark-gap is mightier than the pen'. Seemingly it escaped him that the rhetoric of the Führer had already reduced the scientists of the Third Reich into docile slaves, who demonstrated at his bidding the virtues of a non-existent Aryan race, or forged the weapons that were to force his infernal gospel on the world. Similarly in the Soviet Union we have seen biologists compelled to bow to 'Marxism' and to find once more, like Galileo, orthodoxy mightier than science.

And, again, Señor de Madariaga has quoted a pleasant

item on Darwin from a catechism current in Franco's Spain: 'This so-called scientist was born in Shrewsburg [*sic*], England. Endowed by God with a considerable gift of observation, but with very little intelligence. . . .'

Our grandfathers hopefully chanted 'Great is the truth, and shall prevail'; they knew little of propaganda. Mankind has not yet mastered language; often it has mastered *them*—scientists and all. Few of them realize this. And that only makes it worse.

True, it is not always by excellence of style that books exert this appalling power. It was not by beauty of language that the writings of Marx became a new gospel. Flaubert himself, that saint and martyr of style, felt driven to confess that the greatest writers were pre-occupied with greater things than perfect words. 'Ce qui distingue les grands génies, c'est la généralisation et la création. . . . Est-ce qu'on ne croit pas à l'existence de Don Quichotte comme à celle de César? Shakespeare est quelque chose de formidable sous ce rapport. Ce n'était pas un homme, mais un continent; il y avait des grands hommes en lui, des foules entières, des paysages. Ils n'ont pas besoin de faire du style, ceux-là; ils sont forts en dépit de toutes les fautes et à cause d'elles. Mais nous, les petits, nous ne valons que par l'exécution achevée. Hugo, en ce siècle, enfoncera tout le monde, quoiqu'il soit plein de mauvaises choses; mais quel souffle! quel souffle! Je hasarde ici une proposition que je n'oserais dire nulle part: c'est que les très grands hommes écrivent souvent fort mal, et tant mieux pour eux. Ce n'est pas là qu'il faut chercher l'art de la forme, mais chez les seconds (Horace, la Bruyère).'[1]

There seems to me much truth in this; but not quite

---

[1] *Correspondance*, 25 September 1852. Contrast Voltaire: 'Sans le style, il est impossible qu'il y ait un seul bon ouvrage en aucun genre d'éloquence et de poésie.' But here Flaubert is surely more reasonable.

enough. Granted that Scott, or Dickens, or Balzac may often write carelessly, even badly, surely at their greatest moments they owe much of their greatness to their style.[1] Granted that Hugo is often dull, and sometimes grotesque, his triumphs seem to me to depend less on his characters, or his ideas, than on his language, music, and imagery.[2]

[1] For example, in Scott the appeal of Jeanie Deans to Queen Caroline, or the malediction of Meg Merrilies (see A. W. Verrall, *Literary Essays*); in Dickens, the description of Chancery at the beginning of *Bleak House*. Balzac might indulge in fatuities like 'Un torrent de pensées découla de son front', 'Le général se tourna pour jeter à la mer une larme de rage', 'Voilà deux ans que mon coeur se brise tous les jours'; but he could also write things as trenchant as Vautrin's advice to Rastignac on success: 'Il faut entrer dans cette masse d'hommes comme un boulet de canon ou s'y glisser comme une peste. L'honnêteté ne sert à rien'; or the description of Rastignac after the burial of Goriot: 'Rastignac, resté seul, fit quelques pas vers le haut du cimetière, et vit Paris tortueusement couché le long des deux rives de la Seine, où commençaient à briller les lumières. Ses yeux s'attachèrent presque avidement entre la colonne de la place Vendôme et le dôme des Invalides, là où vivait ce beau monde dans lequel il avait voulu pénétrer. Il lança sur cette ruche bourdonnante un regard qui semblait par avance en pomper le miel et dit ces mots grandioses: "A nous deux maintenant".

'Et pour premier acte du défi qu'il portait à la Société, Rastignac alla dîner chez Mme de Nucingen.'

[2] As in *Gastibelza*:

> Dansez, chantez, villageois, la nuit tombe.
> Sabine un jour
> A tout vendu, sa beauté de colombe
> Et son amour,
> Pour l'anneau d'or du comte de Saldagne,
> Pour un bijou . . .
> Le vent qui vient à travers la montagne
> Me rendra fou.

The theme is common: the style is not. Flaubert himself, writing to George Sand in December 1875, becomes juster to Hugo's style: 'Je donnerais toutes les légendes de Gavarni pour certaines expressions et coupes des maîtres comme "l'ombre était *nuptiale*, auguste et solennelle", de Victor Hugo.'

[21]

Shakespeare himself has been accused of feeble plots, shallow characterization, superficial ideas—not always with injustice; but even those who brought such charges have admitted the mysterious magic of his 'verbal abracadabra'. And when Flaubert denied style to the greatest, did he remember Homer?

In reality, I think, he is only repeating the simple point of 'Longinus' two thousand years before—that faulty greatness in a writer stands above narrower perfections; Pindar, for example, above Bacchylides. Most of us would agree. But then how amazing it remains that this perfection of style can still do so much to immortalize writers of the second magnitude, like Horace and Virgil, Pope and Racine, and Flaubert himself!

In short, I do not know which is more striking—the clumsy inadequacy of words, or their world-shaking power. So long as men remain emotional creatures, they will continue to be taken, like rabbits, by the ears.

But you may still be feeling, with some impatience, 'What is all this to us? We are not proposing to be great statesmen, nor great writers. It is unlikely that most of us will compose so much as a pamphlet, or sway the passions even of a parish council.' True. Yet we all talk—often more dully than we need. We all write letters—though it seems likely that, in this age of turmoil and telephones, the art of writing them has declined; which is a great pity. We all have personal relations, which at times depend vitally on a sense of what to say, how to say it, and what to leave unsaid. And even the most utilitarian will find that there are few careers where it does not sometimes become important to be able to put a case with persuasiveness, or facts with precision. For instance, I have wartime memories of congested signals-communications, where messages had to be clear if they were not to be disastrous, yet brief if they were to get sent at all. That was an unlooked-for, but unforgettable lesson. And finally, since a good deal of literature owes its power largely to its style, without a sense of style how can it be fully enjoyed?

When Phoenix was chosen by Peleus as tutor for his young son Achilles, he was to teach the boy two things:

> Therefore he set me by thee, to guide thee and to teach,
> To make thee a doer of deeds, and *a master too of speech*.[1]

That ideal is not yet out of date.

What, after all, are the objects of education? Knowledge? That is only one, and not the greatest. Look forward ten years. Most of the facts and dates so laboriously accumulated will have slipped away. Sooner or later, most of us find that our memories are sieves.

The Danaïds in Hell filled sieves for eternity; we do the same through our lives on earth. Even through Cambridge Lethe flows, as well as Cam.

There are, if I may cite my own experience, minor plays by Webster, or partly by Webster, that I have read and re-read two dozen times, written about, annotated, corrected and recorrected in proof—and yet today I have forgotten even their plots. I had in the First War to memorize the organization of the German Army—yet today that knowledge has vanished from my brain almost as completely as *that* German Army faded from the earth. Such acquisitions may survive in the Unconscious; no doubt they could quickly be revived; but meanwhile they are gone. And perhaps better so. A too good

[1] *Iliad*, IX, 442–3.

> τοὔνεκά με προέηκε διδασκέμεναι τάδε πάντα,
> μύθων τε ῥητῆρ᾽ ἔμεναι πρηκτῆρά τε ἔργων.

Certainly Achilles had learnt those lessons. I know no eloquence in all literature that can surpass his replies to Agamemnon (*Iliad* I), to the envoys of Agamemnon (*Iliad* IX), and to the aged Priam at his feet (*Iliad* XXIV).

memory can become like a crowded lumber-room, where it grows hard to move and *think*; there are better things to do than to ride through life like the White Knight, clattering with saucepans and mousetraps. In any case most of us know accurately only what we constantly relearn; memory is a dipsomaniac, needing to be perpetually refreshed.

For this reason, if I may say so, many educators astonish me. It is not only that they often do not seem to know what is worth knowing. They constantly forget how much we forget. But a skill once acquired—for example, the power to speak and write and enjoy one's own language, or another—is less easily lost, more quickly recovered, than mere accumulations of facts. And it seems to me more important to go out into life able to think straight and communicate clearly than even to know—and remember—the contents of every English book since Caedmon. Then, like Medea, even if you lose everything else, you can still feel 'Myself remains'. Whereas stuffed geese, even if stuffed with the Universe, remain geese.

One might have thought, then, that a prime object of education in English would be to learn to write it. If you read Q's *Art of Writing*, you will see how passionately he hoped that would happen here. And I remember how he would grunt with wistful irritation over some of the abstruser critics then in fashion: 'But the fellows can't write!' *He* could. And partly for that reason I suspect that some of those who thought him 'out of date' will be far sooner out-of-date themselves.

Since then, English has taken a wider place in our schools and Universities. But quantity is not quality. And one may sometimes wonder whether this vast increase is really serving either English literature or the English character.

One disastrous mistake, I cannot help thinking, is the

fantastic stress now laid on reading and writing 'criticism'. The critics are often blind guides—and in any case there are many more valuable activities, for which the longest life is all too brief. And criticism is not a science whose elements can be mass-taught to adolescents —it is a difficult art, at which even adults are seldom a notable success. With the young the result is often that they either just regurgitate the judgements they have been taught, or else, if they have a natural and healthy rebelliousness, the opposite of what they have been taught. Thence it is possible to arrive by easy stages at the happy notion, not uncommon among 'intellectuals', that taste consists of distaste, and that the loftiest of pleasures is that of feeling displeased; and thus to end by enjoying almost nothing in literature except one's own opinions, while oneself incapable of writing a living sentence.

> So by false learning is good sense defac'd:
> Some are bewilder'd in the maze of schools,
> And some made coxcombs Nature meant but fools.

Constantly and incorrigibly we forget how much harder it is to create, even with mediocre results, than to criticize. We can all criticize Napoleon's folly in lingering so late into the autumn at Moscow; but how many of us would ever have got there? I conclude, not that we should fear to criticize frankly, but that it might often be done with rather more modesty by those who have created nothing themselves.

At the University, English seems to me a good subject for a gifted few—perhaps as many as take Moral Science. Instead, it becomes thought a soft subject and attracts six times as many. The numbers could at least be reduced by demanding a sound knowledge of one ancient and one modern language besides one's own. But, above all, what matters at school, at the University, and in after-life is not new interpretations of Shakespeare—they are usually false; not new theories of criticism—they are usually futile; but a knowledge of the best that has been said or written, and the power—I admit the limited extent to which this can be taught—to speak and write.

If all this seems needless anxiety, listen to some results of that new specialization in English even at school, which I regard with particular misgiving. Thus writes a recent scholarship candidate.

'To be a poet, a man must have a particular *frame of receptivity* in his contact with the outer world. His medium may be prose, poetry, blank verse, or doggerel. If the essence is there, *the formal ectoplasm* slips off unnoticed.'

(Of inspiration.) 'The *spark* which achieves it cannot be superseded by a rule, but something must be its *vehicle*. In many cases the vehicle must be that of a prose-form. We now feel satisfied that temperament cannot be *such a tortuously circuitous state of health as to pursue this figure eight*, and are justified in concluding that external factors are *the vital cog-wheels in determining the writer's "niche"*.'

('I could have gnawed it better with my teeth,' cried William Morris once, in superb rage at some sculptural deformity; but 'niches' carved with '*vital* cog-wheels'!)

Or, finally, of the close of *The Tempest*: 'This is made possible by *the veneer of contented bewilderment and the soaring moral ceiling* of the whole play, the treasure-house of fulfillment [*sic*].'

You see why one may have doubts about too much 'English Literature' in schools? Had this luckless youth, with his 'veneer of contented bewilderment', done Greek, his mind might have had something to bite on and acquired something of Greek grace and Greek self-control; had he done Modern Languages, he might at least have gained something useful; had he done Mathematics, he might have been forced to think; had he done History or Science, he might have realized something of the relentless need for evidence, and the implacability of facts. But he has learnt only to express worthless thought in worthless language. I often remember the smiling remark made to me by a veteran and famous Professor of English Literature: 'Well, I'm thankful I didn't do it myself at the University. *I* did Classics.'

Take a more serious type of mind; give it six further years of English study; and it may produce a Ph.D. thesis written in this fashion: 'It is clear that the later poem was designed for delivery to audiences of mixed character and education, and it is addressed specially to the unlearned, for the better occupation of their minds in the place of secular entertainment, and therefore employing the same conventions and presented in the same manner and context: framed verbally and structurally to be recited aloud and attractively to chance as well as prepared gatherings of people of varying interests, by anyone able or accustomed to it, whether familiar (as a local curate, domestic clerk, or other member of a secular or religious community), or a stranger (casual visitor, mendicant, or other migrant by profession), usually by reason of motive and capacity one of the clergy.'

Such a research-student may turn his life into a concentration camp; he may amass in his own field an erudition to stagger Dr. Casaubon; but he cannot write. And where the words are so muddled, I suspect that the mind is muddled too.

The two main objects, then, of education in English, I take to be, first, to get English well written; secondly, to get English writers appreciated and enjoyed. Now persons who write so ill have clearly failed in the first of these objects; but I am also doubtful if they can have much success in the second. It is, of course, true that to appreciate poetry, or painting, or music, one need not be able to write poetry, or to paint, or to play. When Whistler, in his law-suit against Ruskin, argued to the Attorney-General that a man who had not passed his life in the practice of painting could no more judge its technique than the ordinary citizen could instruct the Attorney-General on points of law, Whistler was indulging in sophistry. Clearly men may be connoisseurs of wine without being wine-growers; they may be gourmets without knowing how to boil an egg.

Literary criticism is, however, not quite analogous. The critic of painting does not paint his criticism; but the critic of literature must also write himself. And if he shows no sense of handling words, it is as if an artist who could only draw and daub vilely should set up to pass judgement on others. He *might* be right; but his judgements would be highly suspect. There is therefore a good deal to be said for refusing to read literary critics who cannot write decently; though they may, of course, do valuable historical or textual research.

My conclusion is that English students who write as ill as those I have quoted are not very likely to get much from their English studies; since those who possess so little style themselves can hardly judge it in others.

'Ah,' you may reply, 'all this only shows, what we have always believed, that style cannot be taught.'

I am afraid that this is often true. I will go further and admit that education often, so far from doing good in this respect, does positive harm. In real life, as in Scott, in Dickens, or in Hardy, the uneducated sometimes speak a far more living language than their social superiors. And they may likewise relish vivid speech in others, with the delighted zest of Hardy's milkman. '"More know Tom Fool—what rambling canticle is it you say, Hostler?" inquired the milkman, lifting his ear. "Let's have it again—a good saying well spit out is a Christmas fire to my withered heart."'

When Bruce had stabbed John Comyn in the Church
of the Minorites at Dumfries, at the church-door he ran
into Sir Thomas Kirkpatrick and cried, it is said, 'I doubt
I have killed the Comyn.' 'Ye doubt!' replied Kirkpatrick. '*I* mak siccar.' And, entering, he finished off
the wounded man. These grim brevities Hume in his
history (governed despite his genius by eighteenth-
century sophistication) thought it necessary to polish—
and destroy. 'Sir Thomas Kirkpatric, one of Bruce's
friends, asking him soon after, if the traitor was slain,
"I believe so," replied Bruce. "And is that a matter,"
cried Kirkpatric, "to be left to conjecture? I will secure
him." '[1]

Or take a typical passage from Synge. (Christy, in *The
Playboy of the Western World*, has just begged Pegeen
to marry him.)

PEGEEN (*backing away from him*). You've right daring
to go ask me that, when all knows you'll be starting to
some girl in your own townland, when your father's rotten
in four months, or five.

CHRISTY (*indignantly*). Starting from you, is it? (*He
follows her.*) I will not, then, and when the airs is warming,
in four months or five, it's then yourself and me should
be pacing Neifin in the dews of night, the times sweet smells
do be rising, and you'd see a little, shiny new moon, maybe,
sinking on the hills.

PEGEEN (*looking at him playfully*). And it's that kind
of a poacher's love you'd make, Christy Mahon, on the
sides of Neifin, when the night is down?

CHRISTY. It's little you'll think if my love's a poacher's,
or an earl's itself, when you'll feel my two hands stretched
around you, and I squeezing kisses on your puckered lips,
till I'd feel a kind of pity for the Lord God is all ages sitting
lonesome in His golden chair.

[1] See J. M. Robertson, *Essays towards a Critical Method* (1889),
p. 25.

PEGEEN. That'll be right fun, Christy Mahon, and any girl would walk her heart out before she'd meet *a young man was your like for eloquence, or talk at all.*

CHRISTY (*encouraged*). Let you wait, to hear me talking, till we're astray in Erris, when Good Friday's by, drinking a sup from a well, and making mighty kisses with our wetted mouths, or gaming in a gap of sunshine, with yourself stretched back unto your necklace, in the flowers of the earth.

PEGEEN (*in a low voice, moved by his tone*). I'd be nice so, is it?

CHRISTY (*with rapture*). If the mitred bishops seen you that time, they'd be the like of the holy prophets, I'm thinking, do be straining the bars of Paradise to lay eyes on the Lady Helen of Troy, and she abroad, pacing back and forward, with a nosegay in her golden shawl.

PEGEEN (*with real tenderness*). And what is it I have, Christy Mahon, to make me fitting entertainment for the like of you, that has *such poet's talking,* and such bravery of heart.[1]

I confess that each time I re-read this, I could claw myself for pleasure, like the Cook of Chaucer (another writer whose common characters speak with a robust vitality beyond their 'betters'). Had Wordsworth's Westmorlanders talked with such zest, one could listen with more resignation to his tedious harpings on the speech of common men. You may of course answer that Synge's Irish are mere literary rustics, as artificial as the scented shepherds of some pastoral Arcadia. But Synge himself did not think so.

In writing *The Playboy of the Western World*, as in my other plays, I have used one or two words only that I have not heard among the people of Ireland, or spoken in my own nursery before I could read the newspapers. . . . Anyone who has lived in real intimacy with the Irish peasantry will know

[1] *Plays* (1924 ed.), pp. 269–71.

that the wildest sayings and ideas in this play are tame indeed, compared with the fancies one may hear in any little hillside cabin in Geesala, or Carraroe, or Dingle Bay. . . . When I was writing *The Shadow of the Glen*, some years ago, I got more aid than any learning could have given me from a chink in the floor of the old Wicklow house where I was staying, that let me hear what was being said by the servant girls in the kitchen. This matter, I think, is of importance, for in countries where the imagination of the people, and the language they use, is rich and living, it is possible for a writer to be rich and copious in his words, and at the same time to give the reality, which is the root of all poetry, in a comprehensive and natural form. In the modern literature of towns, however, richness is found only in sonnets, or prose poems, or in one or two elaborate books that are far away from the profound and common interests of life. One has, on one side, Mallarmé and Huysmans producing this literature; and, on the other, Ibsen and Zola dealing with the reality of life in joyless and pallid words. . . . In a good play every speech should be as fully flavoured as a nut or apple, and such speeches cannot be written by anyone who works among people who have shut their lips on poetry. In Ireland, for a few years more, we have a popular imagination that is fiery, and magnificent, and. tender; so that those of us who wish to write start with a chance that is not given to writers in places where the springtime of the local life has been forgotten, and the harvest is a memory only, and the straw has been turned into bricks.[1]

Not a very gay picture of the results of education. Yet, I am afraid there is much truth in it—that towns, schools, and newspapers have done vast harm as well as good. We should face the unpleasant truth that civilization and education, while they sharpen the mind, often blunt the tongue; while they brighten the intelligence, often tarnish the imagination. Primitive language seems often a kind of magic; intellectual language, a kind of algebra. Remember Bunyan.

[1] Preface to *The Playboy* (in *Plays*, 1924 ed., p. 183).

This, I suppose, is partly why Montaigne was well content with the phrases of 'les halles à Paris' and 'les rues françaises'; and why the purist Malherbe (1555–1628), ardent to perfect the French tongue, listened with serious attention to the porters of the Porte Saint-Jean (just as 'Melancholy' Burton listened for his diversion to the cursing bargees of Oxford). Again Vaugelas (1585–1650), continuing the search for pure French, made it his rule that 'il vaut mieux d'ordinaire consulter *les femmes et ceux qui n'ont point étudié* que ceux qui sont bien savants en la langue grecque et en la latine'. And Diderot, on the wider question of style in general, is more downright still: 'C'est que le bon style est dans le coeur; voilà pourquoi tant de femmes disent et écrivent comme des anges, sans avoir appris ni à dire ni à écrire, et pourquoi tant de pédants diront et écriront mal toute leur vie, quoiqu'ils n'aient cessé d'étudier sans apprendre.'

Whether women still speak better I do not know (though I think they tend to write better letters); to say that 'le bon style est dans le coeur' seems to me an exaggeration typical of the warm-hearted Diderot, though I believe it to be based none the less on a vital truth; but that education, learning, and research, instead of making men speak and write better, often make them do both worse, remains, I am afraid, a matter of simple observation. When Professor Gilbert Murray, if I remember rightly, confesses to sometimes wishing that the inhabitants of University towns were rather more like Polynesians, I know what he means. But at this point prudence enjoins silence.

Am I suggesting, then, that we should despair of education, and try to go back to some illiterate Arcadia or Connemara of noble rustics? Of course not. There is no going back. But one can have the courage to admit that modern civilization has not been pure gain, without falling into the sentimental regrets of Rousseau. Nor have I any wish to belittle what we *have* gained. If we feel, for example, that there is more poetry in the primitive legends of Hellas or Eire, or in our own Northern Ballads, than in all the verse of the eighteenth century (which was yet, for the happy few, perhaps the most civilized of European centuries), that need not make us forget the splendour, delight, and charm in the prose of that great age. If Malherbe listened to porters, he was far from being one. And the Synge who immortalized peasants went himself both to Trinity College, Dublin, and to Paris. Most English writers, indeed, have been of the middle class, and many of them have been to Universities (though they have seldom written there). My point is merely that the sophisticated (ready though they may be to suppose so) do not necessarily express themselves better than the simple—in fact, may often have much to learn from them.

Educators, indeed, are prone to believe too blindly in education. Chesterfield, for example, had the extraordinary notion that anyone could train himself to become 'a model of eloquence' and indeed anything else, except (he admits) a poet—'a drayman is probably born with as good organs as Milton, Locke, or Newton; but by culture they are much more above him than he is above his horse'. Similarly I once knew a clever man who fervently imagined that he could turn any normal child, if caught young enough, into a Trinity scholar. But my own experience is that firsts are born rather than made. In the same way, though painters have been and still are trained in schools, writers of value are not *taught* to write (though I believe something of the sort is advertised in London and in the United States)—they appear to teach themselves. The authors you read in 'doing English', from Chaucer to Virginia Woolf, never 'did English'.

It is true that Antiquity made efforts, persisting for

centuries, to train orators. But the results seem significantly insignificant. It began when some of the Greek sophists professed to make men eloquent; they were followed by generations of rhetoricians who eventually swarmed over the whole Greco-Roman world, till Juvenal could speak of them as finding employment even in furthest Thule. But in practice not even Aristotle's *Rhetoric* could prolong the great age of Attic oratory, then nearing its end; just as his *Poetics* brought no new life to dying Tragedy. As usual, critical theory could not procreate, it could only dissect. Cicero produced treatises on oratory, but no new Cicero. Writers like 'Longinus' or Quintilian, often interesting, often admirable, seem to have been equally barren of practical effect. And in the upshot, for the English (though not for the Scots) 'rhetoric' has become, ironically enough, a term of abuse. I cannot believe, despite Matthew Arnold, that critics have ever done very much good to the creative; though sometimes they have done a good deal of harm.

One is too often reminded of the man in Chekhov who set out to teach his kitten an improved method of catching mice, till it cowered at sight of one; or of that wise apologue uttered by Prince Mou of Wei, about the child from Shou-ling who was sent to Han-tan to learn the Han-tan walk—'he failed to master the steps, but spent so much time trying to acquire them, that in the end he forgot how one usually walks, and came home to Shou-ling on all fours'.

None the less, though education may be less infallible and more perilous than sanguine souls assume, it remains an inescapable necessity. It spoilt Chekhov's kitten: but it has to be imposed on every horse and hawk and hound. You cannot turn glass into diamonds; but diamonds can be polished; even glass can be cut. No one is born a writer. The greatest have had to learn. Only one learns most from trying to do things oneself; and my purpose is simply to make some suggestions, and provide some illustrations from the experience of others, which may perhaps help to shorten that painful process.

But besides these two aims—a deeper enjoyment of the good writing of others, and a better ability to speak, write, and think clearly oneself—the study of style has also a third object: to preserve the purity of the English tongue.

It is unlikely that many of us will be famous, or even remembered. But not less important than the brilliant few that lead a nation or a literature to fresh achievements, are the unknown many whose patient efforts keep the world from running backward; who guard and maintain the ancient values, even if they do not conquer new; whose inconspicuous triumph it is to pass on what they inherited from their fathers, unimpaired and undiminished, to their sons. Enough, for almost all of us, if we can hand on the torch, and not let it down; content to win the affection, if it may be, of a few who know us, and to be forgotten when they in their turn have vanished. The destiny of mankind is not governed wholly by its 'stars'.

Part of our heritage—you are now coming into it—is the English tongue. You may not be among the few in whose hands it becomes an Excalibur; but you can do your part to pass it on, clean, unrusted, undefiled.

England no longer holds the place as a world-power that was hers fifty years ago. We no longer need a Kipling to warn us, as in the days of Queen Victoria's Diamond Jubilee, against blind and blatant arrogance:

> For frantic boast and foolish word
> Thy mercy on Thy People, Lord!

Indeed, the essays I read sometimes give me an impression of the opposite kind—of a certain alarm and despondency among the young at seeing England overshadowed by two super-states to east and west. But I can really see no cogent reason for talking in the disheartened tones of an Athenian of the third century before Christ, or a Roman of the third century after. The England of the first Elizabeth, the England of Queen Anne, lived likewise in the shadow of more powerful and more populous rivals; that did not prevent the English of those days from enriching civilization to a degree surpassed by none; alike in literature and in thought. For they had two vital assets—the English character and the English tongue.

Both remain.

Granted, our position is difficult and dangerous. Yet, were it safer, it might be really more dangerous. For the English tend to be lazy—lazy in thought and lazy in effort, till a crisis comes. We need east winds.

But our present concern is with language. On the quality of a nation's language depends to some extent the quality of its life and thought; and on the quality of its life and thought the quality of its language. This can be seen, I think, without being fanciful, in the grace and subtlety of the best Greek, the lapidary strength of the best Latin, the bright clarity of the best French; and again in the stark brevity of the Icelandic sagas, or the oratorical melody of Italian, which half sings even when it speaks.

Great writers may better a language; but they cannot remake it. There were times when Goethe groaned that he had to write in German. And one of the weaknesses of Roman literature under the Empire was the widening gap between the Latin of authors and the Latin of the common man. The language of a nation, like the land it lives by, needs constant cultivation and weeding. Degeneration can go far. Modern Greek has lost its infinitive and its future (now replaced by awkward periphrases); and degraded three vowels and three diphthongs to a single sound—'ee'. So that the Goddess of Health—'Hygieia'—has been reduced to the cacophony of 'Ee-yee-ee-a'. Such indeed is the common law of life. It is only too easy to go downhill. Oysters and barnacles once had heads.

Here, I think, we have something to learn from the French. In poetry, and in the more poetic kinds of prose, English literature need fear no comparisons; but in more normal prose the French seem to me to keep a higher general level. And that I suspect to be partly because educated Frenchmen, and French educators, think, and care, more about it. When will you hear an Englishman exclaim 'But that isn't English' in the tone of scorn and passion with which a Frenchman protests 'Mais ce n'est pas français'?

More than two centuries ago the Abbé Le Blanc, visiting England, was struck by the same contrast— 'Aussi notre façon de louer un Ouvrage est aujourd'hui de dire: *C'est un Livre bien fait, une Pièce bien écrite, un Discours bien arrangé.* Les Anglois au contraire disent: *C'est un Livre plein de bonnes, ou d'excellentes choses.*'[1] The French even invented an Academy to keep them straight. How far it has succeeded, I cannot say. But it remains one symptom of a conscious concern about language which the ordinary Englishman would think fussy, precious, or pedantic, and worthy only of more serious matters like Test Matches.[2]

---

[1] J. B. Le Blanc, *Lettres d'un François* (1745). I quote from the 1749 edition, III, p. 17 (Letter LXVII).

[2] At times, indeed, this purism has been carried to lengths where it becomes comical. 'An hour before his death,' says Racan of Malherbe (1555–1628), 'he suddenly revived to rebuke his hostess, who was nursing him, for some word that to his mind was not good French; and when reprimanded by his confessor, replied that he could not help it—that to his last moment he was set on upholding the purity of the French tongue.' Père Bouhours is said to have expired (1702) with the words: 'Je vas, ou je vais, mourir; l'un ou l'autre se dit.' And of the purist Prince de Beauvau some ironic wit remarked, according to Chamfort: 'Quand je le rencontre dans

Now if the French have preserved in their prose this high average of excellence, it is not, I think, because they were born with a silver spoon of a language in their mouths. Many find French less melodious than Italian. Alfieri detested the very sound of it—its nasal whine. And a French writer has complained that it is pestered with swarms of little midge-like words—not only such forms as *y*, *en*, *se*, *ne*, *le*, *la*, but also 'les auxiliaires *avoir* et *être*, le verbe *faire*, les conjonctions encombrantes; toute cette pouillerie de notre prose française'.[1]

Yet, as John Addington Symonds has pointed out, by assiduous cultivation the French have produced a finer harvest than some more favoured lands. Just as they cook better dishes than ours with inferior meat—or meat that used to be inferior: just as their women, often with less natural beauty than those of some other nations, can yet contrive a style and charm and grace that are unsurpassed. Hence, strangely enough, Goethe himself preferred in old age to read his own Faust in French;[2] and the French translation of Strauss's *Leben Jesu* is said to have sold more copies in Germany than in France. I suggest that from reading French prose you may learn a good deal about writing English; and I feel, though this must remain a matter of taste, that English prose suffered badly when, in the early nineteenth century, French influence was replaced by German.

mes promenades du matin et que je passe dans l'ombre de son cheval . . . j'ai remarqué que je ne fais pas une faute de français de toute la journée.' My point is that these fantastic tales are typically French, and not easy to match in English.

[1] J. A. Symonds, *Essays Speculative and Suggestive* (1907 ed.), p. 199.

[2] In Gérard de Nerval's version. 'En allemand je ne peux plus lire le *Faust*, mais dans cette traduction française chaque trait me frappe comme s'il était tout nouveau pour moi.' (Sainte-Beuve, *Nouveaux Lundis*, III, p. 311.) Of *Hermann and Dorothea* Goethe similarly preferred the Latin version to the original German.

On the other hand, I believe—though it may be prejudice—that among the causes and effects of the sometimes unhappy history of the German mind are certain qualities of the German tongue; a language that can lend itself splendidly to poetry, but in prose (with great exceptions like Schopenhauer or Nietzsche) seems prone at times to lose itself in a kind of ponderous *Götterdämmerung* of drifting obscurities and cloudy abstractions. Take an example from Hitler himself (on Judaism): 'Eine von infernalischer Unduldsamkeit erfüllte Weltanschauung wird nur zerbrochen werden durch eine vom gleichen Geist vorwärtsgetriebene, vom gleichen stärksten Willen verfochtene, dabei aber in sich reine und durchaus wahrhaftige neue Idee.'[1] To the ordinary English mind the idea of reading an eight-hundred-page book composed in such sentences is a nightmare; that it should be read with enthusiasm remains flatly incomprehensible. There was current in my War Department a jesting quotation, perhaps apocryphal, to express this side of the German mind: 'Warum denn so einfach? Können Sie es nicht komplizierter machen?'[2] We did not underestimate the formidable efficiency, pertinacity, and courage of our opponents. None the less, if you wish to talk imposing twaddle of an abstruse and abstract kind, though wonders can be done even in English, you will find it hard to equal German.

Or consider a more particular point. One of the most important things, to my mind, in English style is word-order. For us, the most emphatic place in clause or sentence is the end. This is the climax; and, during the momentary pause that follows, that last word continues,

---

[1] *Mein Kampf* (1936 ed.), pp. 506–7. Literally, 'A with infernal intolerance filled view of life will only be shattered by a by the like spirit impelled, by the like strongest will championed, but in itself pure and fundamentally truthful new idea.'

[2] 'Why then so simple? Can't you make it more complicated?'

as it were, to reverberate in the reader's mind. It has, in fact, the last word. One should therefore think twice about what one puts at a sentence-end. But in a German sentence this final position may be reserved, by a most curious grammatical convention, for an infinitive or past participle; or, in a subordinate clause, for the main verb. Thus logical emphasis, unless particularly strong, tends to be sacrificed to mere grammar. One can see this happening even in the eloquence of Nietzsche: 'Ich lehre Euch den Übermenschen. Der Mensch ist Etwas, das überwunden werden soll.' The essential words are *Übermenschen* and *überwunden*; but, though *Übermenschen* gets its rightful pride of place, *überwunden* does not.[1] Here it may not much matter. But in longer sentences or clauses, German has a tendency to lose clarity and point. Hence the pleasant story of the man who, entering a foreign café where there sat groups of English, French, and Germans, noted that the English were of course entrenched round their table in solid silence; the French all gabbling at once; but the Germans listening to each other in turn with a tense concentration that for a moment astonished him. Then he realized— they were waiting for the verb! The curious thing is how rules so misguided could ever arise. They date, I am told, from a naïve Renaissance idea of capturing for German the excellence of Latin prose. The Romans had a marked tendency to put their verbs last;[2] that

---

[1] Cf. 'Ach, es giebt so viel Dinge zwischen Himmel und Erde, von denen sich nur die Dichter Etwas *haben träumen lassen.*' 'Und verloren sei uns der Tag wo nicht Ein Mal getanzt *wurde!* Und falsch heisze uns jede Wahrheit, bei der es nicht ein Gelächter *gab!*' The important words are 'getanzt' and 'Gelächter'; but they are elbowed away from the end by the colourless 'wurde' and 'gab'.

[2] But of course they were not enslaved by it. Cf. the close of Caesar, *Gallic War*, II: 'Ob easque res ex litteris Caesaris dies quindecim supplicatio decreta est, quod ante id tempus accidit *nulli*'—'which till then had happened to *none!*'

Roman tendency, it seems, became in German hands an iron law. Arminius might have laughed bitterly in his grave.

Here English has been more fortunate. Like a rock smoothed by a glacier, it got rid of many a useless excrescence while our peasant forefathers groaned under their Norman conquerors. On the other hand, it has been constantly enriched from foreign sources, especially from French and, partly through French, from Latin. But it cannot now be left to look after itself, unless we are content to see it gradually become a kind of debased Basic. There are things that need to be taught; others, that need to be fought. We face plenty of dangerous influences —cheap newspapers, cheap books, giant towns, ubiquitous bureaucrats. Never were so many functionaries employed in packing so little meaning into so many words; partly from the natural pompousness of the official mind, partly from the need for legal or political caution. Of nineteenth-century democracy a wise politician observed, 'We must educate our masters': that applies no less urgently to twentieth-century bureaucracy.

Like our coastline, our language changes slowly but ceaselessly under the stress of time. Indeed, the change is not so slow as not to be noticeable at certain points within a lifetime. Take one example. 'Not one Londoner in ten thousand', wrote Macaulay in 1837, 'can lay down the rules for the proper use of *will* and *shall*. Yet not one Londoner in a million ever misplaces his *will* and *shall*.' This, indeed, seems typical Macaulay. Admirably clear; trenchant; and yet surely exaggerated? Can we seriously believe that there were less than half-a-dozen persons in that happy London of 1837 who 'ever' fell into grammatical error on this point? But it may be doubted, without falling into Macaulay's rashness, whether one Londoner in a hundred observes those rules today. Nearly all of us, so far as I can notice, whether high or low, whether writing or speaking, have come to say, for example, 'I will go tomorrow from London to Cambridge'. We do not mean, 'I am willing to go'; we do not mean, 'I am resolved to burst through Bishop's Stortford or die'; we mean simply 'I *shall* go'. I still think it would be better to say so.

In my childhood one was taught that, in the first person singular or plural, 'will' implied willingness or determination;[1] 'shall', simple statement. Everybody knew that; except, of course, the uneducated, or Scots (evidently not including Macaulay), or Irishmen. Indeed, there was adduced to us in warning, as the drunken Helot before the young Spartans, that comic Irishman who fell into the sea and unwittingly discouraged rescue by bawling 'No one shall save me. I will be drowned.' Today, however, this poor Irishman seems vanished beneath the waters; and everybody, almost, has adopted his use of '*will*'.

It seems to me rather a pity. If 'I will see her tomorrow' becomes a mere statement of fact, not of willingness or iron resolve, then willingness or resolve must, at least in writing, be expressed by some circumlocution, such as 'I am willing, or am resolved, to see her tomorrow'. We shall have lost brevity. Or else we must italicize: 'I *will* see her tomorrow.' To some, italics are anathema; in moderation, I cannot see why a legitimate stress of the voice should not be marked by an equally legitimate convention in print; still, italics can easily be abused.[2]

It may be argued on the other side that the older usage of 'shall' to express fact, and of 'will' to express willingness or determination, in the first person, whereas in the second and third persons it was the other way about,

---

[1] Cf. Shakespeare, *Venus and Adonis*, 409: 'I know not love (quoth he) nor will not know it.'

[2] See p. 77.

remained vilely complicated;[1] in now using 'will' to state mere fact, for all three persons alike, English laziness may be continuing that sensible process of simplification which has proved so valuable in the past, ridding us of things like case-endings and arbitrary genders.

It is a nice point. I suspect that the ignorant will win, and that their incorrectness in this matter will end by becoming correct English. One cannot tell. But meanwhile I shall, and will, continue to fight a rearguard action in defence of the older use of 'will' and 'shall'.

Another, worse example of language changing before our eyes is provided by 'as if'. We now hear and read on every side such phrases as 'It looks as if negotiations are breaking down'. This seems to me detestable. 'It looks as if' is used as if it were equivalent to 'it seems that'. But it is *not* equivalent. The full statement would be— 'It looks as it would look if negotiations *were* breaking down.' To use 'are' here, instead of 'were', is quite illogical. And if the French tend to be too logical, the English, I think, tend not to be logical enough.

Style is my subject, not grammar. But bad grammar can spoil style; and a language can deteriorate till it becomes difficult for style to exist. If English ever reached, in the course of centuries, the condition once imagined by Professor Gilbert Murray in which it said things like 'When 'e met 'e, 'e took off 'e 'at', our Miltons would be likely to remain, if not mute, at least inglorious. There are dangers to which more of us, I think, might well be more awake; those who have had the good fortune to be most carefully educated, must accept in return the heaviest responsibility.

It is not a question of banning all linguistic changes, as some writers on pure English are too apt to do. That is merely imitating King Canute and Mrs. Partington.

[1] *E.g.* 'You shall see her' (*i.e.* 'You will be allowed to'); or 'You *shall* see her' (*i.e.* 'You must').

[43]

In general I am, I own, a conservative in literature. I have seen too many leaders of literary revolts—and revolting most of them were. But since language cannot stand still, the main thing for the public interest is that alterations in vocabulary and idiom should not become too rapid, reckless, and wanton; as for the individual writer, I do not know where he will find better advice than Pope's:

> Be not the first by whom the new are tried,
> Nor yet the last to lay the old aside.[1]

That Britain, the Dominions, and the United States speak the same tongue means that English has a growing chance of becoming ultimately a world-language.[2] But

[1] Cf. p. 127. A like principle applies, I think, to idioms. For example, shall we split infinitives? Older writers did; including Johnson himself. Then a taboo developed—like many taboos, not very rational. One may argue: 'I see no reason to consistently avoid split infinitives. "Consistently to avoid split infinitives" is strained: "to avoid consistently split infinitives" reads as if "consistently" belonged to "split".' It may, however, be replied that, as things are, any split infinitive distracts the attentive reader; who begins asking, "did he split it on purpose, or from ignorance?" Therefore the cautious will see here a psychological reason against split infinitives; these jolt some readers; and it takes no great ingenuity to avoid them.
Similarly 'due to' is now becoming a prepositional phrase, equivalent to 'owing to'—'They stopped work, due to the rain.' To this new usage there are two objections. First, it can be ambiguous (was the stoppage, or the work, 'due to' the rain?). Secondly, it has not yet established itself; it can irritate; and it may never establish itself. 'Wait and see.'
[2] Contrast the situation at the beginning of the eighteenth century, when English literature was still little known outside England and, as Jespersen points out, Veneroni's *Dictionary* (1714) covered, as 'die 4 europäischen Hauptsprachen', Italian, French, German, and Latin; not English. But already Hume foresaw the future, when he advised Gibbon against writing in French (24 October 1767): 'Let the French, therefore, triumph in the present

[44]

this common language might easily grow common in a less desirable sense; it would be a pity if English, in gaining the whole world, were to lose its soul. By the beginning of our era, Greek had become a common tongue for the Near East; but it was not the Greek of Sophocles.

I conclude, then, that the study of style in education has three main objects—the appreciation of English; the mastery of English; and the purity of English. If anyone does not find these three important enough, he seems to me greedy.

You may be thinking: 'All this is very magnificent and grandiloquent. But these fine or gloomy prospects of the English language are very remote; we shall be dead long before; and meanwhile we have our own gardens to cultivate. We grant your truism that it is excellent to be a master of one's tongue. But how do we do it? In Ireland it was once thought enough to kiss the Blarney Stone. What is your recipe?'

I have no Blarney Stone in my pocket. I offer only a few principles; a number of examples; and a few warnings.

I must end (perhaps I should have begun) by asking your indulgence. For 'Style' is a most terrible subject to discourse upon. I am haunted by the mocking eighteenth-century lines:

> Rules for good verse they first with pain indite,
> Then show us what is bad, by what they write.

To indite rules for good prose may seem just as pretentious. But I take shelter behind the massive bulk of Johnson. When Lady Macleod objected that a writer did not practise what he preached, 'I cannot help that,

diffusion of their tongue. Our solid and increasing establishments in America, where we need less dread the inundation of Barbarians, promise a superior stability and duration to the English language.' (One may not feel quite so sure of the 'stability'.)

madam,' was his reply. 'That does not make his book the worse. .... I have, all my life long, been lying till noon; yet I tell all young men, and tell them with great sincerity, that no one who does not rise early will ever do any good.'

II

THE FOUNDATION OF STYLE—
CHARACTER

MOST discussions of style seem to me to begin at the wrong end; like an architect who should disregard foundations, and give his mind only to superstructure and decoration. They plunge into the tricks of the trade—the choice of words, the employment of epithets, the build of paragraphs. Yet here their rules seem often arbitrary, their precepts often capricious; and I grow as bored and rebellious as, I take it, Laertes did while listening to the injunctions of Polonius (even though some of the injunctions are excellent, and Laertes himself shared only too fully his father's fondness for lecturing). I begin to damn all tricks of all trades; to forswear tricks of any sort; to wish I were away on a Scottish hillside, or among Greek peasants who have never heard of such coxcombries; in fact, to feel very like Samuel Butler in his continuation of that passage I quoted at the beginning:[1]

A man may, and ought to take pains to write clearly, tersely and euphemistically:[2] he will write many a sentence three or four times over—to do much more than this is worse than not rewriting at all:[3] he will be at great pains to see that he does not repeat himself, to arrange his matter in the way that shall best enable the reader to master it, to cut out superfluous words and, even more, to eschew irrelevant matter: but in

[1] P. 13.
[2] I suppose Butler meant, and perhaps wrote, 'euphoniously'— few men have been less given than he to euphemism—that is, calling unpleasant things by pleasant names.
[3] But contrast pp. 269–73.

each case he will be thinking not of his own style but of his reader's convenience. Men like Newman and R. L. Stevenson seem to have taken pains to acquire what they called a style as a preliminary measure—as something they had to form before their writings could be of any value. I should like to put it on record that I never took the smallest pains with my style, have never thought about it, do not know nor want to know whether it is a style at all or whether it is not, as I believe and hope, just common, simple straightforwardness. I cannot conceive how any man can take thought for his style without loss to himself and his readers.

As I have already said, I suspect that Butler really knew he had an excellent style; but chose, aggressive creature, to misuse 'style' to mean 'elegant mannerism', in order then to damn it. But my point is this. Literary style is simply a means by which one personality moves others. The problems of style, therefore, are really problems of personality—of practical psychology. Therefore this psychological foundation should come first; for on it the rules of rhetoric are logically based. These are *not* (when they are sound) arbitrary or capricious. And when they are seen to be neither arbitrary nor capricious, but rational and logical, they may then cease to be irritating or boring.

The primary question, therefore, is how best to move and direct men's feelings. For even the most factual writing may involve feeling. Even the coldest biological monograph on the habits of flatworms, or the most detached piece of historical research into the price of eggs under Edward I, may be written so lucidly, argued so neatly, as to stir pleasure and admiration. Even mathematical solutions (though here I speak with trembling) can have aesthetic beauty.

Further, apart from the charm of neatness and lucidity, the influence of personality intrudes itself even into subjects where men try to be dispassionately judicial.

You may have a new theory of trade-cycles; your evidence may be excellent; but, though the truth may in the end prevail anyway, no matter how personally repellent its advocate, you are likely to make it prevail much more quickly if you know not only how to state, but how to state *persuasively*.

In less scientific and more literary forms of writing or speaking, the element of emotion becomes far larger; and so does the importance of persuasiveness.

A nation, for example, has to be persuaded that though Hitler is at Dunkirk, there can be no question of white flags (then, fortunately, little persuasion was needed); or a reader has to be persuaded that a skylark is not a bird, but 'a blithe spirit' (to which, I own, I remain somewhat recalcitrant).

But persuasion, though it depends partly on the motives adduced for belief—how plausibly they are put, how compellingly they are worded—depends also, and sometimes depends still more, on the *personality* of the persuader. Just as, when we are advised in real life, we are often influenced as much by the character of the adviser as by the intrinsic merits of his advice.

Style, I repeat, is a means by which a human being gains contact with others; it is personality clothed in words, character embodied in speech. If handwriting reveals character, style reveals it still more—unless it is so colourless and lifeless as not really to be a style at all. The fundamental thing, therefore, is *not* technique, useful though that may be; if a writer's personality repels, it will not avail him to eschew split infinitives, to master the difference between 'that' and 'which', to have Fowler's *Modern English Usage* by heart. Soul is more than syntax. If your readers dislike you, they will dislike what you say. Indeed, such is human nature, unless they like you they will mostly deny you even justice.

Therefore, if you wish your writing to seem good,

your character must seem at least partly so. And since in the long run deception is likely to be found out,[1] your character had better not only *seem* good, but *be* it. Those who publish make themselves public in more ways than they sometimes realize. Authors may sell their books: but they give themselves away.

Does this, I wonder, seem very far-fetched? Yet it is not so new a view, after all. I find something not very different in that dry-minded person Aristotle (though he is talking, of course, only of oratory). 'But since the art of speech aims at producing certain judgements . . . the speaker must not only look to his words, to see they are cogent and convincing, he must also present himself as a certain type of person and put those who judge him in a certain frame of mind. . . . For it makes all the difference to men's opinions whether they feel friendly or hostile, irritated or indulgent. . . . To carry conviction, a speaker needs three qualities—for there are three things that convince us, apart from actual proof—good sense, good character, and good will towards his hearers.'[2] Such stress on sympathy and personality may seem to come a little strangely from the cold and detached Aristotle. But it is only the more telling for that.

Some three centuries later, the less prosaic 'Longinus' glimpsed essentially the same truth (though I wish he had not mixed his metaphors): 'Height of style is the echo of a great personality.'[3] And when the noble

---

[1] Cf. Sainte-Beuve on Victor Cousin: 'Le style de Cousin est *grand*, il a *grand* air, il rappelle la *grande* époque à s'y méprendre; mais il ne paraît pas original, rien n'y marque l'homme, l'individu qui écrit. Bossuet, par moments, ne parlerait pas autrement, et Cousin n'est pas Bossuet.' (*Causeries du Lundi*, XI, p. 469.) In short, borrowed plumes fall off. [2] *Rhetoric*, II, 1.

[3] IX, 2. Compare the Roman definition of a good orator—'Vir bonus, dicendi peritus'—'A good man with practice in speech.' Optimistic perhaps; but, in the long run, not without truth; and truer of literature, which has a longer run than oratory. (This

simplicity of Vauvenargues uttered its corollary as
applied to the critic: 'Il faut avoir de l'âme pour avoir du
goût'; when Buffon penned his much quoted, and misquoted, 'Le style est l'homme même';[1] when Yeats des-

definition is said to be Cato the Elder's. See Seneca the rhetorician,
Controv., I, 9; Quintilian, XII, 1, 1.) Compare too Anatole France
—'Les grands écrivains n'ont pas l'âme basse. Voilà, M. Brown,
tout leur secret.' (Though 'tout' is too much.)

[1] Sometimes cited as 'Le style, c'est l'homme'; sometimes in the
form 'le style est *de* l'homme'. But it is weakened both by the
addition of 'de' and by the omission of 'même'. Needless difficulties,
I think, have also been made over the meaning. Gosse, for
example, (*s.v.* 'Style' in *Encyclopædia Britannica*, 1910 edition)
reminds us that Buffon was a biologist and that the sentence comes
from his *Natural History*; therefore, he says, Buffon really meant
that style 'distinguished the language of man (*homo sapiens*) from
the monotonous roar of the lion or the limited gamut of the bird.
Buffon was engaged with biological, not with aesthetic ideas.'

But I doubt if Buffon would have stooped to the platitude of
telling us that man has style, birds not. It too much recalls *The
Anti-Jacobin*:

> The feather'd tribes on pinions skim the air,
> Not so the mackerel, and still less the bear.

Actually, Buffon's phrase comes, not from his *Natural History*,
but from his *Discours sur le Style*, his inaugural address to the
French Academy. It seems to me not in the least 'biological'. And
I take Buffon to be saying with classic calm very much what Victor
Hugo proclaimed with romantic fervour:

> Quiconque pense, illustre, obscur, sifflé, vainqueur,
> Grand ou petit, *exprime en son livre son coeur*.
> Ce que nous écrivons de nos plumes d'argile,
> Soit sur le livre d'or comme le doux Virgile,
> Soit comme Aligieri sur la bible de fer,
> Est notre propre flamme et notre propre chair.

Or, as Gibbon put it, more briefly and clearly: 'Style is the image of
character' (*Autobiographies of E. Gibbon*, ed. J. Murray, 2nd ed.
1897, p. 353). The idea itself goes back far further. Socrates is
credited with the saying: 'As a man is, so is his speech'; similar
maxims occur in Plato and Menander; and Seneca discusses it at
length in *Epistle* 114.

cribed style as 'but high breeding in words and in argument', they were all restating this constantly forgotten point.

Napoleon was no sentimental aesthete. But even he, when asked to appoint some person to a post, replied, if I remember, 'Has he written anything? Que je voie son style!'

The wisdom of China, indeed, realized this truth long ago. The *Book of Odes*, preserved for us by Confucius, includes popular ballads of the feudal states, which were periodically forwarded to the Son of Heaven so that, we are told, the Imperial Musicians might infer from them the moral state of the people. Plato would have approved. Confucius himself (says a fanciful tradition) thus studied a certain tune on his lute. After ten days he observed, 'I have learned the tune, but I cannot get the rhythm'; after several days more, 'I have the rhythm, but not the composer's intention'; after several days more, 'I still cannot visualize his person'; and finally, 'Now I have seen one deep in thought gazing up to far heights, with intense longing. Now I see him—dark, tall, with whimsical eyes and the ambition of a world-ruler. Who could he be but King Wen the Civilized?'[1] Even in judging calligraphy and painting, according to Lin Yutang, 'the highest criterion is not whether the artist shows good technique, but whether he has or has not *a high personality*'.[2]

All this may seem strangely remote from modern ideas. But it has a foundation of fact too often forgotten by most criticism; though Johnson and Sainte-Beuve kept it always in mind.

Return to Aristotle. The orator, he says, has to consider three things: the statements he utters; the attitude of his audience; the impression made by himself. This

---

[1] Tsui Chi, *Short History of Chinese Civilization* (1942), p. 53.
[2] *Importance of Living* (1938), p. 384.

analysis can easily be extended from oratory to literature at large. Any literary writer is concerned with (A) statements, (B) feelings. (A) He makes his statements in a certain way. (B) (1) He arouses certain feelings in his audience[1] about his statements (a) intentionally, (b) unintentionally.

(2) He reveals certain feelings of his own (a) intentionally (unless he is deliberately impersonal), (b) unintentionally.

(3) He arouses certain feelings in his audience about himself and his feelings (a) intentionally, (b) unintentionally.

In short, a writer may be doing seven different things at once; four of them, consciously. Literature is complicated.

Consider, for example, Mark Antony's speech in the Forum. (A) Statements. Caesar has been killed by honourable men, who say he was ambitious.

(B) Feelings. (1) While pretending deference to the murderers, Antony rouses his hearers to rage against them.

(2) He reveals his own feelings. (a) (Intentionally): loyal resentment. (b) (Unintentionally): secret ambition.

---

[1] In the most subjective forms of writing, such as the personal lyric, the writer's own feelings may become the main thing, and the audience may recede into the background. In Mill's phrase, the poet is less heard than overheard. Yet this convention contains a good deal of fiction. The poet may, indeed, proclaim as proudly as Hafiz:

> From the east to the west no man understands me—
> The happier I that confide to none but the wind!

Yet even modern poets, of whom the first of these lines would be far truer than of Hafiz, still seek publishers and read proofs. Whatever is published invites a public. And most prose-writers, at all events, are not much less conscious than the orator of addressing an audience.

(3) He arouses feelings in his audience towards himself. (a) (Intentionally): he poses as the moderate statesman, yet loyal friend. (b) (Unintentionally): he moves the more knowing theatre-audience to ironic amusement at his astuteness.

The theatre-goer who knows the play, or Roman history, has Antony at a disadvantage. But even among Antony's audience in the Forum one can imagine a shrewd observer here and there seeing through his splendid rhetoric. For a writer, likewise, such shrewder minds are always there in wait. The readers who read between the lines, are the readers worth winning. But if the writer forgets them, if his mood in writing is mean or peevish or petty or vain or false, no cleverness and no technique are likely, in the end, to save him. That is why I repeat that the first thing in style is character. It is not easy to fool all one's readers all the time.

Consider side by side these two passages—letters to noble lords. (The first has become a lasting part of English Literature.)

Seven years, My Lord, have now past since I waited in your outward Rooms or was repulsed from your Door, during which time I have been pushing on my work through difficulties of which It is useless to complain, and have brought it at last to the verge of Publication without one Act of assistance, one word of encouragement, or one smile of favour. Such treatment I did not expect, for I never had a Patron before.

The Shepherd in Virgil grew at last acquainted with Love, and found him a native of the rocks.

Is not a Patron,[1] My Lord, one who looks with unconcern on

---

[1] Cf. the definition of 'Patron' in Johnson's *Dictionary*—'commonly a wretch who supports with insolence, and is paid with flattery'; and the couplet in *The Vanity of Human Wishes*:

> There mark what ills the scholar's life assail,
> Toil, envy, want, the Patron, and the jail.

('The Patron' was substituted by Johnson, after his affray with Chesterfield, for 'the garret' of the original version.)

a Man struggling for Life in the water and when he has reached ground encumbers him with help? The notice which you have been pleased to take of my Labours, had it been early, had been kind; but it has been delayed till I am indifferent and cannot enjoy it, till I am solitary and cannot impart it, till I am known, and do not want it.

I hope it is no very cynical asperity not to confess obligation where no benefit has been received, or to be unwilling that the Public should consider me as owing that to a Patron, which Providence has enabled me to do for myself.

Having carried on my work thus far with so little obligation to any Favourer of Learning I shall not be disappointed though I should conclude it, if less be possible, with less, for I have been long wakened from that Dream of hope, in which I once boasted myself with so much exultation,

My Lord,
Your Lordship's most humble,
Most Obedient Servant,
Sam: Johnson.

And now for a different picture.

My Lord,

I feel that I am taking a liberty for which I shall have but small excuse and no justification to offer, if I am not fortunate enough to find one in your Lordship's approbation of my design; and unless you should condescend to regard the writer as addressing himself to your Genius rather than your Rank, and graciously permit me to forget my total inacquaintance with your Lordship personally in my familiarity with your other more permanent Self, to which your works have introduced me. If indeed I had not in *them* discovered that Balance of Thought and Feeling, of Submission and Mastery; that one sole unfleeting music which is never of yesterday, but still remaining reproduces *itself*, and powers akin to itself in the minds of other men:—believe me, my Lord! I not only could not have hazarded this Boldness, but my own sense of propriety would have precluded the very Wish. A sort of pre-established good will, like that with which the Swan instinctively takes up the weakling cygnet into the Hollow between its wings, I knew I might confidently look for from one who is indeed a Poet: were I but assured that your Lordship had ever thought of me as a fellow-laborer in the same vineyard, and as not otherwise unworthy your notice. And surely a fellow-laborer I *have* been, and a co-inheritor of the same Bequest, tho' of a smaller portion; and tho' your Lordship's ampler Lot is on the sunny side, while mine has lain upon the North, my *growing* Vines gnawed down by Asses, and my richest and raciest clusters carried off and spoilt by the plundering Fox. Excuse my Lord! the length and 'petitionary' solemnity of this Preface, as attributable to the unquiet state of my spirits, under which I write this Letter, and my fears as to its final reception. Anxiety makes us all ceremonious. . . .

The contrast is surely startling. One passage seems superb; the other, abject. Yet each is from the hand of genius.

Johnson's statement of fact is simple: Chesterfield is claiming gratitude for helping him too little and too late. The feelings Johnson seeks to stir in his audience are also simple. (By 'his audience' I do not mean Chesterfield, whom he merely wished to put in his place, but the public to whom, in fact, he is appealing against aristocratic arrogance. For his letter became 'the talk of the town'.) His readers are to feel anger towards a neglectful patron, and admiration for worth which no poverty could depress. It is, in fine (much as Johnson would have disliked being compared to Americans or republicans) a Declaration of Independence in the republic of letters.

As for Johnson's own feelings, what he reveals is the sturdy resentment of an honest man; and if one senses between the lines certain other feelings—satisfaction that Chesterfield's ill-treatment has relieved him of any obligations; pride, that he has accomplished his great work alone; triumph, that he can so trenchantly settle an old score—after all, these are perfectly human, and do him no discredit.

[56]

Therefore the letter as a whole is brilliantly effective. Full of art, it yet seems natural—for art has become second nature. Those balanced antitheses remain as much a part of Johnson as the majestic see-saw of his body when he perused a book; the irony vibrates; and the reader exults each time he reaches that sonorous Roman triplet—'cannot enjoy it . . . cannot impart it[1] . . . do not want it'. It is hardly a very Christian letter, nor a very humble one; but it is the anger of a very honest man.

Only one note in it, to me, rings false. What is this shepherd doing here, who found Love a native of the rocks? What possessed Johnson, that contemner of *Lycidas*, that ceaseless mocker at the falsetto absurdities of the pastoral, to pose himself here with Arcadian pipe and crook? Drum and cudgel would have been more in *his* line. And Lord Chesterfield as a fickle Amaryllis?— Chesterfield, who looked more like a dwarf Cyclops!

But this false note, if false note it is, lasts only for one sentence. Contrast the second letter, written to Byron by Coleridge in March 1815.[2] Coleridge was, I suppose, as clever a man as Johnson—many would say cleverer; he was, at rare intervals, a finer poet; how could he here write so ill? So miscalculate his whole effect? For Byron, one imagines, must have read it with a pitying smile. No doubt it is easier to write with dignity letters refusing help than begging it. Yet it *can* be done. Read the appeal written—not in vain—by the despairing Crabbe to Burke. But this fulsome twaddle about weakling cygnets chirping for the hollow of his lordship's wings was surely not only feeble but also false and

---

[1] A reference to the death of his dear, queer Tetty.

[2] *Unpublished Letters*, ed. E. L. Griggs (1932), II, pp. 131–2. (Coleridge wanted Byron to recommend his poems to 'some Publisher', in the hope that Byron's influence would obtain him better terms.)

foolish.[1] Heep and Pecksniff. Perhaps Coleridge dimly felt that, and was ashamed, and thereby grew demoralized in his style. Whether or no, my point is simply that this piece of writing is ruined, above all, by the personality behind—by Coleridge's weaker self. A good deal of difference between these two Samuels. No need to dwell on it—'look and pass'.[2]

Naturally no fineness of character is likely to make an ungifted man write well (though I think that even this sometimes happens); but it can make a gifted one write far better. It is, I believe, personality above all that sets Virgil and Horace higher than Catullus and Ovid;

[1] In the margin of his *Pepys* (1825 edition) Coleridge expressed a franker opinion of Byron's work: 'W. Wordsworth calls Lord Byron the mocking bird of our Parnassian ornithology, but the mocking bird, they say, has a very sweet song of his own, in true notes proper to himself. Now I cannot say I have ever heard any such in his Lordship's volumes of warbles; and in spite of Sir W. Scott, I dare predict that in less than a century, the Baronet's and the Baron's poems will lie on the same shelf of oblivion, Scott be read and remembered as a novelist and the founder of a new race of novels, and Byron not be remembered at all, except as a wicked lord who, from morbid and restless vanity, pretended to be ten times more wicked than he was.'

So far from being 'a swan', Byron had not 'ever', apparently, seemed to Coleridge even so much as a mocking bird. It is rash to pass judgement on the animosities of authors; one never knows all the facts; though sometimes, as here, one may seem to know pretty well. At all events, in 1816 Coleridge had accepted £100 from Byron; in 1824, while Coleridge sat safe in Highgate, Byron had died for Greece in the marshes of Missolonghi. Coleridge's marginal note, like his letter, might have been better left unwritten.

[2] It is pleasant to contrast the refusal by Leconte de Lisle, though very poor, of a pension of 300 francs a month from Napoleon III on condition that he would dedicate his translations to the Prince Imperial. 'Il serait sacrilège,' he replied, 'de dédier ces chefs d'oeuvre antiques à un enfant trop jeune pour les comprendre.' To the honour of the Second Empire, Leconte de Lisle got his pension none the less.

Chaucer than Dryden;[1] Shakespeare than his contemporaries. Many Elizabethans could write at times blank verse as enchanting as his; but he alone could conceive a Hamlet or an Imogen. Or again we may read of Goldsmith's Vicar or Sterne's Uncle Toby with simple pleasure and amusement; but, if we stop to think, we must surely recognize also that, whatever faults or foibles Goldsmith and Sterne displayed in real life, yet they had characters fine enough to imagine these types of human nature at its most lovable. And it is for this above all that they are remembered.[2]

Again, though these are more questionable and more personal preferences, I find myself preferring Montaigne to Bacon, Flaubert and Hardy to Wilde and Shaw, as being fundamentally more honest characters; Sterne and Voltaire to Swift and Rousseau, as having more gaiety and good humour; Tennyson and Arnold to Browning and Meredith, as personalities more sensitive and more self-controlled. Or, to take a more recent example, amid the criticism of the last half-century, with all its acidulated sciolists and balderdashing decadents, dizzy with their own intellectual altitude, why is it, for me, such a relief to turn back to Desmond MacCarthy? Because his writing was not only witty and amusing, but also wise and good.

'And yet,' you may exclaim, 'think of the good writers who have been bad men—Villon, Rousseau, Byron, Baudelaire. . . .'

But I do not find this matter quite so simple. It is surely a little summary to dismiss a man in a monosyllable as 'bad'. No doubt Kingsley, when asked by one

[1] For a detailed comparison, from this point of view, between two typical passages of Chaucer and Dryden, see my *Decline and Fall of the Romantic Ideal* (1948 ed.), pp. 214–18.

[2] Cf. Goethe to Eckermann: 'To Shakespeare, Sterne, and Goldsmith my debt has been infinite'—'Ich bin Shakespeare, Sterne, und Goldsmith unendliches schuldig gewesen.'

of his children who Heine was, is said to have replied, 'A bad man, my dear, a bad man.' And Carlyle, if I remember, dismissed Heine as 'that blackguard'. But do we take such judgements very seriously?

On ethics, as on aesthetics, men's judgements have varied wildly from age to age, without appearing any nearer to agreement. On certain points, indeed, there has been, since history began, surprising unanimity. Avarice, treachery, cowardice have had few admirers at any time. But in the Middle Ages, for instance, one of the deadliest sins was a refusal to believe certain abstruse theological details, hard to comprehend and impossible to establish; or to believe differently about them. Again in nineteenth-century England some people almost reduced sin to sex—a hazardous simplification, in reaction from which many of their grandchildren made sex their only god. Therefore I should myself prefer to keep the term 'bad' for moral qualities or actions that cause suffering to others without any justifying counter-balance of good.

Secondly, every man is many-sided—as Whitman said of himself, 'I am large, I contain multitudes.' Nor does this complicated blend of good and bad remain static. Character is not only a compound of extremely various qualities, but the qualities themselves vary from year to year, even from hour to hour. The Spaniards will wisely say of a man, 'He was brave *that day*.' We are all at war with ourselves; if an 'individual' meant one literally 'undivided', no such creature would exist.

Clearly Coleridge wrote *The Ancient Mariner* in a mood very different from that in which he wrote his miserable letter to Byron (which Johnson, indeed, could not have written in any mood).

For all these reasons, judgements of character must remain extremely precarious. Yet it is often necessary to make them. A man with no sense of values is as crippled as a man cramped with prejudice.

Thirdly it has to be remembered in judging writers, that they often do—and indeed should—write with the best side of their character, and at their best moments. (It is indeed a commonplace that authors seem often less admirable and less interesting than their books.) Thus Montaigne confesses that his *Essays* kept him up to the mark in life, lest he should seem to live less uprightly than he wrote. Again, the Arabic poet al-Mutanabbi (d. 965), returning from Persia, was attacked near Kufa by the Beni Asad, and worsted; as he wheeled to flee, his slave said, 'Never be it told that *you* turned in flight, you that wrote:

> I am known to the horse-troop, the night, and the desert's expanse;
> Not more to the paper and pen than the sword and the lance.'

And al-Mutanabbi, shamed by his own verses, rode back into the battle, and fell. *Poésie oblige.*

No doubt a writer's worse qualities also are likely to get into his work—and to betray themselves there. But what still lives in Villon, ne'er-do-well as he may have been, is his bitter honesty of mind; his pity for his comrades swaying bird-pecked on the gallows, for his old mother shuddering before the fires of Hell, for the withered hags regretting their lost April, for the faded beauty of women dead long ago. What still lives in Rousseau, that walking museum of pathological curiosities—Narcissist, exhibitionist, and persecution-maniac—is his vivid sense for Nature, for simplicity, for the injustice and falsity of a decadent 'civilization' riding on the necks of the poor. The histrionic melancholy and melodrama of Byron are long dead; but not the prose and verse he wrote in blazing scorn of shams and in detestation of tyranny. The carrion-side of Baudelaire is rotten; but not his tragic compassion for human waste and suffering and shame.

[61]

In short, where good writers have been commonly judged bad characters, one may sometimes answer that the code by which they were judged was narrow; or that the writers were better men in their studies than in the active world; or that they were better men at the moments when they wrote their best work.

On the other hand, when Croker in his review of Macaulay, as Rogers put it, 'attempted murder and committed suicide', that was because the malicious feelings Croker betrayed in himself more than neutralized those that he tried to rouse in his readers. Well did Bentley say that no man was demolished but by himself; though unfortunately he also did his best to demonstrate it by his own edition of Milton.

In his *Commentaires*—'la Bible du Soldat' Henri IV called them—Blaise de Montluc (1502–77) describes his famous defence of Siena, against the forces of Charles the Fifth, in 1554–5, and the account he afterwards gave of it to Henri II. Montluc, a fiery Gascon famous for his choler, who might have been a ruder grandfather of d'Artagnan, and showed perhaps a touch of our own Montgomery, had yet astonished men by the patience and *finesse* with which, through those long months of famine and peril, he had steadied the Sienese to resist. How had he done it?

Je lui dis que je m'en étais allé un samedi au marché, et qu'en présence de tout le monde j'avais acheté un sac et une petite corde pour lier la bouche d'icelui, ensemble un fagot, ayant pris et chargé tout cela sur le col à la vue d'un chacun; et comme je fus à ma chambre, je demandai du feu pour allumer le fagot, et après je pris le sac, et là j'y mis dedans toute mon ambition, toute mon avarice, ma paillardise, ma gourmandise, ma paresse, ma partialité, mon envie et mes particularités, et toutes mes humeurs de Gascogne, bref tout ce que je pus penser qui me pourrait nuire, à considérer tout ce qu'il me fallait faire pour son service; puis après je liai fort la bouche du sac avec la corde, afin que rien n'en sortît, et mis tout cela dans le feu; et alors je me trouvai net de toutes choses qui me pouvaient empêcher en tout ce qu'il fallait que je fisse pour le service de Sa Majesté.[1]

A most vivid revelation of character; most graphically written. For, fire-eater as he was, Montluc knew the importance of being able to marshal words as well as troops. 'Je crois que c'est une très belle partie à un capitaine que de bien dire'—'Plût à Dieu que nous qui portons les armes prissions cette coutume d'écrire ce que nous voyons et faisons! Car il me semble que cela serait mieux accommodé de notre main (j'entends du fait de guerre) que non pas des gens de lettres; car ils déguisent trop les choses, et cela sent son clerc.'

Yet I quoted this passage about the siege of Siena, not for its vivid style, but because it seems to me an admirable summary of what those who wish to attain style would be wise to do, each time they took pen in hand.

You may say that you came for a lecture, not a sermon. If so, I am sorry; but I speak the truth as I see it. The beginning of style is character. This discovery was not first made by me, but by others better able to judge; and since I made it, I have been surprised to find confirmation even where one might least have looked for it. None had believed more passionately than Flaubert in the vain cry

[1] 'I told the King that I had gone off one Saturday to the market, and in sight of everybody bought a bag, and a little cord to tie its mouth, together with a faggot, taking and shouldering them all in the public view; and when I reached my room, I asked for fire to kindle the faggot, then took the bag and stuffed into it all my ambition, all my avarice, my sensuality, my gluttony, my indolence, my partiality, my envy and my eccentricities, and all my Gascon humours—in short, everything that I thought might hinder me, in view of all I had to do in his service; then I tightly tied the mouth of the bag with the cord, so that nothing should get out, and thrust it all in the fire. And thus I found myself clear of everything that could impede me in all I had to do for the service of His Majesty.'

of 'Art for Art's sake'; yet at fifty-seven, the year before he died, he writes to Madame Sabatier: 'Une théorie esthético-morale: le coeur est inséparable de l'esprit; ceux qui ont distingué l'un de l'autre n'avaient ni l'un ni l'autre.'[1] And Samuel Butler, having begun by denying style, yet comes full circle before he ends: 'I have also taken much pains, with what success I know not, to correct impatience, irritability and other like faults in my own character—and this not because I care two straws about my own character, but because I find the correction of such faults as I have been able to correct makes life easier, and saves me from getting into scrapes, and attaches nice people to me more readily. But I suppose this really is attending to style after all.' It is, indeed.

My conclusion is: If you want to write decently, do not begin by reading up all about Synecdoche and Metonymy and the other pretty figures that dance in the rhetoricians' manuals—you can meet them later; but always remember the bag of Montluc.

'But,' you may object, 'you have said that the problem of style was concerned with the impact of one personality on many. You have gone on and on about the character of the writer. But what about the character of his public? Is that not also important?'

Yes, it is: sometimes to an unfortunate degree. One can sympathize with the anger of Schopenhauer, asking if ever man had so detestable a set of contemporaries as he; or with Flaubert's 'Mon Dieu, dans quel âge m'avez-vous fait naître!' But the writers I most admire have not considered too much the tastes of their immediate public.

The arts of speaking or writing, like some sciences, can be either pure or applied. The applied form aims at some practical purpose—as in addressing a jury, canvassing a constituency, composing official memoranda or propaganda, writing for money. Here, obviously, a style is not

1 *Correspondance* (1926), VIII, p. 209 (February 1879).

good if it is not good for its audience. But the writer of
pure literature hopes to be read by men whom he does
not know—even by men unborn, whom he cannot know.
He must therefore write more to please himself, trusting
so to please others; or he may write for an ideal audience,
of the kind that he values—for *les âmes amies*. He may—
I think he should—show this unknown audience the
courtesy due to any audience, of communicating as clearly
as he can what he thinks and feels; but he may well
consider that to set about satisfying tastes not his own
would be a betrayal and a prostitution.

No doubt great writers have sometimes acted otherwise. Shakespeare seems to have contrived to serve both
God and Mammon, both his own ideals and popular taste
—though not, to judge from some bitter phrases in the
Sonnets, without moments of revulsion and shame.
Dryden, again (in contrast to the inflexible Milton) offers
a striking instance of the terrible pull exerted by public
taste, or lack of it. If much Restoration Drama is poor,
or worse, that could hardly have been otherwise with the
type of audience whose tone was set by the Whitehall of
Charles II—men and women who were largely rakes, or
brutes, or both, thinly veneered with French polish and
Spanish rhodomontade—as shallowly cynical as the bright
young of the nineteen-twenties, yet at moments as
foolishly romantic as the intoxicated young of the
eighteen-twenties. The surprising thing, then, is not
that *All for Love* should be shallower than *Antony and
Cleopatra*, but that it contains as fine things as it does.
Dryden can here be praised for not being more subdued
than he was, to what he worked in.

And then there is Scott; who, never making an idol of
literature as compared with still more important things
in life, felt no hesitation about consulting his sales-
returns to see what the public liked.

But though in judging past writers it is vital to remember the character of their audiences, I confess that my preference in this matter is for those who have never given in to the world—who have remained as proud as Lucifer, as unbending as Coriolanus. When Wordsworth, or Hopkins, follows his own crotchets to the limit, Wordsworth seems to me at times rather stupid, and Hopkins downright silly; but I respect their independence. I like the aloofness of Landor, and Stendhal's acceptance of being unappreciated for half a century to come, and Flaubert's disdain for both critics and public. And when Ibsen said that, if *Peer Gynt* were not the Norwegian idea of poetry, then it was going to become so, this seems finely consistent with his brave contempt for all 'compact majorities'.

In fine, I think the author of character will not bow too much to the character of his audience. Courtesy is better than deference. Confucius, as so often, hit the mark, when he said that the gentleman is courteous, but not pliable; the common man pliable, but not courteous.

But if character is important for style, what characteristics are most important? There are, I think, several human qualities that, despite all the variations in ethics from time to time and place to place, men have generally agreed to value; and have especially valued, whether consciously or not, in writers or speakers. I mean such things as good manners and courtesy towards readers, like Goldsmith's; good humour and gaiety, like Sterne's; good health and vitality, like Macaulay's; good sense and sincerity, like Johnson's. These are the opposites of some of the failings Montluc burnt in his bag. And I propose to treat them one by one in the chapters that follow.

III

COURTESY TO READERS—
(1) CLARITY

One should not aim at being possible to understand, but at
being impossible to misunderstand.
QUINTILIAN

Obscurité . . . vicieuse affectation.
MONTAIGNE

CHARACTER, I have suggested, is the first thing
to think about in style. The next step is to consider what characteristics can win a hearer's or a
reader's sympathy. For example, it is bad manners to
give them needless trouble. Therefore clarity. It is bad
manners to waste their time. Therefore brevity.

There clings in my memory a story once told me by
Professor Sisson. A Frenchman said to him: 'In France
it is the writer that takes the trouble; in Germany, the
reader; in England it is betwixt and between.' The
generalization is over-simple; perhaps even libellous; but
not without truth. It gives, I think, another reason why
the level of French prose has remained so high. And
this may in its turn be partly because French culture has
been based more than ours on conversation and the
salon. In most conversation, if he is muddled, wordy, or
tedious, a man is soon made, unless he is a hippopotamus,
to feel it. Further, the salon has been particularly influenced by women; who, as a rule, are less tolerant of
tedium and clumsiness than men.

First, then, clarity. The social purpose of language is
communication—to inform, misinform, or otherwise
influence our fellows. True, we also use words in solitude

[67]

to think our own thoughts, and to express our feelings to ourselves. But writing is concerned rather with communication than with self-communing; though some writers, especially poets, may talk to themselves in public. Yet, as I have said, even these, though in a sense overheard rather than heard, have generally tried to reach an audience. No doubt in some modern literature there has appeared a tendency to replace communication by a private maundering to oneself which shall inspire one's audience to maunder privately to *themselves*—rather as if the author handed round a box of drugged cigarettes of his concoction to stimulate each guest to his own solitary dreams. But I have yet to be convinced that such activities are very valuable; or that one's own dreams and meditations are much heightened by the stimulus of some other voice soliloquizing in Chinese. The irrational, now in politics, now in poetics, has been the sinister opium of our tormented and demented century.

For most prose, at all events, there is a good deal in Defoe's view of what style should be: 'I would answer, that in which a man speaking to five hundred people, of all common and various capacities, idiots or lunatics excepted, should be understood by them all.' This is, indeed, very like the verdict of Anatole France on the three most important qualities of French style: 'd'abord la clarté, puis encore la clarté, et enfin la clarté.' Poetry, and poetic prose, may sometimes gain by a looming mystery like that of mountain-cloud or thunderstorm; but ordinary prose, I think, is happiest when it is clear as the air of a spring day in Attica.

True, obscurity cannot always be avoided. It is impossible to make easy the ideas of an Einstein, or the psychology of a Proust. But even abstruse subjects are often made needlessly difficult; for instance, by the type of philosopher who, sometimes from a sound instinct of self-preservation, consistently refuses to illustrate his

[68]

meaning by *examples*; or by the type of scientific writer who goes decked out with technical jargon as an Indian brave with feathers. Most obscurity is an unmixed, and unnecessary, evil.

It may be caused by incoherence; by inconsiderateness; by overcrowding of ideas; by pomp and circumstance; by sheer charlatanism; and doubtless by other things I have not thought of.

The obscurity of incoherence may come from fumbling with thoughts, or from fumbling with words; but generally the two go together. After all, even our unspoken thinking is largely done with words. 'J'ai toujours tâché,' says the ironic Fontenelle, 'de m'entendre.' But some men have not much wish, and some not much power, to understand themselves. It is not impossible that even these should write well; but it is unlikely. Nor is it enough that individual sentences should be clear; the result may still be chaos, unless they are also clearly connected.

The obscurity of inconsiderateness is often due to egotism—to an absent-minded assumption that one's own knowledge *must* be shared by others. Browning, having familiarized himself, for *Sordello*, with the state of medieval Lombardy, tended to take for granted a like familiarity in his readers. The use of too technical language may arise from a similar reason; or from the baser one of mere pretentiousness.

The obscurity of overcrowding arises from trying to say too many things at once. It may come from having too many ideas and, like Juliet's Nurse, too little sense of relevance. A writer, I think, should be prepared ruthlessly to reject even his brightest inspirations, if they lure him off his line of argument[1]—unless, of course, like

[1] Cf. Metternich's practice: 'If there is any obscurity in what I have written . . . I follow the precept of an old and tried expert, Baron Thugut, who once advised me in such cases not to look for

Montaigne he is deliberately letting his mind ramble in an easy chair. There the result can be happy; but with Coleridge, for example, fertile in associations but weak in self-control, too often it is not. His conceptions become, to use his own image, like Surinam toads flopping along with toadlets sprouting all over them. Meredith, again, used metaphor 'to avoid the long-winded'; but it was not always very good for the metaphors. Or trouble may spring from being, not too fond of one's own ideas, but too unsure of them. This is often noticeable in young writers. After launching out into a sentence, they are seized by sudden misgivings and add qualification after qualification, in subordinate clauses, as they go. It would often be better to think again; to put aside the second thoughts that are not really necessary; and to postpone those that *are* necessary, to separate sentences.[1] Hitler's principle of 'One at a time' may often serve as well in writing as

a different wording, nor to change the thought, nor to try a different approach, but simply to concentrate on ridding the obscure passage of everything superfluous; then what is left usually gives, completely and reliably, the sense required.' (Varnhagen von Ense, *Denkwürdigkeiten* (1859), VIII, pp. 112–3.)

[1] For this reason (apart from the intrinsic ugliness, to most ears, of words like 'which', 'welches', 'qui', 'que') it seems to me a wise rule to be sparing of relative clauses. As for relative clauses within relative clauses, their effect is usually elephantine. For example: 'The prose style in *which* this method *is* embodied *is* marked by that sustained perspicuity and even tenor *which* we noticed in connection with the passage from *The Sacred Wood*, as well as by that rare intellectual delectation *which* comes from the sense of surprise and satisfaction *which* we experience at finding so many discrete facts subsumed under one theory.' Pascal himself provides a specimen still more extraordinary: 'Mais si je ne craignais aussi d'être téméraire, je crois *que* je suivrais l'avis de la plupart des gens *que* je vois, *qui*, ayant cru jusqu'ici, sur la foi publique, *que* ces propositions sont dans Jansénius, commencent à se défier du contraire, par un refus bizarre *qu'*on fait de les montrer, *qui* est tel, *que* je n'ai encore vu personne *qui* n'ait dit les y avoir vues.' (Quoted in A. Albalat, *Le Travail du Style*, p. 125.)

it served him in politics (till he broke it by invading the East before he had finished with the West). Many Renaissance writers, indeed, emulous of Cicero and Livy, were tempted to build their sentences into mazes and labyrinths, where they sometimes lost both themselves and their readers. No doubt a long period can show fine architecture; but there may be more ease, clarity, and point in more compact constructions, like Voltaire's. Besides, as he so wisely said, 'l'art d'ennuyer est de *tout dire*'.

Il y avait dans le voisinage un derviche très fameux qui passait pour le meilleur philosophe de la Turquie; ils allèrent le consulter; Pangloss porta la parole, et lui dit: Maître, nous venons vous prier de nous dire pourquoi un aussi étrange animal que l'homme a été formé.

De quoi te mêles-tu? lui dit le derviche; est-ce là ton affaire? Mais, mon révérend père, dit Candide, il y a horriblement de mal sur la terre. Qu'importe, dit le derviche, qu'il y ait du mal ou du bien? Quand sa hautesse envoie un vaisseau en Égypte, s'embarrasse-t-elle si les souris qui sont dans le vaisseau sont à leur aise ou non? Que faut-il donc faire? dit Pangloss. Te taire, dit le derviche. Je me flattais, dit Pangloss, de raisonner un peu avec vous des effets et des causes, du meilleur des mondes possibles, de l'origine du mal, de la nature de l'âme et de l'harmonie préétablie. Le derviche, à ces mots, leur ferma la porte au nez.[1]

To some simple folk this may seem contemptibly simple. Let them try to equal it. The sentences frisk past like little goblins, with eyes as bright as fire; as lively today as the day they were born. It is not, thank Heaven, the only way of writing; variety is a virtue of prose less important only than clarity; but what a good way of writing it is! Only you will not find much of it in the critical journals that guard, like long-tailed and scaly dragons, the golden fruit of literature.

[1] Voltaire, *Candide*, ch. XXX.

Paragraphs, too, like sentences, can cause obscurity by being overloaded or overlong. But whereas a long sentence, if well built, may have a certain dignity, few readers are likely to seek, or find, any particular dignity in a *long* paragraph. Indeed, paragraphs, at least in prose, seem usually things of convenience rather than of beauty. At each paragraph-end the reader can draw breath for an instant, and rest. The essential is that he should also feel it a rational place to rest—that the paragraph, in other words, should seem a unity. The considerate writer will not make such rests too rare. Short paragraphs make for ease and clarity. No doubt, if they are too short, the effect tends to become snippety, and the reader may feel he is being treated as a half-wit. And, here too, monotony can only be avoided by variety. But in case of doubt it is safer, I think, to risk making paragraphs too short than too long. '*Divide et impera.*'

The obscurity of pomp, though often pretentious, is not always so; the author may be striving, like Sir Thomas Browne, to dignify, not himself, but his theme. For me, criticism is lost in delight when I read in his *Christian Morals* such curiosities as 'move circumspectly, not meticulously, and rather carefully sollicitous than anxiously sollicitudinous'; or 'forget not how assuefaction unto anything minorates the passion from it, how constant Objects loose their hints, and steal an inadvertisement upon us';[1] or 'he who thus still advanceth in Iniquity deepeneth his deformed hue; turns a Shadow into Night, and makes himself a *Negro* in the black Jaundice'. For these are sublime absurdities; one sees Sir Thomas rubbing his hands with delight at that vision of an Ethiop made yet inkier by a 'black Jaundice'. One may, indeed, doubt if *Christian Morals* ever added a millimetre to anyone's moral stature; the homeliest adage on a porridge-bowl might be more effective. But this

[1] A wonderful disguise for 'familiarity breeds contempt'.

queer genius who imagined himself moralist, scientist, and antiquarian, was really an artist to the bone; it mattered little what he wrote about; vulgar errors, urns, quincunces—all turned in his hands to the music and fantasy of an enchanted island.

Still, one *Christian Morals* is enough for a literature. Sir Thomas is hardly for imitation; and with most writers, whether philosophers, scientists, lawyers, or critics, the obscurity of pomp becomes merely a tiresome and ridiculous nuisance—like Addison's pedant: 'Upon enquiry I found my learned friend had dined that day with Mr. Swan, the famous punster; and desiring[1] him to give me some account of Mr. Swan's conversation, he told me that he generally talked in the Paronomasia, that he sometimes gave in to the Plocé, but that in his humble opinion he shone most in the Antanaclasis.'

Similarly when some modern expounder of the beauties of literature tells us that 'the whole object of studying poetry is the reader's imaginative integration', or that 'we can only speculate on the steps by which James moved from the more limited thematic substance of *The Golden Bowl* to the more extreme polarisation of *The Princess Casamassima*', it is usually wise to shut the book. Half the essays that I read can never say that a work has 'unity'; ritual demands that it should have '*organic* unity'. I do not know how many of the writers understand what 'organic' means; not, I suspect, very many. But it seems to me by now a tired metaphor and tedious formula, which might well enjoy a rest. Why not say simply 'unity'?

The obscurity of pomp is, indeed, next neighbour to the obscurity of charlatanism, which has so long thrived,

---

[1] A somewhat pendent participle—as often in our older writers. It is easy to be more correct than they—and yet to write far worse. All the same, one may feel that Addison's use of 'he', 'him', and 'his' is here unduly casual.

and no doubt will long continue to thrive, on the human passion for being mystified; as with the parish-beadle who was asked his opinion of a sermon: 'I watna, sir, it was rather o'er-plain and simple for me. I like thae sermons bae that joombles the joodgement and confounds the sense.' Similarly Coleridge's father delighted his flock with Biblical texts in Hebrew, 'the authentic language of the Holy Ghost'; and preachers less erudite have made shift at least with Latin—even if they were only Latin rules for gender from the grammar-book. 'Mascula quae maribus' rang just as sonorously in rustic ears. We may recall, too, how a parish-clerk applied to Cowper to write some verses for the Christmas bill of mortality, because the local bard, a monumental mason, 'is a gentleman of so much reading, that the people of our town cannot understand him'.

Far earlier, in ancient Alexandria, Lycophron had produced his enigmatic *Alexandra*, a poem employing some three thousand words of which 'five hundred and eighteen are found nowhere else and one hundred and seventeen appear for the first time'. And in the first century of the Roman Empire Quintilian mocks at the obscurantism fashionable in his day: 'We think ourselves geniuses if it takes genius to understand us.' He records a teacher of rhetoric whose watchword to his pupils was 'σκότισον'—'make it dark'; and whose highest praise was the climax, 'Splendid! I can't understand it myself!' But it would be sanguine to assume that modern man has grown less gullible. 'Eh! mon Dieu,' the Goncourts record Zola exclaiming, 'je me moque comme vous de ce mot "naturalisme", et cependant je le répéterai, parce qu'il faut un baptême aux choses, pour que le public les croie neuves.'

Clarity, of course, has its limitations and its dangers. First, do not count on your readers to be grateful. I remember how, after taking a good deal of pains to make as lucid as possible a small manual on Tragedy, I had from a spy in Girton a report of the verdict of one of its readers there: 'Quite good, you know; but so simple!'

Secondly—and more important—both poetry and poetic prose may, as I have said, loom larger in a dimmer light; as *Macbeth* gains by scene after scene of literal darkness. Who could better the horror of 'To lie in cold obstruction, and to rot'? Indeed it is one of the difficulties of translating Aeschylus or Dante that the translation tends, by being clearer, to lose the more shadowy grandeur of the original.

Mallarmé, again, could come to Heredia with the disarming appeal: 'Je viens de faire une pièce superbe, mais je n'en comprends pas bien le sens, et je viens vous trouver pour que vous me l'expliquiez.' But when I read of him also asking for a copy of the notes taken down during one of his discourses, in order to 'put a little obscurity into it', I must own that, if this remark was meant seriously, I cannot take it very seriously. It remains always a little too easy to be difficult.

Yet even for ordinary prose there may sometimes be, as Burke suggested, a lack of strength in a language too lucid. It may seem dull, uninspired, prosaic. The less conscious levels of the mind may remain unstirred. Corot, it is said, would knock off work at nine in the morning—'Everything can be seen now—so there's nothing to see.' Certainly it is not much use making your reader see, if you also make him yawn; therefore it is necessary not only to make all things clear, but also, if possible, to make all things new.

Still, after all, this challenge has often been met. The verse of Milton and Racine, the prose of Burke himself and Chateaubriand can hardly be called obscure;[1] but

[1] Cf. Marmontel: 'Il n'y a peut-être pas un vers dans Racine, dans Massillon une seule phrase, dont l'intelligence coûte au lecteur ni à l'auditeur un moment de réflexion.'

still less can they be called mean. There is nothing insipid in the clarity of Goldsmith or Landor or Macaulay[1] at their best; or in the talk of Johnson; or in the letters of Dorothy Osborne and Horace Walpole. If lucid prose seems sometimes too prosaic, as with Locke and hundreds of smaller men, it is probably because the writer's personality was itself prosaic.

Prose may not have the measured march of poetry; it uses poetic diction only at its peril; but one essential resource of poetry it *can* share—metaphor. No doubt, too poetic metaphors are dangerous; and worn-out metaphors, dying of old age, are deadening; but it is for the prose-writer's imagination to find images that are neither. Purists and puritans who would deny these to prose are shearing the locks of Samson. Already Aristotle saw this (*Rhetoric*, III, 2): 'The most powerful thing both in verse and in prose, as we have already said in the *Poetics*,[2] is metaphor. And there is the more need to take loving care about this in prose, because prose has fewer resources than verse. Metaphor gives, above all, three advantages—clarity, delightfulness, unfamiliarity. And none can borrow this gift from another.' But metaphor—with simile—seems to me so much the life of style that it must be dealt with later at more length.[3]

And how is clarity to be acquired? Mainly by taking trouble; and by writing to serve people rather than to impress them. Most obscurity, I suspect, comes not so much from incompetence as from ambition—the ambition to be admired for depth of sense, or pomp of sound, or wealth of ornament. It is for the writer to think and rethink his ideas till they are clear; to put them in a clear order; to prefer (other things equal, and subject to the law of variety) short words, sentences, and paragraphs

[1] Macaulay's press-reader found only one obscure sentence in the whole *History of England*: Macaulay had good reason to be pleased.
[2] See p. 191.　　　　　　　　　[3] Ch. IX.

to long; not to try to say too many things at once; to
eschew irrelevances; and, above all, to put himself with
imaginative sympathy in his reader's place. Everyone
knows of Molière reading his plays to his cook; eight
centuries before him, in distant China, Po Chu-i had
done the like; and Swift's Dublin publisher, Faulkner,
would similarly read Swift's proofs aloud to him and two
of his men-servants—'which, if they did not comprehend, he would alter and amend, until they understood it
perfectly well'. In short, it is usually the pretentious and
the egotistic who are obscure, especially in prose; those
who write with wider sympathy, to serve some purpose
beyond themselves, must usually be muddy-minded
creatures if they cannot, or will not, be clear.

A Note on Italics

Italics are, in their small way, a contribution to
clarity; yet they sometimes incur disapproval. 'One
should so arrange one's sentences', it is argued, 'that the
meaning is clear without these contrivances'. By parity
of reasoning we should abolish marks of interrogation or
exclamation ('shriek-marks' I have heard them called);
for one *can* so arrange one's sentences that the meaning
is clear without these contrivances either. Indeed, why
not dispense with commas too? The ancients did; and
modern lawyers do, when they draft a will.

The answer seems to me that writing is merely a
substitute for speech. (Indeed, Goethe called it 'an abuse
of speech'.) It is, then, simply a matter of commonsense
convenience what symbols we use in writing to indicate
how the words should be spoken.

There is all the difference in tone between 'You are
satisfied with what you have done?' and 'You are satisfied
with what you have done!' In speech, this difference is
conveyed by the voice; in writing, by the punctuation.

But if exclamation-marks had not been invented, it might become necessary, unless the context made all clear, to replace the second by some clumsy periphrasis like 'You surely do not mean to say that you are satisfied with what you have done?'

It might indeed be argued that we could usefully have still more typographical devices to bring writing closer to speech, and the reader nearer to the writer's intentions. Thus Dr. Erasmus Darwin suggested that irony might be indicated by some symbol like 'a note of admiration inverted'! And it is perhaps surprising that fastidious poets have not evolved more of a notation to mark exactly how their verses should be recited; as musicians have, to mark how they should be sung. I do not myself hanker in the least for either of these additions to our stock of symbols; but I should be sorry to see that stock diminished by the abolition of italics as a mark of emphasis.

'We look at that familiar old tomb,' writes Thackeray, 'and think how the seats are altered since we were here, and how the doctor—not the present doctor, the doctor of *our* time—used to sit yonder, and his awful eye used to frighten us shuddering boys,[1] on whom it lighted; and how the boy next us *would* kick our shins during service time, and how the monitor would cane us afterwards because our shins were kicked.' And when Wells's hero sees asleep the plump lady at the Potwell Inn, '"*My* sort," said Mr. Polly.' To remove the italics in these passages would lose clarity: to reword them would lose brevity.

No doubt, it is dangerously easy to fall into excess; as Arnold sometimes employed in his verse an excess of exclamation-marks; and Queen Victoria in her letters,

[1] The sense, I think, would be better without this comma. (The only boys that shuddered were those on whom the doctor's eye lighted.)

an excess of underlining.[1] But this occasional abuse of useful things seems to me far from justifying their general abolition.

[1] Thackeray, though using italics more freely than many writers, realized their danger. He smiles in *The Newcomes* at the excesses of his Lady Clara: '"*Dearest, kindest* Mrs. Pendennis,"* Lady Clara wrote, with many italics, and evidently in much distress of mind, "your visit *is not to be*."' (Perhaps I am pedantic. But as Lady Clara can hardly have set her correspondence up in type, I should have thought it truer to say, not 'with many italics', but 'with many underlinings'.)

IV

COURTESY TO READERS—
(2) BREVITY AND VARIETY

> Then nothing can be nattier or nicer
>   For those who like a light and rapid style
> Than to trifle with a work of Mr. Dreiser,
>   As it comes along in waggons by the mile.
> He has taught us what a swift selective art meant
>   By descriptions of his dinner and all that,
> And his dwelling which he says is an Apartment,
>   Because he cannot stop to say 'a Flat'.
>   G. K. CHESTERTON, *Ballad of Abbreviations*

'**B**REVITIE', says the prolix Polonius, 'is the Soule of Wit.' He does not mean, of witticisms—true though that would be. He means, the soul of *intelligent discussion* (in this case, discussion of Hamlet's sanity). And, as so often, that foolish senior speaks very wisely. It surprises me that books on style usually say so little of brevity. Most poems, said Tennyson, are too long, including *Tintern Abbey* and *Mr. Sludge, the Medium.* (He might perhaps also have included *In Memoriam.*) The same is true, I think, of most prose.

Brevity is first of all a form of courtesy. 'What did you think of my speech?' Alfred de Vigny is said to have asked a friend after his reception into the Academy. 'Superb! —perhaps a little long?' 'Mais je ne suis pas fatigué!' Vigny was a noble mind; yet, like Carlyle, finely though he praised silence—'Seul le silence est grand, tout le reste est faiblesse'—he found it less easy to practise.

But it is not only ill-mannered in the individual author to waste his hearers' time; it is also a public problem.

[80]

With nearly twenty thousand volumes published yearly in Britain alone, there is a danger of good books, both new and old, being buried under bad. If the process went on indefinitely, we should finally be pushed into the sea by our libraries. Yet there are few of these books that might not at least be shorter, and all the better for being shorter; and most of them could, I believe, be most effectively shortened, not by cutting out whole chapters, but by purging sentences of their useless words, and paragraphs of their useless sentences. When Mme de Sergeville read Fontenelle's works to him in old age, 'il l'interrompit quelquefois en lui disant: cela est trop long'. And similarly Chekhov came to write: 'Odd, I have now a mania for shortness. Whatever I read—my own or other people's work—it all seems to me not short enough.' I suspect that they were both right.

In the passage that follows I have rashly attempted the kind of abbreviation I mean; putting in square brackets the words that seem to me needless. (The few changes of wording entailed by these omissions are italicized.)

When the highest intelligence [enlisted] in [the service of the higher] criticism has done all it can [ever aim at doing] in exposition of the highest things in art, there remains always something unspoken [and something undone which never in any way can be done or spoken]. The full cause of the [full] effect achieved by poetry of the first order can (*cannot*) be defined and expounded [with exact precision and certitude of accuracy by no strength of argument or subtlety of definition. All that exists of good in the best work of a Byron or a Southey can be defined, expounded, justified and classified by judicious admiration, with no fear lest anything noticeable or laudable should evade the analytic apprehension of critical goodwill]. No one can mistake what there is to admire[, no one can want words to define what it is that he admires,][1] in the [forcible

---

[1] To say that *everyone* can admire *The Isles of Greece* seems to me false; to say that *everyone* who admires it can put his admiration into words seems even falser.

and fervent][1] eloquence of [a poem so composed of strong
oratorical effects arranged in vigorous and telling succession as]
Byron's *Isles of Greece*. There is not a [single] point missed
that an orator [on the subject][2] would have aimed at making:
[there is] not a touch of rhetoric that would not[, if delivered
under favourable circumstances,][3] have brought down the
house [or shaken the platform[4] with a thunder-peal of prolonged and merited[4] applause]. It is almost as effective[, and
as genuine in its effect,] as anything in *Absalom and Achitophel*, or *The Medal*, or *The Hind and the Panther*. It is Dryden
—and Dryden at his best—done [out of couplets][5] into stanzas.
That is the [very][6] utmost [that] Byron could achieve; as the
[very][6] utmost [to which] Southey could attain was the noble
and pathetic epitome of history[, with its rapid and vivid
glimpses of tragic action and passion, cast into brief elegiac
form] in his monody on the Princess Charlotte. And the merits
of either are as easily definable as they are obvious [and un-
mistakable]. The same thing may be said of Wordsworth's
defects: it cannot be said of Wordsworth's merits. The test
of the highest poetry is that it eludes all tests. Poetry in which
there is no element at once perceptible and indefinable [by
any reader or hearer of any poetic instinct][7] may have every
other good quality; it may be as nobly ardent [and invigorating]

[1] Eloquence that is not 'forcible' is hardly eloquence; and most
readers can see for themselves that *The Isles of Greece* is 'fervid'.
Swinburne was, I think, overfond of what he might have called
'accumulative and alliterative aggregations of adjectives'.

[2] If the orator had chosen a *different* subject, he could hardly
have made the same points.

[3] Surely one may take the 'favourable circumstances' for
granted.

[4] After 'bringing down the house' (a somewhat tired metaphor),
it seems an anticlimax merely to 'shake the platform'. And unless
the applause *was* 'merited', it would be beside the point.

[5] The reader of this type of criticism may be expected to know
that Dryden's satires are in couplets. (Not that Byron's *Isles of
Greece* seems to me much like Dryden.)

[6] 'Very' is a facile means of emphasis that easily becomes a
tic. It occurs here thrice in eighteen lines.

[7] Readers *without* poetic instinct would be irrelevant.

[82]

as the best of Byron's, or as nobly mournful [and contempla-
tive] as the best of Southey's: if all its properties can [easily or
can ever][1] be [gauged and] named [by their admirers], it is
not poetry—above all it is not lyric poetry—of the first water.
There must be something in the mere progress and resonance
of the words, some secret in the very motion and cadence of the
lines, (*that remains*) inexplicable [by the most sympathetic
acuteness of criticism]. [Analysis may be able to explain how
the colours of this flower of poetry are created and combined,
but never by what process its odour is produced.[2] Witness the
first casual[3] instance that may be chosen from the high wide
range of Wordsworth's.[4]]

> Will no one tell me what she sings?
> Perhaps the plaintive numbers flow
> For old, unhappy, far-off things,
> And battles long ago.

If not another·word were left of the poem [in which] these
two last lines [occur,[5] those two lines] would suffice to show
the hand of a poet differing not in degree but in kind from the
tribe of Byron or [of] Southey. [In the whole expanse of poetry
there can hardly be two verses of more perfect and profound
and exalted beauty.[6] But if anybody does not happen to see

[1] If all the properties of the best poetry cannot 'ever' be named,
a fortiori they cannot be named '*easily*'. 'Can ever' makes 'can
easily' superfluous.

[2] Literary men are often, I think, rashly fond of scientific
analogies. It is not clear why the colours of flowers should be any
easier to explain than their scent.

[3] Critics are apt to talk as if any example taken at random must
be truly representative. Clearly it may quite well be exceptional—
the first marble pulled out of a bag may be white, and yet ninety-
nine others in it be black. Such random choices seem to me a
lazy and irritating habit—why not take the trouble to *choose* an
example that really is typical?

[4] Wordsworth's what? His poetry? But, if so, 'poetry' has to
be supplied from a good way back. For once, there seems a word
too few.

[5] No other poem would be relevant.

[6] This habit of saying that something is the most something in
all literature seems tiresome: (a) one knows the critic has not read

this, no critic of all that ever criticised from the days of Longinus to the days of Arnold, from the days of Zoilus to the days of Zola,[1] could succeed in making visible the certainty of this truth to the mind's eye of that person][2]. And this[, if the phrase may for once be used without conveying a taint of affectation[3] —this] is the mystery of Wordsworth: that [none of all great poets][4] (*no great poet*) was ever so persuaded of [his capacity to understand and] his ability to explain how his best work was done[, his highest effect attained, his deepest impression conveyed]; and yet there never was a poet whose power[, whose success, whose unquestionable triumph] was more independent of all his theories, more inexplicable by any of his rules.[5]

For the reader's convenience it is perhaps worth repeating the passage as curtailed. (A very few further changes have been made, and are italicized.)

When the highest intelligence in criticism has *said* all it can, there remains always something unspoken. The full cause of the effect achieved by poetry of the first order cannot be defined and expounded. No one, *indeed*, can mistake what

all literature; (b) if he had, he could not remember it; (c) his statement could only be true, even for him, if he had read all literature with this comparison constantly in mind (and one knows he has not); (d) it would also be necessary that the relevant qualities of all the works compared should be commensurable (which is most improbable); (e) since tastes so differ, it is certain that others would disagree.

[1] The reader naturally suspects that this odd pair is only coupled together because there are three letters common to both; a reason that seems inadequate.

[2] This is merely a roundabout way of saying 'If you disagree with me, you are imbecile'; which, even if true, would be a little dictatorial.

[3] This kind of apology seems to me a mistake. If the writer has any doubts whether a phrase is affected, he should not use it; if he is sure it is *not* affected, he should offer no excuses. *Qui s'excuse, s'accuse.*

[4] 'None of all great poets' seems to me not English; nor do I see why it should become so.

[5] Swinburne, *Miscellanies* (1911 ed.), pp. 125-7.

there is to admire in the eloquence of Byron's *Isles of Greece*.
There is not a point missed that an orator would have aimed
at making; not a touch of rhetoric that would not have brought
down the house. It is almost as effective as anything in
Absalom and Achitophel, or *The Medal*, or *The Hind and the
Panther*. It is Dryden—and Dryden at his best—done into
stanzas. That is the utmost Byron could achieve; as the utmost
Southey could attain was the noble and pathetic epitome of
history in his monody on the Princess Charlotte. And the
merits of either are as easily definable as they are obvious. The
same thing may be said of Wordsworth's defects: it cannot be
said of Wordsworth's merits. The test of the highest poetry
is that it eludes all tests. Poetry in which there is no element
at once perceptible and indefinable may have every other
good quality; it may be as nobly ardent as the best of Byron's, or
as nobly mournful as the best of Southey's: if all its properties
can be named, it is not poetry—above all it is not lyric poetry
—of the first water. There must be something in the mere
progress and resonance of the words, some secret in the very
motion and cadence of the lines, that remains inexplicable.

> Will no one tell me what she sings?
> Perhaps the plaintive numbers flow
> For old, unhappy, far-off things,
> And battles long ago.

If not another word were left of the poem, these two last lines
would suffice to show the hand of a poet differing not in degree
but in kind from the tribe of Byron or Southey. And this is
the mystery of Wordsworth: that no great poet was ever so
persuaded of his ability to explain how his best work was done;
and yet there never was a poet whose power was more independent of all his theories, more inexplicable by any of his rules.

The passage has been cut from sixty-seven lines to
thirty-one;[1] and no doubt some readers will feel that its
not very new or abstruse ideas could have been put more
shortly still. My point is that every book written in this

[1] Excluding in each case the four lines of Wordsworth.

kind of style is more than twice as long as it need be. A monstrous waste of life.

It is not that I wish to join those who decry Swinburne's genius. I retain a deep admiration for the musical prodigy who wrote parts of *Atalanta* and some of the pieces in *Poems and Ballads I*. But he suffered badly both from dearth of ideas, even of sense, and from this incurable dysentery of words.

If Swinburne had been an orator addressing a public meeting where some could only half hear, and some could only half understand the obvious; or if his object had been to work them all into a passion (for which there seems little occasion); then there might be some ground for all these rhetorical repetitions and amplifications. In fact, he is simply saying that some passages of literature move us inexplicably; they have a magic we cannot explain; and if we could explain it, they would cease to be magic. There is, of course, a similar mystery of charm about some people. It much impressed the all-explaining minds of the eighteenth century; they called it the 'Je ne sais quoi'.[1] Surely all this could have been

[1] The psychologist might add that the reason lies in unconscious or half-conscious memories and emotions; as in Hazlitt's tale of the man who in 1794, looking out of a window at Llangollen, found he had unaccountably lost his appetite, and only realized later that among the faces outside he had seen, though not consciously recognized, a government spy.

Take that, to me, enchanting verse—

And we in dreams behold the Hebrides.

It is easy enough to enumerate the chiming vowel-sounds and alliterated consonants; to point out how blessed the corruption that turned the dull ancient name 'Ĕbudes' into 'Hebrides', with its ringing 'r'; and to talk about their associations with Thomson and Collins and the '45 and Johnson and Wordsworth. Yet, after all, does it help much? Indeed one may ask if the modern critical mania for such analyses does not at times do positive harm, by trying too much to drag the unconscious up into consciousness, like

said in less than sixty-seven lines? Indeed, it perhaps need not have been said at all. For it has been said before.

Why do people talk or write like this? Mainly, I suppose, because any abundance of words, thoughts, or knowledge may tempt its possessors to abuse it. They enjoy functioning. Thus in talk, one gathers, Coleridge and Macaulay could not help spouting like Niagaras (though the best verse of the one and the prose of the other do not seem to me verbose). Then again there are differences of taste. To some, prodigality seems wealth; and flamboyance, beauty. But even if I felt so, the terrible brevity of life would demand more brevity of language; there are so many fascinating things to know, that one dare not waste time being extravagant with words. And, lastly, some have an idea that directness is not dignified enough; as with the famous Alderman who objected to the phrase, in Canning's inscription for a Pitt Memorial, 'He died poor', and wished to substitute 'He expired in indigent circumstances'.[1] That Alderman is dead; but his posterity abounds like Abraham's. Even so good a writer as Leslie Stephen can say of Young's *Annals of Agriculture* (in the very manner of Micawber), 'the pecuniary results were mainly negative'. Even so clever a critic as Saintsbury can write of Collins's poems: 'In Chalmers's large pages and compressed printing, they barely exceed the half-score, and do not reach the dozen.'[2] Which means, I suppose, 'eleven'?

There are also persons for whom, in print, quantity is itself a quality. Both pedants and simpletons can be impressed by mere bulk. Some publishers, I am told,

ancient prophets divining from entrails. Their divinations were imposture; they destroyed a living thing; and they made of it a mess.

[1] T. L. Kington Oliphant, *The New English* (1886), II, p. 232.
[2] *The Peace of the Augustans* (1948 ed.), p. 302.

dislike slim volumes of fiction, because their public likes to be well-provisioned with a fat novel for the week-end. 'Ich dehne diesen Band mehr aus,' writes Marx to Engels on 18 June 1862, 'da die deutschen Hunde den Wert der Bücher nach dem Kubikinhalt schätzen.'[1] But it does not seem a very admirable reason.

Every author's fairy godmother should provide him not only with a pen but also with a blue pencil. A good writer is one who knows also what not to write. Too many books (like some of Wells's novels) are large simply from lack of patience—it would have taken too long to make them short. One is stupefied by the energy of authors like Lope de Vega, writing eighteen hundred plays and four hundred and fifty autos, with over seventeen thousand characters, or like Balzac, George Sand, and Trollope[2] filling shelf after shelf; yet one feels it would have been better to write less and rewrite more. (Only to temperaments like theirs it was probably impossible.) No doubt to be fertile is sometimes a sign of vigorous genius; no doubt there is something valetudinarian about a costiveness like Gray's. But if there is a brevity of weakness, there is also a brevity of strength and restraint. Sappho's poems were 'few, but roses'; and of her fellow-poetess Erinna it was written long ago:

> Terse-tongued and sparely-worded was the singing of
>   Erinna,
>   And yet on those brief pages the Muses' blessing came;
> Therefore the memory fails not, that her words had power
>   to win her,
>   No shadowy wing of darkness casts night upon her
>   name;

[1] 'I am further expanding this volume, as those hounds of Germans judge the value of books by their cubic content.'

[2] Balzac produced an average of four to five volumes annually for nineteen years; Trollope lists forty-five books written from 1847 to 1879 (receipts £68,939 17s. 5d.).

Whilst we, earth's latter singers, O stranger, are left
   lying
To moulder unremembered, in heaps past numbering.
Better the muted music of the swan than all the crying
  Of jackdaws chattering shrilly across the clouds of
    spring.[1]

Tacitus' life of his father-in-law Agricola occupies
only twenty-four pages. Johnson in his *Lives*, Sainte-
Beuve in his *Causeries*, have often covered their subjects
more effectively in fifty pages, or less, than subsequent
critics in monographs ten times the size. There is, indeed,
a fine and trenchant brevity (though he had not always
practised it himself) in the dictum of the ageing Chateaubriand: 'I have written enough if my name will last:
too much, if it will not.'

But the value of brevity is not so much to make writers
write less (we can always cut them short by not reading
them), as to make them write better. It is not only a
practical, but also an artistic economy. Brevity can give
grace, force, speed.

Grace comes largely from effects produced without
apparent effort, from that subtle simplicity which has
sometimes specially distinguished the Greeks and the
French, and can be seen in the Temple of Wingless
Victory, or in the best epigrams of the Anthology; in La
Fontaine and La Rochefoucauld and La Bruyère; or
even in those three wistfully witty words with which the
Vicomtesse d'Houdetot took leave of life: 'Je me regrette.'

Says this gravestone sorrow-laden: 'Death has taken to
  his keeping,
  In the first flower of her springtide, little Theódotē.'
But the little one makes answer to her father: 'Cease from
  weeping,
  Theódotus. Unhappy all men must often be.'
     (PHILITAS OF SAMOS; *Palatine Anthology*, VII, 481.)

[1] Antipater of Sidon (*Palatine Anthology*, VII, 713).

May! Be thou never grac'd with birds that sing,
    Nor Flora's pride!
In thee all flowers and roses spring,
    Mine only died.
          (WILLIAM BROWNE, *In Obitum M. S.*)

Mais elle étoit du monde, où les plus belles choses
    Ont le pire destin;
Et, rose, elle a vécu ce que vivent les roses,
    L'espace d'un matin.
          (MALHERBE, *Consolation à M. du Périer.*)

The grace of all these is so living largely because they too, like the rose, are brief. The first two pieces are complete as they stand; the third is accompanied by seventeen other stanzas—but I am inclined to feel it would be better without them.

Similarly with the Chinese preference for short poems; where, as they put it, even after the reader has finished, 'the thought goes on'.[1]

The snow has gone from Chung-nan; spring is almost
    come.
Lovely in the distance its blue colours, the brown of the
    streets.
A thousand coaches, ten thousand horsemen pass down
    the Nine Roads;
Turns his head and looks at the mountains—not one man!
          (PO CHU-I, 772–846; tr. A. Waley.)

The red tulip I gave you, you let fall in the dust. I picked
    it up. It was all white.
In that brief moment the snow fell upon our love.
          (CHANG-WOU-KIEN, b. 1879.)

[1] According to H. A. Giles, *Chinese Literature* (1901), p. 145, the ideal length for poems in the T'ang period (A.D. 600–900) was thought to be twelve lines; though others were only eight or four. None exceeded a few hundred.

And yet despite this brevity the 1707 collection of T'ang poetry alone comprised (appalling thought!) no less than forty-eight thousand nine hundred poems, in thirty good-sized volumes.

Briefer still the Japanese *haiku*:

> A shower in spring, where an umbrella
> And a raincoat walk conversing;

or:

> A morning-glory[1] had entwined the well-bucket:
> I begged for water;[2]

or:

> My barn is burnt down—
> Nothing hides the moon;

or (of rural silence):

> A butterfly sleeps on the village bell.

A Japanese writer in this form, contemporary with Milton, Yasuhara Teishitsu, for the sake of posterity destroyed all of his poems but three. *There* was brevity indeed!

Naturally I am not suggesting that writers should all try to sail down to posterity in an armada of nutshells; I am only giving examples of 'gracious silences'. And brevity can bring not only grace but force. The unlovely communism of ancient Sparta contributed little to art or thought; but one quality of that iron race so struck the imagination of antiquity that the name of their country, Laconia, has added a word to the tongues of modern Europe—'laconism'. To the menaces, for example, of Philip of Macedon, they replied: 'The Lacedaemonians to Philip. Dionysius is at Corinth.'[3] And when he threatened, 'If I enter Laconia, you shall be exterminated', they wrote back the one word 'If'. It was, indeed, fitting that Simonides should limit to two lines his epitaph

---

[1] A beautiful creeper.

[2] *I.e.* rather than disturb the plant.

[3] Five words in the original. (Dionysius the Younger, who succeeded his father as despot of Syracuse, fell from power in 345 B.C. and ended his days in exile at Corinth, by one account as a schoolmaster.) See Plutarch, *On Garrulity*.

on the Spartans fallen in the most glorious of Greek defeats, Thermopylae:

> Tell them at Lacedaemon, passer-by,
> That here obedient to their laws we lie.

A land of iron coinage and of iron speech.

If the Spartans provide a classic example of the power gained by compression, I feel that their Athenian rivals, alike in tragedy and oratory, tended on the contrary to lose strength by wordiness. When at the end of *The Iliad* Andromache, Hecuba, and Helen mourn over the dead Hector, the three of them together speak only forty-seven lines—and it is perfect; an Attic dramatist would have lamented far longer—and moved me less.

But it was Rome, nearer in temper to Sparta, that bred two writers who seem to me among the first great literary examples of the strength of brevity; though she produced also the somewhat verbose abundance of Cicero and the amplitude of Livy. I am not thinking of 'Caesars Thrasonicall bragge of I came, saw, and overcame' (though his *Commentaries* are also an excellent example of clarity and brevity); nor of the clever, yet too snippety wisdom of Seneca: I am thinking of Horace, in those *Odes* where the sparingly chosen words stand bright and imperishable, like stones of a mosaic set in Roman cement itself as hard as stone; and of Tacitus. For I do not know any work whose first chapters surpass in tense concentration that opening of his *Histories* where he unveils his theme, and the state of the Empire in the January of A.D. 69, the Year of the Four Emperors.[1]

Opus adgredior opimum casibus, atrox praeliis, discors seditionibus, ipsa etiam pace saevom. Quattuor principes ferro interempti. Trina bella civilia, plura externa, ac plerumque permixta. Prosperae in Oriente, adversae in Occidente res.

---

[1] Cf. Montesquieu: 'Tacite qui abrégeoit tout, parce qu'il voyoit tout.'

Turbatum Illyricum; Galliae nutantes; perdomita Britannia, et statim missa; coortae in nos Sarmatarum ac Suevorum gentes; nobilitatus cladibus mutuis Dacus; mota prope etiam Parthorum arma falsi Neronis ludibrio. Iam vero Italia novis cladibus vel post longam seculorum seriem repetitis afflicta. Haustae aut obrutae urbes fecundissima Campaniae ora. Et urbs incendiis vastata, consumptis antiquissimis delubris, ipso Capitolio civium manibus incenso. Pollutae caerimoniae, magna adulteria. Plenum exsiliis mare, infecti caedibus scopuli. Atrocius in urbe saevitum.

And so to the great rolling climax:

Hic fuit rerum Romanarum status, cum Servius Galba iterum, Titus Vinius, consules inchoavere annum sibi ultimum, rei publicae prope supremum.[1]

Here is a controlled brevity, deadly as the short sword of the Roman legionary; which no uninflected language can rival, and no rendering reproduce. It is interesting to contrast the hysteria of Roman decadence in the centuries

[1] Such a style is really untranslatable; but here is a rough version: 'I am entering on a work rich in disasters, savage wars, civil strife; even its peace was cruel. Four emperors perished by the sword. There were three civil wars; more wars abroad; often both at once. Things went well in the East, ill in the West. Illyricum was troubled; the Gauls wavered; the full conquest of Britain was achieved, but at once abandoned; the Sarmatic and Suevic tribes rose against us; Dacia became famous by heavy blows given and received; Parthia, too, nearly drew the sword, duped by a false Nero. Italy itself was stricken by disasters, either wholly new or unknown for centuries. Cities were swallowed up or over-whelmed on the richest part of the Campanian coast. Rome was wasted with conflagrations; her most ancient shrines destroyed; the Capitol itself kindled by Roman hands. There were profana-tions of religious rites, adulteries in high places. The seas were crowded with exiles; and rocky islets stained with murder. Rome itself saw cruelties yet more savage. . . . Such was the state of the Empire when Servius Galba assumed his second consulship, with Titus Vinius for colleague, in the year that was to be their last, and came near being the last for Rome.' (Tacitus, *Histories*, I, 2, and 11.)

that followed. When the historian's descendant and namesake, Claudius Tacitus, was hailed emperor by the Senate in A.D. 275, it was, says the *Historia Augusta*, in the following terms: '"Trajan too came old to the throne" (repeated ten times). "Hadrian too came old to the throne" (repeated ten times). "Antoninus too came old to the throne" (repeated ten times). . . . "We make you an emperor, not a soldier" (repeated twenty times). "Command the soldiers to fight" (repeated thirty times).' And so on.[1] At the accession of Claudius (A.D. 268) such vain repetitions had been carried even to eighty times![2] As for the hysterically reiterated chants addressed by the Senate to Pertinax after the assassination of Commodus (A.D. 192), they must be read to be believed.[3] The individual phrases keep their Roman brevity; but their hysterical iteration recalls only the 'Sieg-heil' and 'Du-ce-du-ce' of Nazi and Fascist. The reader of this orgy of verbiage feels that a race grown so neurotic was doomed even without the barbarians.

And yet even in the late Latin of St. Jerome's Vulgate (383–405) the Latin tongue still keeps its terse energy. Nothing indeed can surpass the *Job* of our own Authorized Version:

Why died I not from the womb? why did I not give up the ghost when I came out of the belly?

Why did the knees prevent me? or why the breasts that I should suck?

For now I should have lain still and been quiet, I should have slept: then had I been at rest,

With kings and counsellors of the earth, which built desolate places for themselves;

Or with princes that had gold, who filled their houses with silver.

[1] Flavius Vopiscus, *Tacitus*, V.
[2] Trebellius Pollio, *Claudius*, IV.
[3] Lampridius, *Commodus*, XVIII.

But this remains far less concise than the Latin:

Quare non in vulva mortuus sum, egressus ex utero non statim perii?
Quare exceptus genibus? Cur lactatus uberibus?
Nunc enim dormiens silerem, et somno meo requiescerem:
Cum regibus et consulibus terrae, qui aedificant sibi solitudines:
Aut cum principibus, qui possident aurum et replent domos suas argento.

Forty-six words against eighty-one! No wonder Dr. Johnson would not hear of epitaphs in English.

The Dark and Middle Ages do not seem to me to have realized much of the grace or the force of brevity. Their years may often have been 'nasty, brutish, and short'; but their days and evenings must often have seemed intolerably long—so boring that men often became unborable. The absence of printing could not prevent them from writing works like great whales. Catullus and Skelton both produced poems on young ladies' sparrows; but Catullus' poem has eighteen lines; Skelton's one thousand three hundred and eighty-two. Yet at times, even in the Middle Ages, the virtue of terseness reappears in Latin hymn or vernacular lyric:

> Dies irae dies illa,
> Teste David cum Sibylla,
> Solvet saeclum cum favilla.

> The Erth goes on the Erth glittering with gold;
> The Erth goes to the Erth sooner than it wold;
> The Erth builds on the Erth castles and towers;
> The Erth says to the Erth, 'All this is ours.'

> Mais où sont les neiges d'antan?

Or again there is a splendid brevity in the best Ballads:

> May Margaret sits in her bower door
> Sewing her silken seam;
> She heard a note in Elmond's wood,
> And wish'd she there had been.

She loot the seam fa' frae her side,
The needle to her tae,
And she is on to Elmond's wood
As fast as she could gae.

And, then there are the Icelandic Sagas. Iceland gave modern Europe its earliest parliament; but also, curiously enough, some of its first lessons in reticence. Indeed, the best of these tales of men and women who feel so much, and say so little, seem to me in some ways more tragic than any stage-tragedies, where the characters have constantly to unpack their hearts in tirades; since otherwise there could be no play. Few would wish to shorten the last speeches of Antigone, or Othello, or Phèdre; and yet I am not sure that the laconic words of Njal and Bergthora before the burning of Bergthórshvoll do not move me more; or the brief, bitter utterance of Gudrun Oswifs-dottir above the slain Kiartan; or her summary in old age of her life's vicissitudes: 'I did the worst to him I loved the best'—'Theim var ek verst, er ek unna mest.' Such things go deeper and ring truer than all the windy eloquence of actors. I have seen real tragedies happen to those I knew: I found I respected most those that talked the least.

Again, Dante's *Divine Comedy* is not a terse poem; yet it is terseness that gives life to some of its greatest lines. Thanks to that, what poet more leaves his sting in his hearers?

Non ragioniam di lor, ma guarda e passa.

Vuolsi cosi colà, dove si puote
Ciò che si vuole; e più non dimandare.

Cesare armato con gli occhi grifagni.

(Of Semiramis) Che libito fe' licito in sua legge.

Amor che a nullo amato amor perdona.

Quel giorno più non vi legemmo avante.

[96]

E quindi uscimmo a riveder le stelle.

Siena mi fe', disfecemi Maremma.

It is clear that Dante consciously admired brevity (in
which his countrymen have not always followed him);
for he attributes it to his pagan worthies in Limbo:

> Genti v'eran con occhi tardi e gravi,
> Di grande autorità ne' lor sembianti;
> Parlavan rado, con voci soavi.[1]

In medieval England, Chaucer and Malory are not brief
writers; but at least they begin to show some sense of the
value of brevity:

> But flee we now prolixitee best is,
> For love of God, and lat us faste go
> Right to th' effect, withouten tales mo.

The superiority of the best *Canterbury Tales* is partly due
to a growing realization of this need. The *Knight's Tale*
is only a quarter the length of its original in Boccaccio.
Similarly Malory's stories are only from a half to a fifth
the length of *his* sources; had he been as verbose, **he**
might well have been as forgotten.

At the Renaissance men seem at first too delighted with
the new-found capacities of language to be very econo-
mical with it. Few poems are more leisurely than *The
Faerie Queene* (Spenser might have retorted that queens
should not run); and though Elizabethan drama is full
of rapid action, most of it is also gorgeously full of words.
Only seldom does it attain such superb compression as
Webster's

> Cover her face: Mine eyes dazell: she di'd yong.

True, the sonnet spread, and the sonnet is a brief form;
but it does not seem to encourage brevity so much as
might be expected; especially when written in sequences.

---

[1] Figures were there, with glances grave and slow,
   And with a semblance full of majesty;
   Seldom they spoke, with voices calm and low.

And often even a sonnet seems too long for what the sonneteer really has to say.

In Renaissance prose the Ciceronianism which had worshipped that orator's sonorous amplitude produced a natural reaction. His elaboration irritated the good sense of Erasmus, and his wordiness the Gascon energy of Montaigne. A terser rival-model was provided by Seneca; though opponents jeered at his 'pipkins', or at 'the dry chips of short-lunged Seneca', or at the 'hopping' style of his Flemish imitator Lipsius (1547–1606). So developed a long conflict between *le style périodique* and *le style coupé* (a partly needless conflict,[1] I think, since a good writer has occasions for both); until the close of the seventeenth century in England brought victory to neither, but to the gentlemanly ease of Dryden, the honest plainness of Tillotson, the scientific precision of the Royal Society.

As a thinker, Bacon condemned the over-copious fluency of Cicero; but he also condemned as only 'a little healthier' the brevity of Seneca and Tacitus, because too artificially epigrammatic. As an essayist, on the other hand, he learnt from the style of Seneca's *Epistles*. He bettered his model, however; and his epoch can show no more striking monument of concentrated brevity.

Iterations are commonly loss of time: but there is no such gain of time, as to iterate often the state of the question; for it chaseth away many a frivolous speech as it is coming forth.[2]

[1] For interesting examples see G. Williamson, *The Senecan Amble*, 1951. (The metaphor of 'ambling' comes from Shaftesbury's *Characteristics*; but it hardly seems very apt. Seneca's pointed style suggests to me less an easy-paced palfry than a, not fretful, but suavely philosophic porcupine.)

Fronto (Loeb edition, II, 102) better compares his jerky, staccato movement to 'a trotting horse that never breaks into full gallop'.

[2] How seldom really practised by chairmen! All this essay, 'Of Despatch', and that 'Of Discourse', are admirable, and relevant to our subject.

Long and curious speeches are as fit for despatch, as a robe or
mantle with a long train is for a race. Prefaces, and passages,
and excusations, and other speeches of reference to the person,
are great wastes of time; and though they seem to proceed of
modesty, they are bravery.[1] ... Above all things, order and
distribution, and singling out of parts, is the life of despatch:
so as the distribution be not too subtile; for he that doth not
divide will never enter well into business; and he that divideth
too much will never come out of it clearly. To choose time, is
to save time; and unseasonable motion is but beating the air.
(Of Despatch.)

There are also good brevities in Burton's *Anatomy of
Melancholy*; but his book rambles—though it rambles
delightfully, if taken in small doses.[2] Perhaps it is only
after 1660 that brevity, like wit, comes at last into its
own—in work like the maxims of La Rochefoucauld, the
Pensées of Pascal, the Theophrastian characters of La
Bruyère, the verse of Pope, the prose of Voltaire and
Montesquieu, or parts of Sterne and Burke and Landor.
A few examples will suffice here, as reminders of that
great age.

La véritable éloquence consiste à dire tout ce qu'il faut et
à ne dire que ce qu'il faut.[3] (LA ROCHEFOUCAULD)

Words are like leaves; and where they most abound,
Much fruit of sense beneath is rarely found. (POPE)

Yes I am proud; I must be proud to see
Men not afraid of God, afraid of me.[4] (POPE)

[1] *I.e.* ostentation.   [2] See p. 103.
[3] Briefer still in MS.—'L'éloquence est de ne dire que ce qu'il
faut.'
Cf. the effectiveness of another of La Rochefoucauld's shorten-
ings, cited by Lanson—the MS. version 'Celui qui vit sans folie
n'est pas si raisonnable qu'il voudrait le faire croire' becomes 'Qui
vit sans folie n'est pas si sage qu'il croit'.
[4] The first of these two couplets is one of those precepts of mere
good sense that have made men deny Pope the name of poet; but
if the second, with its daemonic concentration (and truth) is not
poetry, I do not know what is.

'I have left Trim my bowling-green,' said my uncle Toby.
My father smiled. 'I have also left him a small pension.' My
father looked grave. (STERNE)

Pour bien écrire, il faut sauter les idées intermédiaires; assez
pour n'être pas ennuyeux; pas trop, de peur de n'être pas
entendu. Ce sont ces suppressions heureuses qui ont fait dire
à M. Nicole que tous les bons livres étoient doubles.
(MONTESQUIEU)

Jamais vingt volumes in-folio ne feront de révolutions: ce
sont les petits livres portatifs à trente sous qui sont à craindre.
Si l'Évangile avait coûté douze cents sesterces, jamais la
réligion chrétienne ne se serait établie. (VOLTAIRE)

The present question is not how we are to be affected with
it in regard to our dignity. That is gone. I shall say no more
about it. Light lie the earth on the ashes of English pride!
(BURKE)

I had avoided him; I had slighted him; he knew it; he did
not love me; he could not.[1] (LANDOR, of Byron)

Whom should we contend with? The less? It were inglorious. The greater? It were vain. (LANDOR)

Johnson offers a curious mixture. With him, as with
Gibbon, Burke, and Rousseau, followed by Chateaubriand and the Romantics, prose reverts to an ampler
style. Johnson himself became notorious as a portent of
circumlocution: '*Network*. Anything reticulated or de-
cussated, at equal distances, with interstices between the
intersections.' Here Sir Thomas Browne might have
bestowed a ghostly smile on his pupil. On the other hand
Johnson's best things, both in his talk and in his later
writing, are admirably brief.[2] How did he feel at the

---

[1] The view has been expressed that 'to be emotive' (to me, a
horrible phrase—let us say, 'to stir emotion'), prose must be
written in *long* rhythms. Often, no doubt. But why 'must'?
These passages seem passionate enough.

[2] Johnson, to the end of his life, had really two styles—one
rather pompous and ponderous, for general disquisitions; the other

failure of his *Irene?* 'Like the Monument.' A Mr. Pot
had called his *Irene* 'the finest tragedy of modern times'
—'If Pot says so, Pot lies.' And after hearing *Irene* read
aloud in later years, he said only, 'Sir, I thought it had
been better'—and left the room. His summary of 'the
two most engaging powers of an author'—'New things
are made familiar, and familiar things are made new'—
embodies in eleven words perhaps the most essential
difference between Classic and Romantic. His dictum on
poetic diction, 'Words too familiar, or too remote, defeat
the purpose of a poet', seems to me more to the point than
all the laboured pages of dispute that were devoted to the
question by Wordsworth and Coleridge. And it was
Johnson who imagined that all books might one day be
written 'aphoristically' (as Nietzsche was, indeed, to
write much of his philosophy).

Of nineteenth-century English writers few so loved
brevity as, at times, Macaulay. Naturally he had sense
enough to choose his times; but when the moment called,
he could be as headlong as the eccentric Peterborough
whom he describes in his *War of the Succession in Spain*:
'The English government could not understand him. He
was so eccentric that they gave him no credit for the judg-
ment which he really possessed. One day he took towns
with horse-soldiers; then again he turned some hundreds
of infantry into cavalry at a moment's notice. He obtained
his political intelligence chiefly by means of love affairs,
and filled his despatches with epigrams.' You may call
this 'snip-snap'; but I think they are rather sheep who
object to those brilliant shears. I find his breathlessness
often admirably suited to the impetuous pace of war. The
Spanish treasure-fleet has run into Vigo; yet Spanish

light and lively for narrative, or for lighter moods, in letters. The
average *length* of his sentences, however, drops by two-fifths
between the early *Ramblers* and the *Lives*. (See W. K. Wimsatt,
Prose Style of Johnson, 1941.)

red-tape allowed treasure-fleets to unlade only at Cadiz.

The Chamber of Commerce at Cadiz, in the true spirit of monopoly, refused, even at this conjuncture, to bate one jot of its privilege. The matter was referred to the Council of the Indies. That body deliberated and hesitated just a day too long. Some feeble preparations for defence were made. Two ruined towers at the mouth of the bay of Vigo were garrisoned by a few ill-armed and untrained rustics; a boom was thrown across the entrance of the basin; and a few French ships of war, which had convoyed the galleons from America, were moored within. But all was to no purpose. The English ships broke the boom; Ormond and his soldiers scaled the forts; the French burned their ships, and escaped to the shore. The conquerors shared some millions of dollars; some millions more were sunk. When all the galleons had been captured or destroyed came an order in due form allowing them to unload.

With Macaulay there comes into my mind—oddly, it may seem—another nineteenth-century master of brevity, though of a graver and more iron kind. I mean that often admirable writer and talker, the Duke of Wellington.

(To an officer asking reinforcements.) 'Tell him to die where he stands.'

(To an officer asking an inordinate prolongation of leave from the Cape.) 'Sell[1] or sail.'

(When French Marshals turned their backs on him in Paris.) 'I have seen their backs before.'

And when the Duke was asked to suggest three possible names for the post of C.-in-C. India, he simply took a piece of paper and wrote three times 'Napier'.

Here was a man whom the ancient Spartans might have honoured with the freedom of Lacedaemon.[2]

[1] *I.e.* his commission.

[2] Characteristic, therefore, is Wellington's admiration for Pitt's last and shortest public speech, in reply to the Guildhall toast of 'the Saviour of Europe'—'I return you many thanks for the honour you have done me, but Europe is not to be saved by any

In our own time I know no better example to illustrate the virtues I mean than the concision of Lytton Strachey's *Portraits in Miniature*. On the whole I think we are less wordy than Victorians, yet often wordier than we need be. One would expect broadcasting, with its narrow time-limits, to encourage succinctness; but I cannot say that I see, or hear, many signs of this. Even with only twenty minutes before them, speakers ramble round their theme instead of springing at its throat. It was a very wise Scottish professor who always asked his pupils, when they brought their essays, 'Now did ye remember to tear up that first page?' Indeed, I sometimes wonder whether books would not gain if their authors had first to tele-graph them at their own expense.[1]

Brevity can give grace; it can give force; but it can also give rapidity—a more innocent form of that exhilara-tion of speed to which we sacrifice five thousand lives a year on our roads. To watch a film that moves too slowly, to follow a speaker or writer who thinks too slowly, can be both boring and exhausting; just as walking two miles at two miles an hour can be more tiring than thrice the distance at twice the speed. Here is an admirably rapid little sketch from the sardonic Burton.[2]

But to your farther content, Ile tell you a tale. In *Moronia pia*, or *Moronia faelix*, I know not whether, nor how long since,

single man. England has saved herself by her exertions, and will, as I trust, save Europe by her example.' 'That was all,' commented Wellington. 'He was scarcely up two minutes; yet nothing could be more perfect.'

[1] Even Proust might sometimes have learned from the curtness of his own Duc de Guermantes; who, it will be remembered, used to evade invitations by wiring: 'Impossible venir. Mensonge suit.'

[2] Quoted in G. Saintsbury, *History of English Prose Rhythm*; but it is remarkable not only for the briskness of its *rhythm*, but also for the tripping liveliness of its wording. Like Saintsbury, I have modernized the punctuation, which is confusingly light in the original.

nor in what Cathedrall Church, a fat Prebend fell void. The carcasse scarce cold, many sutors were up in an instant. The first had rich friends, a good purse; and he was resolved to out-bid any man before he would lose it; every man supposed he should carry it. The second was My Lord Bishops Chaplain (in whose gift it was); and he thought it his due to have it. The third was nobly born; and he meant to get it by his great parents, patrons, and allies. The fourth stood upon his worth; he had newly found out strange mysteries in Chymistry, and other rare inventions, which he would detect to the publike good. The fifth was a painfull preacher, and he was commended by the whole parish where he dwelt; he had all their hands to his Certificate. The sixth was the prebendaries son lately deceased; his father died in debt (for it, as they say), left a wife and many poor children. The seventh stood upon fair promises, which to him and his noble friends had been formerly made for the next place in his Lordships gift. The eighth pretended great losses, and what he had suffered for the Church, what pains he had taken at home and abroad; and besides he brought noble mens letters. The ninth had married a kinswoman, and he sent his wife to sue for him. The tenth was a forrain Doctor, a late convert, and wanted means. The eleventh would exchange for another; he did not like the formers site, could not agree with his neighbours and fellows upon any termes; he would be gone. The twelfth and last was (a suitor in conceit) a right honest, civil, sober man, an excellent scholar, and such a one as lived private in the Universitie; but he had neither means nor money to compasse it; besides he hated all such courses; he could not speak for himself, neither had he any friends to solicite his cause, and therefore made no suit, could not expect, neither did he hope for, or look after it. The good Bishop amongst a jury of competitors thus perplexed, and not yet resolved what to do, or on whom to bestow it, at the last, of his own accord, meer motion, and bountifull nature, gave it freely to the University student, altogether unknown to him but by fame; and, to be brief, the Academical Scholar had the Prebend sent him for a present. The newes was no sooner published abroad, but all good students rejoyced, and were much cheered up with it, though some would not beleeve it; others, as men amazed, said it was a miracle; but one amongst the rest thanked God for it, and said, '*Nunc juvat tandem studiosum esse, et Deo integro corde servire.*' You have heard my tale; but alas, it is but a tale, a meer fiction; 'twas never so, never like to be; and so let it rest.[1]

Such speed is not only stimulating in itself; it also makes the reader or hearer collaborate—instead of gaping passively as an oyster, he has to get up and run. He is challenged to be quick in the uptake; and, provided the challenge is not too severe, he enjoys it.

A similar reason underlies a fourth advantage of brevity—its power to imply things. The reader has to supply what is missing; and he relishes the result all the more because it seems partly his own.[2] Hobbes, attacking Popish priests, becomes the smiler with the knife. He draws a parallel between priests and fairies. 'Fairies marry not; but there be among them Incubi, that have copulation with flesh and blood. The Priests also marry not.'

More savage is the poisoned stab at Milman, in a letter of Beddoes: 'Mr. Milman (our poetry professor) has made me quite unfashionable here by denouncing me as "one of a villainous school". I wish him another son.' Or there is Talleyrand's thrust at the too masculine Madame de Stael who had portrayed him, along with herself, in *Delphine*: 'I hear that Madame de Stael has put us both

---

[1] *Anatomy of Melancholy*, Part II, Section III, Member VII.

[2] Herbert Spencer ('The Philosophy of Style' in *Essays Scientific, Political, and Speculative*) suggested that the essential principle of good style was economy of effort. This principle does, I think, partly explain why we value clarity, variety, and some forms of brevity. But it seems over-simple. Readers do not always wish to be as indolent as possible. On the contrary, many of them welcome, if it seems worth while, a challenge to use their wits. Indeed some, as we have seen, can take a perverse pleasure even in obscurity.

in her novel, *disguised as women.*' Or there is the
brilliant Chinese proverb (corresponding to our 'penny-
wise, pound-foolish'): 'It is useless to go to bed to save
the light, if the result is twins.'

The extreme case of this effectiveness in things left
unsaid comes when nothing is said at all—in the eloquence
of silence. In 1814, after the fall of Paris, Napoleon at
Fontainebleau assembled the officers and N.C.O.'s of the
Division Friant and announced that he would march on
the capital: 'Je compte sur vous.' This desperate proposal
was received, not with the expected acclamations, but
in complete silence. The Emperor was perturbed. But
he did not know his Old Guard. They were silent, it
turned out, merely because they accepted the plan as a
matter of course. They saw nothing to say. Yet what
words could have said so much as that silent acceptance?

Finally, besides grace and force, rapidity and sugges-
tiveness, there is sometimes a fifth advantage in brevity—
clarity. This may seem a paradox; for it is a commonplace
that brevity risks obscurity. But one has to consider not
only how much the reader or hearer grasps at the time,
but how much he still grasps afterwards. For *then* the
half may prove far more effective than the whole. Lord
Abinger (1769–1844) attributed his success at the bar to
concentration on one vital point, without dwelling overmuch on others: 'I find if I exceed half an hour, I am
always doing a mischief to my client: if I drive into the
heads of the jury important matter, I drive out matter
more important that I had previously lodged there.'
Writers are apt to forget this. No doubt their success
depends less than a barrister's on how much their
audience remembers. But their usefulness does not. (It
may be, indeed, that I have tried to pack too much into
this very book.) A good writer is a man who knows not
only what to write, but also what not to write. You can be
clear because you are brief; brief because you are clear.

But though it may be a counsel of perfection never to write a sentence without asking 'Might it not be better shorter?', brevity, like clarity, has its limitations. It is not considerate to the reader to present him continuously with matter so tersely and tensely compressed that his attention can never relax, because if he loses a word he is lost. This becomes truer still with oratory. Ben Jonson says in praise of Bacon that 'His hearers could not cough, or look aside from him, without loss.'[1] Very fine. But hearers do cough, and look aside. They also misunderstand, or forget. It is not good to feed horses on nothing but oats, or human beings on nothing but verbal tabloids. There remains sometimes a certain need of bulk. Though, even so, it may often be better to repeat a thing succinctly in two or three different ways than to say it once wordily.

There is also a further point. If a style is *too* tense, and the reader *too* concentrated, he may never be able to relax—to dream; the less conscious levels of his mind may be too much suppressed; and he may begin, perhaps without knowing it, to long for a vaguer, softer atmosphere, as a traveller among the sharp outlines of Greece grows homesick for the mistier contours and more brooding distances of northern lands.

Again, variety is a law more important even than brevity. There are few good things that one cannot have too much of, just as Athens sickened of Aristides 'the Just'; and brief sentences (which, of course, are only one form of brevity), forcible though they may be, can easily grow deadly monotonous. Hence, in part, the contempt heaped by Milton on an asthmatic opponent, who 'sets me out half a dozen phthisical mottoes, wherever he had them, hopping short in the measure of convulsion-fits; in which labour the agony of his wit having escaped

[1] The passage is imitated from Seneca the Elder on Cassius Severus. Significantly Seneca adds that Cassius was *not* a successful declaimer. He may have overdone his brevity.

[107]

narrowly, he greets us with a quantity of thumb-ring posies'.[1]

The following passage from Bentham's preface to the second edition (1822) of his *Fragment on Government*, though lively and amusing, may serve as an example of brevity carried too far, till it jerks.

Such being the tendency, such even the effects of the work, what became of it? how happened it, that, till now, not so much as a second edition has been made of it? Questions natural enough; and satisfaction, such as can be, shall accordingly be given: words as few as possible.

Advertisements, none. Bookseller did not, Author could not,[2] afford any. Ireland pirated. Concealment had been the plan: how advantageous has been already visible. Promise of secrecy had accordingly been exacted: parental weakness broke it. No longer a great man, the Author was now a nobody.[3]

[1] On this point P. B. Ballard (*Thought and Language* (1934), p. 152) gives some interesting figures for the first one hundred and fifty sentences of Macaulay's *William Pitt* and an equivalent passage of Gibbon.

Macaulay

Number of sentences with three to four words	7
Number of sentences with five to nine words	25
Number of sentences with ten to fourteen words	28
Number of sentences with fifteen to nineteen words	20
Number of sentences with over nineteen words	70

(nearly half)

Ten sentences have over sixty-five words each; and one of these has two hundred and eighteen. The *median* number of words per sentence is eighteen (*i.e.* as many sentences have more than eighteen words as have less; not to be confused with the *average* number).

In the corresponding Gibbon passage no sentence has under ten words; none has over seventy-two; and the median is 34.5. So far as it goes, this greater variety of Macaulay seems to me a gain.

[2] Much as I loathe that ubiquitous pismire of a word—'the', Bentham's omissions of it here too much suggest a telegram.

[3] When first published, the *Fragment* was variously attributed to Lord Mansfield or Lord Camden. When Bentham owned his authorship, sales fell (as happened also when Samuel Butler owned to *Erewhon*).

In catalogues, the name of Lind has been seen given to him. On the part of the men of politics, and in particular the men of law on all sides, whether endeavour was wanting to suppression may be imagined.

Clearly, then, a writer should be able to vary his length; like a bowler. Whether the modern world has much use for leviathan sentences like those of the seventeenth century, filling a page apiece,[1] may be doubted; on the other hand it is very rarely that I see in essays a sentence of less than six words. Why? Mere habit.

Variety, indeed, in a wider sense—variety in mood, feeling, and tone—seems both a necessity for the writer and a courtesy to the reader. No one would entertain a guest on the same dishes for days; and no nervous system can go on responding without fatigue to one sort of stimulus, any more than an electric bell can stand being rung for hours. The 'infinite variety' of Cleopatra (she spoke a dozen languages and, says Plutarch, 'Plato admits four sorts of flattery, but she had a thousand') was probably far more important than the length of her nose. Sincerity, of course, is more important still; one does not trust a human chameleon, like Dryden's Zimri; but a man of one mood, or one manner, tends to be as boring as a man of one book, or of one idea. Many-sidedness, both in life and literature, seems to me one of the great qualities of Chaucer and, in life, of his disciple Morris; on the other hand Morris's *Earthly Paradise*, lovely as it often is, has not the appeal of *The Canterbury Tales*, just because its graceful melancholy lacks their variety. So with Racine beside Shakespeare. A pearl may be perfect,

---

[1] I am thinking of genuinely long periods, which their construction makes indivisible; not of accumulations of short clauses separated by colons, or semicolons, which could as well be full stops. The ear can hardly tell that they are not full stops; and in style the final appeal, I think, should be to ear rather than eye.

yet in some lights it grows dull; where a diamond flashes
its brilliant answer to the least ray, no matter whence.

A Note on Epithets

One frequent transgressor against brevity is the point-
less or banal epithet. Voltaire urged that the adjective,
though it agrees in gender, number, and case, is the
noun's greatest enemy; Daudet, that the epithet should
be to its noun like a mistress, not a long-wedded wife. And
Mr. Somerset Maugham has related how he once planned
to write a book without a single epithet. This last, indeed,
seems too heroically austere. For it would be easy to
multiply examples of passages that derive most of their
magic from happy epithets.

οὔρεά τε σκιόεντα θάλασσά τε ἠχήεσσα.
Shadowy mountains and far-echoing seas.

ῥοδοδάκτυλος ᾿Ηώς.
Rosy-fingered Dawn.

῎Ιλιος ἠνεμόεσσα.
Windy Ilios.

κορυθαίολος ῞Εκτωρ.
Hector of the glancing helm. (HOMER)

Luna, dies, et nox, et noctis signa severa.
Moon, day, and night, and all night's solemn stars.

Altitonans Volturnus et Auster fulmine pollens.
Deep-thundering Volturnus and South Winds
strong with storm. (LUCRETIUS)

Fortuna omnipotens et ineluctabile Fatum.
Almighty Fortune and resistless Fate.

Confusae sonus urbis et inlaetabile murmur.
The sound of a city troubled, and a murmur void
of joy. (VIRGIL)

Wynsynge she was, as is a joly colt,
Long as a mast, and upright as a bolt. (CHAUCER)

[110]

Amelette ronsardelette,
Mignonnelette, doucelette,
Très chère hôtesse de mon corps,
Tu descends là-bas faiblette,
Pâle, maigrelette, seulette,
Dans le froid royaume des morts. (RONSARD)

The belching Whale
And humming Water.

The gilded Puddle
Which Beasts would cough at.

That glib and oylie Art.

To be imprison'd in the viewlesse windes
And blowne with restlesse violence round about
The pendant world. (SHAKESPEARE)

Now came still Evening on, and Twilight gray
Had in her sober Liverie all things clad.

They view'd the vast immeasurable Abyss,
Outrageous as a Sea, dark, wasteful, wilde. (MILTON)

Rolled round in earth's diurnal course,
    With rocks and stones and trees.

Their incommunicable sleep. (WORDSWORTH)

The unplumb'd, salt, estranging sea.[1] (ARNOLD)

Such epithets do not sacrifice brevity. They gain it.
For in one or two words they embody a whole vision or a
whole meditation. But in many writers (as in the Swinburne passage quoted above) the epithets are excessive in
quantity and deficient in quality. And if an epithet does
not really strengthen the effect, it is likely to weaken it.

[1] Perhaps suggested by Horace's 'deus abscidit Oceano dissocia-
bili'.

V

COURTESY TO READERS —
(3) URBANITY AND
SIMPLICITY

URBANITY is an old-fashioned word; perhaps an old-fashioned thing. Some geniuses have been above it; many, not geniuses, have thought themselves above it; or have not thought about it at all. But, for the ordinary writer, it seems to me an important part of being civilized. After all, etymologically, urbanity and civilization are much the same—they cover those qualities that distinguish the better type of *city*-dweller from the boor. Urbanity is that form of true politeness which sets men at ease, as contrasted with the false kind that leaves its victims stiff, red, and bothered; and it is largely based on simple sympathy and unpretentiousness. I find it an embarrassing subject on which to lay down principles; for a lecture on this form of manners finds it hard to avoid an appearance of that very pretentiousness of which it urges the avoidance. Still if one has thought about a subject for years, and hopes that some use to others may perhaps come of it, it is no use being modestly tongue-tied. Enough to admit—as of course one must—that one may be totally wrong.

In speaking, or writing, some flatter; some hector. Writers are less tempted than speakers to flatter, because the reader is out of sight, and solitary; though they have sometimes stooped to flatter particular persons from whom they had hopes. In general, however, the writer's temptation is not so much to flatter as to pontificate.

Most people like being flattered, if it is done well enough; the strange thing is that part of the public likes to be hectored, as much as healthier minds resent it. When I was a shy little boy at school, my benevolent housemaster once said: 'But people, you know, take you at your own valuation.' It is often true; yet in the long run you are likely to be found out. Their prophetic mantles, for example, served Carlyle and Ruskin very successfully for decades; yet those solemn robes look a little moth-eaten now.

But the fatal objection to hectoring, or playing oracle, is just that it entails being charlatan, or fool, or both. Life seems to me to admit only of probabilities, not certainties; and though in crises of action—say, when a ship, or a state, is in danger—dictatorial methods may be vital, in literature or thought I can see no place for dictators. Far better the historic Socrates who knew only that he knew nothing (unlike the self-opinionated personage who wears his name in some of Plato's later dialogues); far better the smiling headshake of Montaigne, tranquil on his pillow of doubt. There have been, no doubt, arrogant geniuses, like Swift, or Blake, or Chateaubriand; but there have also been other, more attractive geniuses free from all such pretentiousness, like Horace or Chaucer, Montaigne or Molière, Goldsmith or Hardy. I can hardly doubt which of these two types is the better model for those not geniuses to follow. And if this seems a platitude, I only wish it were more so in practice.

True, the modern world would hardly tolerate in criticism the vulgar horse-whipping style of the old *Quarterly* and *Blackwood's*; the few twentieth-century writers who have tried it (like D. H. Lawrence, for instance) damaged themselves more than their enemies. But if we have fewer vultures, I doubt if there is any decrease in the owls and peacocks. It is still possible, for example, for a distinguished critic, having compiled an anthology, to preface it by saying that most people will like some things in it and dislike others (which I should have thought true of all the anthologies ever made); but that only the elect few in the world who have trained themselves to appreciate poetry, will like it *all*. Which is really tantamount to saying: 'Do not dare to disagree with me. For my taste happens to be infallible.' In themselves such lapses are trivial enough. This comical dogmatism may be due in part to disinterested enthusiasm as well as to vanity. Still it is a pity when critics become infected with an epidemic itch for sitting on thrones judging the tribes of Israel. It may be endured by a long-suffering public; but it is not very good for the critics themselves. And one,of the least desirable results of too much English in Universities is that it turns out numbers of bright young men and women who will trot off half a dozen pages exposing the 'stupidity' of Tennyson, or the 'insincerity' of Hardy, quite uncramped by their own very indifferent capacity to write English, or even to spell it. No doubt it is right and natural at twenty to have strong feelings; but even at twenty it is well to have learnt some control of them.

Some, I find, are surprised at this suggestion that a writer should consider not only the convenience of his readers, by being clear and brief, but also their feelings, by not laying down the law. But I must say that my personal preference goes to the type of author who realizes that to have read a lot of books, or even to have written them, is not after all very important; that most of the things we debate so hotly are extremely debatable, and anyway will not matter two straws in fifty years' time; that since nothing matters ultimately but good states of mind, and the means to them, many an honest artisan or simple housewife gets more from life, and gives more to it, than many a writer of repute; and that it is better to gain the respect of readers than their admiration—better still, if may be, to gain their gratitude. I was struck by a curious critical quotation set recently in the Tripos:

'Morris was not a great anything—painter, poet, romancer, or philosopher—but he was a very great man.' Is to be 'a great man' not to be 'a great anything', compared with being a great artist or poet? I should have thought it the greatest thing of all. But some literary circles, it seems, judge otherwise.

Newman's portrait of a gentleman has often been admired:

> He has his eyes on all his company; . . . he can recollect to whom he is speaking; he guards against unseasonable allusions, or topics which may irritate; he is seldom prominent in conversation, and never wearisome. . . . He has too much good sense to be affronted at insults, he is too well employed to remember injuries, and too indolent to bear malice. . . . If he engages in controversy of any kind, his disciplined intellect preserves him from the blundering discourtesy of better, perhaps, but less educated minds; who, like blunt weapons, tear and hack instead of cutting clean, who mistake the point in argument, waste their strength on trifles, misconceive their adversary, and leave the question more involved than they find it.[1] He may be right or wrong in his opinion, but he is too clear-headed to be unjust; he is as simple as he is forcible, and as brief as he is decisive.

This portrait reflects the sensitive lines of Newman's own temperament; though I find it a little solemn and Grandisonian. (There seems also—though, of course, I have not quoted the whole passage—overmuch stress on methods of controversy, as if Newman's gentleman, despite his gentleness, were a trifle disputatious; perhaps Newman was remembering the battles of his own career.) But it illustrates some of the points I have tried to make.

There is, however, a companion-picture from the eighteenth century that moves me to far warmer sym-

---

[1] But would really 'better' minds, even if 'less educated', be so very blundering?

[115]

pathy, and renders much better what I imagine by 'urbanity'. Nothing more typical, indeed, was ever written by that most charming person, the Prince de Ligne (1735–1814).

Tout le monde a de l'esprit à présent, mais, s'il n'y en a pas beaucoup dans les idées, méfiez-vous des phrases. S'il n'y a pas du trait, du neuf, du piquant, de l'originalité, ces gens d'esprit sont des sots à mon avis. Ceux qui ont ce trait, ce neuf, ce piquant peuvent encore ne pas être parfaitement aimables; mais si l'on unit à cela de l'imagination, de jolis détails, peut-être même des disparates heureux, des choses imprévues qui partent comme un éclair, de la finesse, de l'élégance, de la justesse, un joli genre d'instruction, de la raison qui ne soit pas fatigante, jamais rien de vulgaire, un maintien simple ou distingué, un choix heureux d'expressions, de la gaieté, de l'à-propos, de la grâce, de la négligence,[1] une manière à soi en écrivant ou en parlant, dites alors qu'on a réellement, décidément de l'esprit, et que l'on est aimable.

Interesting, I think, this contrast between the ideals of the churchman and the soldier, of the nineteenth century and the eighteenth. I respect Newman; but I like the Prince de Ligne. Of course to some he may be irritating. 'What a "petit-maître"!' they may exclaim. 'Airing himself affectedly in his salons, while the Third Estate drudged or starved!' But culture, in the past, could only exist on exploitation. The slaves in the mines of Laurium paid for Pericles; and eighteenth-century hovels for the graces of mansion and château. That price, one hopes (if only the world learns the sense to restrict its population) may cease to be paid. But the Prince de Ligne was no fribble; he was an excellent soldier, though fate denied him opportunities, and—what is no less estimable—an admirable father (though, I am afraid, a less admirable husband); and when the old prince died during the

[1] A strange quality, some may think, to include here; yet there may be a good deal in it.

Congress of Vienna, gay to the last, he symbolized the passing of an era that, with many abuses we have since corrected, possessed certain graces we have largely lost. A circle like that of Madame du Deffand was narrow enough in many ways; it had little feeling, by our standards, for poetry; but that blind old woman, and her like, had keen vision for certain qualities that matter both in prose and in life. It would be piquant to have her comments on some writers who satisfy our own less fastidious age.

No need to exaggerate the importance of urbanity, as if it were any substitute for ideas. It is only a kind of polish. If you are Dante or Milton or Swift, you can afford to be harsh, bitter, even cruel; they lost by it as human beings, but it remains a part of their quality; and one must take rough with smooth. But more ordinary writers on more ordinary themes must keep the sympathy of their readers, if they would produce their full effect, or perhaps any effect at all. Even a scientist discussing neutrons or dwarf stars may damage his case by acrimony or arrogance.

I will conclude with an example of urbanity in practice, from a field where its practice is hardest—controversy. Perhaps the wisest way with controversy is to avoid it. There seems to me admirable wisdom in Buffon's answer to friends who wished him to controvert his critics—'Il faut laisser ces mauvaises gens dans l'incertitude.' But there are times—both in criticism, for example, and in other matters more important—when challenges have to be met; times when it becomes 'base to sit dumb and let barbarians talk'. Of the right tone for such controversy—of the effectiveness of perfect calm, courtesy, and self-control—I know no example to equal the reply of Anatole France to Brunetière.

Brunetière had fallen upon Anatole France as a critical anarchist who believed that beauty was relative, and criticism a mere confession of personal tastes. As regards the pleasure-value of literature, Anatole France seems to me absolutely right; but he seems to me to forget that literature has also influence-value. (For while it is idle to *argue* about the pleasure-value of Milton or Proust, it remains quite rational, and not unimportant, to discuss whether the religion of *Paradise Lost* is somewhat debased, or the philosophy of *À la Recherche du Temps Perdu* touched by neurotic decadence.) The point here, however, is not how far Anatole France was right in his opinion, but how admirably right he is in the tone of his reply.

M. Ferdinand Brunetière, que j'aime beaucoup, me fait une grande querelle. Il me reproche de méconnaître les lois mêmes de la critique, de n'avoir pas de critérium pour juger les choses de l'esprit, de flotter, au gré de mes instincts, parmi les contradictions, de ne pas sortir de moi-même, d'être enfermé dans ma subjectivité comme dans une prison obscure. Loin de me plaindre d'être ainsi attaqué, je me réjouis de cette dispute honorable où tout me flatte: le mérite de mon adversaire, la sévérité d'une censure qui cache beaucoup d'indulgence, la grandeur des intérêts qui sont mis en cause, car il n'y va pas moins, selon M. Brunetière, que de l'avenir intellectuel de notre pays.[1] . . .

Il est donc plus juste que je me défende tout seul. J'essayerai de le faire, mais non pas sans avoir d'abord rendu hommage à la vaillance de mon adversaire. M. Brunetière est un critique guerrier d'une intrépidité rare. Il est, en polémique, de l'école de Napoléon et des grands capitaines qui savent qu'on ne se défend victorieusement qu'en prenant l'offensive et que, se laisser attaquer, c'est être déjà à demi vaincu. Et il est venu m'attaquer dans mon petit bois, au bord de mon onde pure. C'est un rude assaillant. Il y va de l'ongle et des dents, sans compter les feintes et les ruses. J'entends par là qu'en polémique il a diverses méthodes et qu'il ne dédaigne point

[1] Already the irony peeps through. Who but a critic could suppose that the fate of nations hung upon theories of criticism?

l'intuitive, quand la déductive ne suffit pas. Je ne troublais point son eau. Mais il est contrariant et même un peu querelleur. C'est le défaut des braves. Je l'aime beaucoup ainsi. N'est-ce pas Nicolas,[1] son maître et le mien, qui a dit:

Achille déplairait moins bouillant et moins prompt.

J'ai beaucoup de désavantages s'il me faut absolument combattre M. Brunetière. Je ne signalerai pas les inégalités trop certaines et qui sautent aux yeux. J'en indiquerai seulement une qui est d'une nature tout particulière; c'est que, tandis qu'il trouve ma critique fâcheuse, je trouve la sienne excellente. Je suis par cela même réduit à cet état de défensive qui, comme nous le disions tout à l'heure, est jugé mauvais par tous les tacticiens. Je tiens en très haute estime les fortes constructions de M. Brunetière. J'admire la solidité des matériaux et la grandeur du plan. Je viens de lire les leçons professées à l'École normale par cet habile maître de conférences, sur l'Évolution de la critique depuis la Renaissance jusqu'à nos jours, et je n'éprouve aucun déplaisir à dire très haut que les idées y sont conduites avec beaucoup de méthode et mises dans un ordre heureux, imposant, nouveau. Leur marche, pesante mais sûre, rappelle cette manoeuvre fameuse des légionnaires s'avançant serrés l'un contre l'autre et couverts de leurs boucliers, à l'assaut d'une ville. Cela se nommait faire la tortue, et c'était formidable. Il se mêle, peut-être, quelque surprise à mon admiration quand je vois où va cette armée d'idées. M. Ferdinand Brunetière se propose d'appliquer à la critique littéraire les théories de l'Évolution. Et, si l'entreprise en elle-même semble intéressante et louable, on n'a pas oublié l'énergie déployée récemment par le critique de la *Revue des Deux Mondes* pour subordonner la science à la morale et pour infirmer l'autorité de toute doctrine fondée sur les sciences naturelles. . . . Il repoussait les idées darwiniennes au nom de la morale immuable. 'Ces idées, disait-il expressément, doivent être fausses, puisqu'elles sont dangereuses.' Et maintenant il fonde la critique nouvelle sur l'hypothèse de l'évolution. . . . Je ne dis pas du tout que M. Brunetiére se démente et se contredise. Je marque un trait de sa nature, un

[1] Boileau.

tour de son caractère, qui est, avec beaucoup d'esprit de suite, de donner volontiers dans l'inattendu et dans l'imprévu. On a dit un jour, qu'il était paradoxal, et il semblait bien que ce fût par antiphrase, tant sa réputation de bon raisonneur était solidement établi. Mais on a vu à la réflexion qu'il est, en effet, un peu paradoxal à sa manière. Il est prodigieusement habile dans la démonstration: il faut qu'il démontre toujours, et il aime parfois à soutenir fortement des opinions extraordinaires et mêmes stupéfiantes.

Par quel sort cruel devais-je aimer et admirer un critique qui correspond si peu à mes sentiments! Pour M. Ferdinand Brunetière, il y a simplement deux sortes de critiques, la subjective, qui est mauvaise, et l'objective, qui est bonne. Selon lui, M. Jules Lemaître, M. Paul Desjardins, et moi-même, nous sommes atteints de subjectivité, et c'est le pire des maux; car, de la subjectivité, on tombe dans l'illusion, dans la sensualité et dans la concupiscence, et l'on juge les oeuvres humaines par le plaisir qu'on en reçoit, ce qui est abominable. Car il ne faut pas se plaire à quelque ouvrage d'esprit avant de savoir si l'on a raison de s'y plaire; car, l'homme étant un animal raisonnable, il faut d'abord qu'il raisonne; car il est nécessaire d'avoir raison et il n'est pas nécessaire de trouver de l'agrément; car le propre de l'homme est de chercher à s'instruire par le moyen de la dialectique, lequel est infaillible; car on doit toujours mettre une vérité au bout d'un raisonnement, comme un noeud au bout d'une natte; car, sans cela, le raisonnement ne tiendrait pas, et il faut qu'il tienne; car on attache ensuite plusieurs raisonnements ensemble de manière à former un système indestructible, qui dure une dizaine d'années. Et c'est pourquoi la critique objective est la seule bonne.[1]

This smiling Socratic irony, this serene catalogue of Brunetière's accusations, mockingly exaggerated, is far more effective than any airs of injured innocence. I think the honey is laid on a trifle thick; but the reader is attracted to a character seemingly so free from vanity; he is tickled by that grotesque vision of the 'tortoise';

[1] *La Vie Littéraire*, III, Préface.

and, though there are moments when the disarming
smile gives place to a curt cut of the whip ('opinions
extraordinaires et stupéfiantes', 'un système indestructible, qui dure une dizaine d'années'), he is inclined to
feel that Brunetière is a cantankerous and elephantine
pedant, treated by Anatole France with excessive indulgence. Now this is a vital point. For the ordinary reader
is a perverse creature who, if he thinks a critic severe, at
once feels indulgent; but if he thinks the critic indulgent,
tends himself to become much more severe.

Again, the ordinary reader takes far less interest in
theories than in personalities; and there is no question
here which personality seems more charming and amusing. It is all not unlike Mark Antony's triumph in the
Forum over Brutus. As in jujitsu, the cleverer combatant,
seeming to yield, uses the very strength of his more rigid
antagonist to overcome him. You may say this is
demagogic vote-catching, or the cunning of an adroit
barrister. But I do not think it is so superficial. There
really *is* more reason to believe in the reasonableness of a
coolly courteous disputant who does not lose his head, and
with it his case. At all events this seems to me no bad
object-lesson of the value of urbanity in style.

But urbanity is something better than a trick for
giving pain and winning controversies. It is a main
means of strengthening that sympathy between writer
and reader which seems to me one of the most valuable
things in literature. It is not a sort of effeminate ele-
gance; it is that quality by which Marlborough, whom no
one thinks effeminate, won more goodwill even from
men whose requests he refused than they felt towards
others who granted all they asked. It involves, among
other things, an avoidance of vanity—of that self-asser-
tion which imposes one's own ego on others—faults
which the world finds less pardonable than many more
serious sins. The vanity of Cicero, to us merely a half-

endearing foible, yet cost him dear in his own day; and Caesar, though less vain than Cicero (with more grounds for being it), might yet have avoided assassination, and perhaps changed the course of history, had he preserved to the end the seeming modesty of the more prudent Augustus. The vanity of the witty and brilliant Marshal Villars (in contrast to Marlborough) not only left Saint-Simon foaming, but seriously damaged his career, by the enemies it made him at Versailles. 'L'honnête homme ne se pique de rien.' And in style it is curious how self-defeating such self-complacency can be. The ego can seem execrable. To the memory of Erskine clings that deadly gibe of *The Anti-Jacobin*, which apologized for not reporting him in full because the printer had run out of capital I's.[1] Further, by tempting a writer to pompous terminology, pretentiousness can sometimes lead him into obscurity; but the pretentiousness itself quickly becomes all too clear. Sometimes it takes the form of pedantry; which consists in attaching undue importance to scraps of knowledge, and undue importance to oneself for knowing them. Thus De Quincey—in an essay on Style, of all places—slips into the strange phrase, 'The τὸ docendum, the thing to be taught.' A simpler person would merely have said 'The thing to be taught.' If De Quincey *must* show that he knew some Latin, he

---

[1] I am sometimes asked by pupils, 'What shall we do about expressing personal opinions? Should one say "I"?' I do not see what else to say. 'We' sounds like an old-fashioned leader-writer. 'One' is often clumsy, and 'one's' still clumsier. 'The present writer' is pompous; nor was I much drawn to a facetious variation I was once offered—'the present scribe'.

'I' seems the only frank and honest form; it will not make a writer seem egotistic, unless his general tone is that. Actually it is far more modest (and often more truthful) to say 'I cannot admire this poem' than to say 'This poem is worthless', with the assurance of a President of the Immortals conducting the Last Judgement.

could have said (though it is hideous, and adds nothing whatever) 'The docendum', as we say 'The agenda'. But what barbarous whimsy made him clap a Greek definite article on to a Latin gerundive, then stick an English definite article in front of both?[1] A writer should not flap.

Or consider this from Saintsbury: 'It is written ἐν ψιλοῖς λόγοις (to adopt one proposed sense of that disputed Aristotelianism), in simple prose—if anything ever was.' Why not say 'It is written in simple prose'? Why drag in a phrase of Aristotle, of which you then have to explain that no one quite knows what it means? To show you know Greek? If you know Greek, you should know better.

Or again, from the same writer: 'Occasionally some general suggestions, inferences and even provisional axioms have cropped up, which I have endeavoured to summarize in this Conclusion, and to tabulate, more shortly and strikingly to the eye, in a third Appendix. But they are only put up and forward as jury-masts or acting-officers; though I do not take quite such a gloomy view, of at least some of them, as Mr. Midshipman Easy's poor friend, the master's mate, did of his "acting" appointment.'

Why not say, 'I have summarized in this Conclusion, and tabulated in Appendix III, some general principles;

---

[1] Compare the curious self-satisfaction of this passage from De Quincey's *Rhetoric*: 'Our explanation (of Aristotle's view of rhetoric) involves a very remarkable detection, which will tax many thousands of books with error in a particular point supposed to be as well established as the hills. We question, indeed, whether any fulminating powder, descending upon the schools of Oxford, would cause more consternation than the explosion of that novelty which we are going to discharge.' Oxford seems to have stood it pretty well. De Quincey, in Elton's phrase, 'is capable of being dismally jaunty and lamentably vulgar'. Luckily he did not always write like this.

which are, however, only provisional'? Why drag in
Mr. Midshipman Easy's poor friend, the master's mate?
Many readers will not have read Marryat's book—it is not
compulsory; many who have, will have forgotten this
particular passage; why should their time and patience be
wasted? Saintsbury was a genial and generous critic,
with a delightful delight in literature, that neither labour
nor custom could stale. He was far, I think, from the
peacock vanity of De Quincey; but he could not bear to
sacrifice, apparently, the most trivial association that
flashed across his memory as he wrote.

In consequence passages in his work like the two last
seem to me to illustrate all the three types of discourtesy
to readers that we have been discussing—lack of brevity;
lack of clarity; and a touch of pedantry and pretentiousness.

What remedy? The best I know is simple—it is
simplicity. Plain prose, I think, should be not too far from
talk, and not too near. Colloquialism seems to me odious.
'Shan't', 'won't', 'can't',[1] for example, are hateful in
prose, unless it is printed conversation in a play or story;
the later seventeenth century tried introducing them
even into verse—which was worse.[2] But that fashion, fortunately, did not last. On the other hand anyone who
talked in the style of the above quotations from De
Quincey or Saintsbury would create appalled silence or
uproarious mirth; as well sing at a breakfast-party.
Entering a salon one evening, the blind Madame du
Deffand exclaimed, 'What is this bad book you are
reading?' It was a certain wit talking—Rivarol. Now
Rivarol was, actually, a clever creature; and Madame du

---

[1] A proposed variation—'shant', 'wont', 'cant'—seems still more
unpleasant; indeed, the last is indistinguishable from 'cant' in a
worse sense.

[2] *E.g.* Otway: 'Boy, don't disturb the ashes of the dead
　　　　With thy capricious follies.'

Deffand may just have been malicious. But whereas it is no praise to say that a person talks like a book, it seems to me a high compliment to say that a book talks like a living person.

Indeed, really good styles seem to have a voice of their own. You hear it as soon as you begin to read them. For me, the prose of Yeats is one of the best examples—it has a passionate, dreamy Irish voice. In some ways Yeats seems to me a *poseur;* it is hard to be patient with his moonings down the road to Endor after a lot of mystical and mythical hocus-pocus; and his attempts in old age to run with a lot of young hares were a contrast to the quiet dignity of Hardy; none the less, another side of him was very genuine—and it speaks in his best prose.

This, too, is part of the charm of Montaigne as he chats, without ever growing vulgar, in his 'arrière-boutique'; now rambling, now pulling himself up— 'Je m'en vais bien à gauche de mon thème'; and yet justifying himself—'Est-ce pas ainsi que je parle?' Montaigne was no soldier; but he hates bookish unreality as heartily and healthily as his fellow-Gascon Montluc —'Le parler que i'ayme, c'est un parler simple et naïf, tel sur le papier qu'à la bouche; un parler succulent et nerveux, court et serré; non tant delicat et peigné, comme vehement et brusque . . . non pedantesque, non fratesque, non plaideresque, mais plustost soldatesque.' This vivid summary of the clarity, brevity, and simplicity I have been urging seems, literally, to *speak* for itself.

'Proper Words in proper Places,' said Swift, 'make the true definition of Style.'[1] That is simple enough—indeed, to me, too simple. It seems to avoid the pretentious only to fall into the bleak. It suggests, in fact, the liveliness of a blue-book. One might as well define good talk as proper

---

[1] Strictly, of course, he should have said 'makes'; for the subject is not 'Proper Words', but the whole formula 'Proper Words in Proper Places'.

remarks in proper places; or the good life as proper conduct
on proper occasions. Thus might the primmer and
grimmer sort of Victorian governess have admonished
her small victims; frowning with ascetic disapproval on
grace or gaiety. Swift's definition not only rules out the
more coloured and poetic kinds of prose, like Sir Thomas
Browne or Chateaubriand; it makes even plain prose
dull—the last thing any art should be. The truth is, I
think, that Swift had moods of morbid austerity when he
saw the world as a kind of ghastly workhouse with starkly
whitewashed walls (on which, when the fit took him, to
scribble his own obscenities). Luckily for us, the style of
Swift himself was a good deal more than proper—or
improper—words in proper places. Into its ruthlessly
swept and garnished body there entered the spirits of
scorn and hate and pride and indignation, but also of
courage and independence, of frustrated affection and
even of something like compassion. But one would
hardly gather from his definition that literature had
anything to do with feelings, of this or any other
kind.

More to our purpose, I think, is Michelet's comment
on Voltaire and Rousseau: 'Dans Voltaire la forme est
l'habit de la pensée—transparent—rien de plus. Avec
Rousseau, l'art paraît trop, et l'on voit commencer le
règne de la forme, par conséquent sa décadence.' This
admirably illustrates my point about the value of un-
pretentious simplicity; yet it seems not quite fair either
to Voltaire or to Rousseau. Voltaire's style is not just a
kind of transparent cellophane wrapped round his ideas;
others, doubtless, have had ideas as sharp and ironic and
sardonic as his; but who else could phrase those ideas in
words so brisk and crisp, so sparkling and pointed, so
mischievously gay? And, much as I prefer Voltaire to
Rousseau (whose proper coat of arms might have been a
wild man, rampant, embracing a weeping willow sur-

mounted by a March hare), I cannot see that Rousseau is 'decadent' simply because he set out to revive a more poetic kind of prose; which was to lead on to the magnificence of Chateaubriand. Let us rather be grateful that both kinds of prose exist—that the Parnassus of prose has two summits; though for most of us, and for most subjects, the less lofty of those summits seems the safer.

Let us not forget, indeed, that both summits exist. I cannot at all agree with the view of a modern critic: 'One would like to think that all of us will come to the stage of refusing to write what we would not, indeed could not, *say*, though that, of course, is not to limit our writing to what we actually do say.' For this, still more clearly than Swift's definition, cuts out the loftier kinds of prose. Again, those who import a too colloquial tone into writing, are apt to go further and import slang. The objection to this is not only that slang is often ugly, but also that it is often ephemeral. 'I should be glad', says a writer to the *Tatler* for 28 September 1710, 'to see you the Instrument of introducing into our Style that Simplicity which is the best and truest Ornament of most things in Life, which the politer Ages always aimed at in their Buildings and Dress (*Simplex munditiis*), as well as their Productions of Wit. It is manifest that all new affected Modes of Speech, whether borrowed from the Court, the Town, or the Theatre, are the first perishing Parts in any Language; and, as I could prove by many hundred Instances, have been so in ours.' The same thing happened with the linguistic reform of Russian by Lomonósov (1711–65). He drew both on Church Slavonic and on the vernacular; but, in the words of Prince Mirsky, 'because of the later evolution of the colloquial language it is often his boldest colloquialisms that seem to us most antiquated'.

Modern democracy, in many ways admirable, has yet

[127]

reached a stage where many think Pericles inferior to
Cleon, the aristocratic to the vulgar. But I believe that the
future will find two qualities fatally lacking in most
twentieth-century literature—dignity and grace. They
are both, in fact, largely aristocratic qualities. Even our
intellectuals, though they may think themselves an
intellectual aristocracy, are seldom conspicuous for either.
Much of their writing, for me, seems to oscillate between
pompousness and vulgarity—except when it combines
both. I would suggest, then, not that we should look
forward to an extinction of the grander kind of prose, but
merely that for ordinary purposes the simpler kind is
better. (Though even this kind should lack neither
dignity nor grace.)

There are, of course, two forms of simplicity in literature. There is, first, the natural simplicity of the un-
sophisticated, as in our best ballads or in Bunyan. Later,
as life grows more complex, men are apt to be captivated
by artificiality and flamboyance, as in the aureate diction
of the declining Middle Ages, or Lyly's *Euphues*, or
Heroic Drama, or the Aesthetic Movement. But those
who are wiser, I think, return at last from such futile
complexities of too artificial art to the simpler things that
really matter; just as in real life the finest characters may
become simpler as their lives draw towards their close—
not because they have grown less subtle, but because their
values have grown clearer. Such was the ideal of
Traherne:

> An easy Stile drawn from a native vein,
> A clearer Stream than that which Poets feign,
> Whose bottom may, how deep so e're, be seen,
> Is that which I think fit to win Esteem:
> Else we could speak *Zamzummim* words, and tell
> A Tale in tongues that sound like *Babel-hell*;
> In Meteors speak, in blazing Prodigies,
> Things that amaze, but will not make us wise.

The first, naïve kind of simplicity has passed away for the educated of this twentieth century; but the second kind remains.

Many writers, especially of an academic or aesthetic kind (and never more than today), seem to me to stultify themselves because they are neither clever enough to be brilliant, nor honest enough to be simple. Were they translated into Basic English, it would often become evident to everyone that they had said nothing to the purpose, and had nothing to the purpose to say.

To illustrate my meaning, I will end with two quotations. The first is from Landor.

LUCIAN. Timotheus, I love to sit by the side of a clear water, although there is nothing in it but naked stones. Do not take the trouble to muddy the stream of language for my benefit; I am not about to fish in it. . . .

I do not blame the prose-writer who opens his bosom occasionally to a breath of poetry; neither, on the contrary, can I praise the gait of that pedestrian who lifts up his legs as high on a bare heath as in a cornfield. Be authority as old and obstinate as it may, never let it persuade you that a man is the stronger for being unable to keep himself on the ground, or the weaker for breathing quietly and softly on ordinary occasions. . . .

I also live under Grace, O Timotheus! and I venerate her for the pleasures I have received at her hands. I do not believe she has quite deserted me. If my grey hairs are unattractive to her, and if the trace of her fingers is lost in the wrinkles of my forehead, still I sometimes am told it is discernible even on the latest and coldest of my writings.[1]

The other passage, full likewise of the beauty of stainless water, is a version of one of the loveliest poems in the Greek Anthology, by Ánytē of Tégea in Arcadia; an embodiment of that natural, effortless gift for style some women have had.

[1] *Lucian and Timotheus.*

On a Statue of Hermes by the Wayside

Beside the grey sea-shingle, here at the cross-roads'
    meeting,
  I, Hermes, stand and wait, where the windswept
    orchard grows.
I give, to wanderers weary, rest from the road, and
    greeting:
Cool and unpolluted from my spring the water flows.[1]

Here are all the qualities I have pleaded for—clarity;
brevity; freedom from pretentiousness or pretence.

Cool and unpolluted from my spring the water flows.

A Note on Footnotes

It is a minor question of style, and of consideration for
the reader, whether (apart from mere references) a
writer should allow himself to use footnotes.

Against them it can be argued that:

(1) they are distracting;

(2) if the author took more trouble, he could weave
them into his text.

But these arguments do not strike me as very convincing.

(1) In excess, footnotes (like most good things) can
become a nuisance; but it seems no less excessive to ban
them unconditionally.

(2) It is true that by giving himself trouble a writer
could often work his footnotes into his text; but it might
mean a good deal more trouble for the reader too. What
was a clear and lucid line of thought, might become a
labyrinth.

(3) Footnotes can increase brevity, as well as clarity.

(4) Who wants Gibbon shorn of his footnotes?

[1] *Palatine Anthology*, IX, 314.

Therefore, provided they are used with moderation and discretion, footnotes seem often fully justified.

But in recent years, especially in America, there has grown up a system of annotation neither intelligent nor considerate. Instead of putting notes at the foot of pages, it jumbles them in a vast dump at the back of the book. No normal reader much enjoys perusing a volume in two places at once; further, though he may find his way, if he has the patience, from the text to note 345, he may have a tedious search to find his way from note 345 to the relevant passage of the text. For this type of author has seldom the sense, or the courtesy, to prefix his notes with the page-numbers concerned. Consequently it may be suspected that five readers out of six either skip the notes altogether or skim through them in a lump, if they are interesting enough, without looking back at the text.

The case is different with commentaries on great literature, like Homer or Sophocles or Shakespeare. Fine writing deserves fine printing; a page of poetry is not enhanced by a rubble of scholia at the bottom; therefore such commentaries appear better at the end. But footnotes are not commentaries; and most books are not great art. Accordingly there seems much to be said for a return to the older system of putting footnotes at the foot of pages, not in a sort of boothole at the back.

VI

GOOD HUMOUR AND GAIETY

My great ambition is not to grow cross.
HORACE WALPOLE

Caressez longtemps votre phrase, elle finira par sourire.
ANATOLE FRANCE

NO manual of style that I know has a word to say of good humour; and yet, for me, a lack of it can sometimes blemish all the literary beauties and blandishments ever taught.

Good humour is, indeed, a part of urbanity. ('What!' you groan. 'Still more on that tedious topic?') But though one cannot have urbanity without good humour, one may have good humour without the least urbanity. I would suggest that a style is usually much the better for both. Any week you may read reviews that were clearly written in a temper; any year you may watch literary controversialists growing peevish and cross; but it does not make them either more pleasant or more persuasive. Even examination answers are too apt, I think, to grow vituperative and shrill about any writer who has the misfortune to displease the candidates; but they are optimistic if they imagine that most examiners find this either impressive or endearing.

Ill-humoured writing appears to have three main objects. One is to give pain; of that the less said the better. A second, often instinctive rather than reasoned, is to vent one's spleen on paper, and push it at the public. It may be good for the spleen; but less good for the public. A better outlet might have been the wastepaper basket.

[132]

A third object of cross and irritated writing is to make as many other people as possible cross and irritated also. Pope wanted Sporus and Sappho contemned and hated by others, as they were by him. But contempt and hatred do not seem, as a rule, such valuable states of mind that one should attempt to propagate them; nor is the attempt very likely to succeed. For most of our quarrels, grievances, or hates the world cares little; and posterity will care still less. Even if the persons you attack are really as evil as Iago, or as stupid as Caliban, your readers will murmur, 'Oh, exaggerated!' And they are likely either to yawn, or to laugh at you; unless you are clever enough to make them laugh *with* you (but, for that, you need humour rather than ill humour). In short, imagine the greatest man you can think of, in a bad temper—does he still, at that moment, seem great? No. Not even were he Alexander. Real greatness implies balance and control.

True, poets are proverbially irritable. The artistic temperament is apt to be highly strung; and writers, especially in the last three hundred years since they became professionals, have tended to take too little exercise. In most walks of literature you will come now and then on some dishevelled Muse, screaming and scratching. But the effects are seldom very happy. Renaissance scholars snarling at one another, 'May God confound you for your theory of impersonal verbs!' or boasting that they had made opponents die of sheer mortification; Milton hailing an antagonist as 'a pork . . . a snout in pickle . . . an apostate scarecrow'; Pope in *The Dunciad* exchanging kicks with donkeys and wrestling with chimney-sweeps; Swinburne and Furnivall baptizing each other 'Brothelsdyke' and 'Pigsbrook'—all these are hardly inspired, or inspiring. When Housman flayed incompetent scholars, generally Teutonic, he was, indeed, so clever as to be sometimes amusing, but so irritable as to become sometimes puerile; and those who most admire him may most regret that tetchy side of him. Literary Paris, with all its brilliance, has long made itself, I feel, slightly ridiculous as a perfect Corsica of petty vendettas. French writers composing their recollections too often bore one with their enemies; and if Monsieur So-and-so is rejected for the Academy, yelps of *Schadenfreude* may echo through the Press: 'Il a le pif bien défleuri.' The style suits the sentiment. And here are two longer examples of the ill effects of peevishness on men who, in their right minds, could write a good deal better.

I am informed that certain American journalists, not content with providing filth of their own for the consumption of their kind, sometimes offer to their readers a dish of beastliness which they profess to have gathered from under the chairs of more distinguished men. . . .

A foul *m*outh is so ill-*m*atched with a white beard that I would gladly believe the newspaper-scribes alone responsible for the bestial utterances which they *d*eclare to have *d*ropped from a teacher whom such *d*isciples as these exhibit to our *d*isgust and com*p*assion as *p*erforming on their obscene *p*latform the last *t*ricks of *t*ongue now possible to a gap-*t*oothed and hoary-headed ape, *c*arried at first into notice on the shoulders of *C*arlyle, and[1] who now in his *d*otage spits and chatters from a *d*irtier perch of his own *f*inding and *f*ouling: *c*oryphaeus or *c*horagus of his *B*ulgarian tribe of auto*c*opro*p*hagous *bab*oons, who make the *f*ilth they *f*eed on.[2]

It is when he comes to sex that Mr. Galsworthy collapses finally. He becomes nastily sentimental. He wants to make sex important, and he only makes it repulsive. Sentimentalism is the working off on yourself of feelings you haven't really got. We all[3] *want* to have certain feelings: feelings of love, of passionate sex, of kindliness, and so forth. Very few people really feel love, or sex passion, or kindliness, or anything else

---

[1] An irrational 'and'; but the writer was doubtless too angry to notice such trifles amid his orgy of alliteration.

[2] Swinburne, *Letter to Emerson.*   [3] All?

that goes at all deep. So the mass just fake these feelings inside themselves. Faked feelings! The world is all gummy with them. They are better than real feelings, because you can spit them out when you brush your teeth; and then tomorrow you can fake them afresh. . . .

Mr. Galsworthy's treatment of passion is really rather shameful. The whole thing is doggy to a degree. The man has a temporary 'hunger'; he is 'on the heat' as they say of dogs. The heat passes. It's done. Trot away, if you're not tangled. Trot off, looking shamefacedly over your shoulder. People have been watching! Damn them! But never mind, it'll blow over. Thank God, the bitch is trotting in the other direction. She'll soon have another trail of dogs after her. That'll wipe out my traces. Good for that! Next time I'll get properly married and do my doggishness in my own house.[1]

These two specimens seem enough to illustrate my point that peevishness may be no great improvement to a style. It would not be hard to bring similar examples from living writers or periodicals whose utterance constantly recalls the weary monotone of a fretful midge. But that, perhaps, would be ill-humoured.

This is not to suggest that good humour is always in season; or to deny that a healthy hate for certain things may become both good in itself and an excellent source of energy. There are wishy-washy people who mask their indolence or cowardice under an intolerable tolerance— the sort of persons who travelled quite serenely in Fascist Italy, and thought the Nazis had their good points, if only war-mongering liberals would not irritate them. There are times when it is good to be angry; there are things that it is feeble not to loathe. One would not wish Tacitus coolly detached towards Nero and Domitian (as Gibbon could afford to be at the calmer distance of seventeen centuries); and there is no place for good humour in

[1] D. H. Lawrence, *John Galsworthy*, in *Scrutinies*, ed. Edgell Rickword, 1928. One might have thought it impossible to be vulgarer than Swinburne to Emerson; but this, I think, succeeds.

front of Belsen and Buchenwald. But, for the writer, even that hatred and anger should be controlled. This, indeed, is one of the eternal paradoxes of both life and literature—that without passion little gets done; yet, without control of that passion, its effects are largely ill or null. One is told that the abominations of the Inquisition used to enrage Sir Richard Grenville to the point of chewing wine-glasses. Unhealthy, one would have thought; and, despite the immortal *Revenge* (whose last fight was quixotry rather than war), I suspect that Sir Francis Drake, with his good-humoured bowls, did more real good to England and more real harm to Spain.

Hate-literature—satire and invective—has never been thought the highest kind; especially in prose, which has, on the whole, less licence to be daemonic than verse. And when the pen does have to become a sword, even then it is usually more trenchant when its steel remains cold. The laughter of Horace, the indolent scorn of Dryden, the impish smile of Voltaire seem to me more effective, and more attractive, than the rage of Juvenal, the snarl of Swift, the virulence of Pope.

To genius indeed many things are possible which other men are wise to avoid. I most freely admit that great style has been sometimes produced in the worst possible humour; and that in writers a certain strength has often gone with bitterness (though it has then usually been, as with Tacitus or La Rochefoucauld, a general astringency of temper; a bitterness with things in general, rather than with particular people). The most magnificent cursing I know is in the Old Testament prophets; yet in bulk their virulence grows tedious and odious. If anything could make one sympathize with Nineveh, some of *them* would. Some ancient critics, it is true, placed Archilochus, the founder of satire, almost on a level with Homer; but time, perhaps not accidentally, has failed to preserve him; and though his savagery was supposed to have driven its victims to suicide, the best fragments of his work now surviving show pathos or humour rather than gall. Juvenal's writing, says Victor Hugo, was 'au-dessus de l'empire romain l'énorme battement du gypaëte au-dessus du nid de reptiles'. Yet here, I think, Hugo rather romanticizes; picturing himself as just such another eagle above the empire of Napoleon III. And I feel no great longing to re-read *Les Châtiments*. Indeed, if you look more closely, you will find that even Juvenal's best remembered lines come, not from his fulminations against Levantine aliens or learned ladies, but from things like his picture, sorrowful rather than angry, of the vanity of all human wishes except for soundness of body and of mind.

Similarly with the too prolonged railings or wailings of Langland, Jonson, Swift, Junius, Rousseau, Carlyle, Ruskin—it would have harmed none of them to read once a year Molière's *Misanthrope*. For, though Alceste has noble qualities, it is himself he frustrates, rather than the knaves and fools. Even the simple Uncle Toby was wiser. 'I declare, quoth my uncle Toby, my heart would not let me curse the Devil himself with so much bitterness.—He is the father of curses, replied Dr. Slop.—So am not I, replied my uncle.—But he is cursed and damned already to all eternity, replied Dr. Slop.—I am sorry for it, quoth my uncle Toby.' And even the acrid Pope sometimes knew better:

> But since, alas! frail beauty must decay,
> Curl'd or uncurl'd, since locks will turn to grey,
> Since painted, or not painted, all shall fade,
> And she who scorns a man must die a maid;
> What then remains but well our pow'r to use,
> And keep good humour still, whate'er we lose?

Had he but kept it himself! I am glad Pope's portraits of Atticus and Atossa were written; but I should not like to see them written by someone I liked personally; and a little of such things goes a long way.

Therefore, whatever genius may have done, for ordinary mortals good writing is, I believe, more likely to go with good humour. Especially in criticism. Both Sir Arthur Quiller-Couch and Sir Desmond MacCarthy, for example, doubtless made critical mistakes (even Aristotle did); they could be justly severe, when necessary, as MacCarthy was towards Mr. Auden's curious remarks on Tennyson; but nothing they wrote showed petulance, or peevishness, or pique. Anger may be a useful source of power; but it is worse than useless unless under control. And it is strange—not less strange for being not uncommon—that men should so often hope to be agreeable by being disagreeable. 'Les honnêtes gens ne boudent pas.'

Gaiety is a more positive quality than good humour— and more perilous; but equally ignored by authorities on English style (who seldom exhibit much of it). Yet I know nothing more effective than a touch of this for relaxing tension, or restoring a sense of proportion. And those who can never relax tend to become, both in life and in letters, a weariness to themselves and to others. With awkward strangers, or awkward committees, or police-constables awkward in a different sense, there is no ice-breaker to equal a smile (if you can get one)—except a laugh, which is better still. You may remember how when Wilkes was canvassing the electors of Middlesex, some sturdy citizen growled, 'Vote for you, Sir! I'd sooner vote for the Devil'; and how Wilkes smilingly rejoined, 'But in case your friend should not stand?' No wonder he was elected; no wonder he disarmed even the Tory antipathy of Johnson.

When Demeter, says the legend, was mournfully wandering the world to find her lost Persephone, she came at last to Eleusis; there the jests of a Thracian maidservant, Iambē, daughter of Pan and Echo, brought even to her sad lips a smile; and from that Iambē came the iambic metre of Ionian satire and Attic comedy, the ancestor of our own. So, for the Greeks, the consolations of gaiety received divine sanction. Comedy itself was a religious ritual; and the tragic trilogy, equally religious, had to be followed by a mocking satyric drama, 'tragedy at play'. Even philosophy learned to smile, in the dialogues of Plato, and in the tradition of the Laughing Philosopher of Abdera.

> Queen of the phantom faces that no smiles ever brighten,
>   Yet give Democritus welcome, as he comes, Persephone,
> Though dead, still gaily laughing. Laughter alone did
>   lighten
>   Even thy mother's burden, what time she mourned
>   for thee.[1]

I will admit that much ancient gaiety, except the best of Aristophanes, is apt to leave modern minds not much amused. Often it rings as thin as the laughter of ghosts. For though laughter is (fortunately) imperishable, men's ideas of the laughable are very perishable indeed. But in the modern world I think the French have realized better than the Germans or ourselves the value of gaiety, both in life and in that art of persuasion which is so large a part of style. No one has put this truth more vividly and vigorously than my beloved Montaigne, when he says of melancholy seriousness: 'Ie suis des plus exempts de cette passion, et ne l'ayme ny l'estime; quoy que le monde ayt entreprins, comme à prix faict, de l'honnorer de faveur particuliere: ils en habillent la sagesse, la vertu, la conscience; sot et vilain ornement!' And again, of philosophic wisdom: 'On a grand tort de la peindre inaccessible aux enfants, et d'un visage renfrogné, sourcilleux et terrible: qui me l'a masquée de ce fauls visage, pasle et hideux? Il n'est rien plus gay, plus gaillard, plus enioué, et à peu que ie ne die folastre.'

[1] Julianus, Prefect of Egypt; *Anth. Pal.* VII, 58.

The Gil Blas of the less subtle Lesage learns in his adventures a similar lesson: 'L'avarice et l'ambition qui me possédaient, changèrent entièrement mon humeur. Je perdis toute ma gaieté; je devins triste et rêveur, en un mot, un sot animal.' And, on a higher level, Renan remains in the same wise and sane tradition when he observes that, with all his melancholy merits, Marcus Aurelius lacked one vital thing—the kiss of a fairy at his birth; or again that excellent critic Faguet, when he finds a like deficiency in Calvin: 'Une qualité manque à ce grand style sévère, c'est la grâce, le sourire, tous les sourires. Il y en a un qui est de gaîté, il y en a un qui est d'indulgence, il y en a un qui est de sensibilité doucement émue, il y en a un qui est d'imagination brillante qui se plaît à ses découvertes et ses jeux.'

And so, in practice, it was typically French that even in the twelfth century the serious voice of Guillaume de Lorris in the first part of the *Roman de la Rose* should be succeeded by the *gaulois* mockeries of Jean de Meung; that again at the Renaissance the nearest French counterpart to More's serious *Utopia* should be the Gargantuan laughter of Rabelais.

> Mieux est de ris que de larmes escripre,
> Pour ce que rire est le propre de l'homme.

Swift might cry 'Vive la bagatelle!'; but it was Voltaire, not Swift, who practised it in his writing. And when the year 1759 produced those strange twins *Rasselas* and *Candide*, the two were as different in tone as Heraclitus and Democritus. Yet in eighteenth-century Europe the laughing Voltaire produced far more practical effect than Swift or Johnson. And even today more men read *Candide* than *Rasselas*; excellent though *Rasselas* is.

It is not, I think, that the English are fundamentally graver. If foreigners have accused us of taking our pleasures sadly, I suspect it is partly that we are apt to be stiffer and shyer than some other races when we spy strangers. But there is also among the educated English a tendency, as Scott complained, to a certain 'hypocrisy in business'—a certain distrust of public jest or irony on serious subjects; so that Lord Peterborough, it was said, was recalled from Spain because his despatches were wittier than became a general. Hence that grotesque aspiration in Gladstone's Journal: 'May we live as by the side of a grave, and looking in.' Hence, too, that astonishing accusation of frivolity brought against Chaucer by Matthew Arnold (whom others found at times too frivolous himself). For Chaucer, though one of the most English of our great writers, is perhaps also the most French.

I do not think Arnold would have much liked this typically French passage from Renan on the danger that German might perhaps become the universal language before the Day of Judgement.

If German is spoken on that day there will be confusion and many errors. I receive so many letters informing me of my eternal damnation that I have finished by regarding it as a matter of course. . . . I am confident, however, that I shall ameliorate the situation if I can converse with the good God in French. In my sleepless hours of the night I compose petitions. . . . I try nearly always to prove to Him that He is to some extent the cause of our perdition and that there are certain things that ought to have been more clearly explained. Some of my petitions, I think, are sufficiently piquant to make the Eternal smile; but it is very evident that they would lose all their salt if I were obliged to translate them into German. Let French be kept alive until the Day of Judgement. Without it I am lost.

But though this may be frivolous, I find it charming.

The practical conclusion? That must remain, I think, a question of temperament and of tact. There are some people with as little gift for gaiety as Milton's elephant trying to amuse Adam and Eve by twisting his 'lithe proboscis'—or as Milton himself. Heaven forbid that I should tempt any such into the quicksands of facetiousness. Better I were taken by the neck and cast into the Cam.

On the other hand, what life and lightness a graceful gaiety can give! In this tragic farce of a world I do not know of any virtue so underestimated. Johnson has summed up in two words that charm of Falstaff which covers (on the stage at least) all his sins—'perpetual gaiety'. Or consider this passage from Gibbon on the two Gordians: 'With the venerable proconsul, his son, who had accompanied him into Africa as his lieutenant, was likewise declared emperor. His manners were less pure, but his character was equally amiable with that of his father. Twenty-two acknowledged concubines, and a library of sixty-two thousand volumes, attested the variety of his inclinations; and from the productions which he left behind him, it appears that both the one and the other were designed for use rather than ostentation.' 'Is not this pleasant reading?' observed FitzGerald. It is. But you will not find much like it in most modern histories. Because they are written by greater men than Gibbon?

Or again, to take an example from our own field, no history of English literature in the Middle Ages and Renaissance has left such an impression on me as Jusserand's; for Jusserand not only contrived to combine the gifts of scholar and diplomat, but added to both the grace and gaiety of France.

Therefore, if you have the gift of gaiety, thank Heaven and do not be too afraid to use it, like those of whom Fuller speaks: 'some, for fear their orations should giggle, will not let them smile.' Dear Fuller!—as full of conceits as Donne and of quaintness as Sir Thomas Browne, but so much more human and humorous than either—he too got into trouble, like Sterne, for his frivolity;[1] yet it is his jests, not his serious erudition nor his portentous memory, that have kept his own memory alive.

But of course gaiety is dangerous in this country, where the owls nest thick. You must consider your subject, and your hearers. Only experience can show how they will take it. As a civil servant I have found that with one department it was possible to get attention paid to important material by making it amusing; while another department would complain that the important material could not be shown to very important persons because it was mixed with unseemly levity.

You never know.

So Boswell found, when solemn persons took amiss some passages of Johnson's wit in the *Tour to the Hebrides*. And he aptly comments, in dedicating his *Johnson* to Reynolds: 'It is related of the great Dr. Clarke, that when in one of his leisure hours he was unbending himself with a few friends in the most playful and frolicksome manner, he observed Beau Nash approaching; upon which he suddenly stopped—"My boys (said he), let us be grave: here comes a fool."'

Again, gaiety of treatment can easily be overdone. Irony is safer than facetiousness; but, for me, it should be an irony that is kindly rather than cruel. A constant grin can make in the end, as with Voltaire, an unpleasant wrinkle. This is partly, I think, why Strachey's *Queen Victoria* is far better than his *Eminent Victorians*. With the Queen he came, perhaps, to mock; but he learnt in the end to respect her, even to admire. Again, with the brilliant critical essays of Virginia Woolf, I feel that her amused passion for the fantastic became itself too fantastic; she had to heighten the oddities even of real life, as if her pen were a hypodermic syringe injecting yet

---

[1] 'Trencher-jests' (Dr. Heylin); 'style of buffoon pleasantry' (Bishop Warburton).

more alcohol into the reeling drunkenness of reality. Nothing too much.

You may find this praise of gaiety very odd. There is not much about it in most works on rhetoric since Aristotle. Yet I take comfort in the advice of Sir Henry Sidney to his famous son, Philip: 'Give yourself to be merry, for you degenerate from your father if you find not yourself most able in wit and body and to do anything when you be most merry.'

But though gaiety can be perilous, or misplaced, good humour seldom is. At least, I suggest, we can avoid in writing that dreary and portentous solemnity which I often find so oppressive in undergraduate essays, or in 'intellectual' journals, or in 'serious' books. Most that is said, most that is written, most that is done, will be dust within ten years; most of our efforts are the drums and tramplings of a nursery; I do not like nurseries that never laugh. Therefore I would dissuade you, when you write, from resembling that shepherd in Addison who had learnt to keep four eggs in the air at once, and thereby acquired 'the seriousness and gravity of a privy councellor'.

VII

GOOD SENSE AND SINCERITY

For I hold that man as hateful as the very gates of Hell,
Who says one thing, while another in his heart lies hidden well.

HOMER

SINCERITY, curiously enough, seems one of the subjects on which it is hardest to be sincere. And it grows no easier in an age when, among the glib charges which critics fling at authors, two of the commonest are 'insincerity' and 'sentimentality'.

The veriest fool nowadays, when he happens to dislike a book, is apt to reach out for these two pet missiles.

But what precisely do they mean? In practice, just as Wilde once said vulgarity was other people's manners, so 'insincerity' becomes often a mere term of abuse for other people's beliefs, 'sentimentality' for other people's feelings. We may pique ourselves on being a tough-minded generation, with no illusions left; or we may lament it; but I think it would be better if we indulged in less cant about 'sincerity'.

It is commonly taken for granted that all good work must be sincere. It may be so; but I do not know how one is to prove it. We cannot really read the hearts of the living whom we know: how should we be so sure about the hearts of the dead we have never known? Mark Antony's speech in the Forum does not strike me as wholly sincere; but it is a marvellous speech. No, I am not prepared to assume that all good writing has seemed to the writer the truth and nothing but the truth.

[145]

Again, on what evidence are we to condemn a writer as 'insincere'? Because he contradicts himself elsewhere? But we all contradict ourselves; and the man who blurts out each mood as it takes him may be more, not less, sincere than tighter-lipped persons who keep a show of consistency. Or is a man 'insincere' because he does not act according to his words? But this too happens to all of us. We may say a thing in fervid good faith on Monday, and do the opposite on Tuesday. Remember what Johnson said of his own precepts and practice in the matter of early rising.[1]

Or are we to tax a writer with insincerity because he says things which we think he must himself have seen to be preposterous? We know little of human nature if we try to set limits of this sort to its powers of self-deception, of seeing only what it wants to see. The gifted Newman could believe in prodigies like the liquefaction of the blood of Saint Januarius, and the aerial transport of the Virgin's house from Palestine to Loreto.

I would suggest, then, that we should confess a good deal more Socratic ignorance on this question of sincerity.

We may, it is true, have the strongest intuitions that a person is genuine or the reverse. But intuitions are not knowledge. It remains terribly hard to tell. When Donne writes, of Christ and His bride, the Church:

> Betray kind husband thy spouse to our sights,
> And let myne amorous soule court thy mild Dove,
> Who is most trew, and pleasing to thee, then
> When she's embrac'd and open to most men,

this stupid quip about celestial cuckoldry makes me question whether the poet, though he knew more than enough about religious terrors, really knew what religious feeling was. But one cannot be positive. Writers are creatures of mood and madness; and men may have plural

1 P. 45.

personalities, so that their right hand does not know what
their left is doing.

It is no doubt a strong argument for a man's sincerity,
if his conscience appears to make him speak or act against
his own interests. When Zola faced obloquy and exile in
defence of Dreyfus, I have no wish to question his
genuine sense of justice. But even martyrs are not always
what they seem; they may be men of perverse obstinacy;
or they may be masochists. There have been martyrs who
looked forward to the lions.

In fine, the man who seems trying to deceive others has
often first deceived himself. Deliberate hypocrites may
be far rarer than we think. 'Then', you may say, 'such
people are intellectually dishonest.' But 'intellectually
dishonest' seems to me a bad and superficial phrase.
'Dishonest' suggests deliberate cheating; but the process
here may be quite unconscious.

Therefore when a man says something that he could
not possibly say if he thought clearly and courageously
about it, I would rather not beg the question of his
intentions by talking of 'insincerity'. I would rather
use the non-committal term 'falsity': for example, 'there
seems at times a falsity in the work of Sterne'. How far
Sterne knew it, how far he planned it, we cannot know;
and should not pretend to.

I apologize for this long proem. But sincerity is an important question; and it seemed essential to clear up the
quagmire into which modern critics appear to me to have
trodden it. First, then, there seems no doubt that a style
which gives a strong impression of sincerity (like the
best of Herbert, or Johnson, or Hardy) is, to decent
readers, strongly appealing; and any suspicion of falsity,
deliberate or not, correspondingly odious. The letter of
Coleridge that I quoted[1] is one example. I do not believe
that he ever really thought he stood to Byron as a

_____
[1] P. 55.

[147]

'weakling cygnet' to a swan; but whether he did or no, the effect is emetic. Or consider these two passages, spoken above the dead.

And when you shall find that hand that has signed to one of you a *Patent* for *Title*, to another for *Pension*, to another for *Pardon*, to another for *Dispensation*, Dead: That hand that settled Possessions by his *Seale*, in the *Keeper*, and rectified *Honours* by the *sword*, in his *Marshall*, and distributed relief to the *Poore*, in his *Almoner*, and *Health* to the *Diseased*, by his *immediate Touch*, Dead: That hand that ballanced *his own three Kingdomes* so equally, as that none of them complained of one another, nor of him; and carried the *Keyes* of all the Christian world, and locked up, and let out *Armies* in their due season, Dead; how poore, how faint, how pale, how momentary, how transitory, how empty, how frivolous, how Dead things, must you necessarily thinke *Titles*, and *Possessions*, and *Favours*, and all, when you see that Hand, which was the *hand* of *Destinie*, of *Christian Destinie*, of the *Almighty God*, lie dead! It was not so *hard* a hand when we touched it last, nor so *cold* a hand when we kissed it last: That hand which was wont *to wipe all teares from all our eyes*, doth now but presse and squeaze us as so many spunges, filled one with one, another with another cause of teares. Teares that can have no other banke to bound them, but the declared and manifested *will of God*: For, till our teares flow to that heighth, that they might be called a *murmuring* against the declared will of God, it is against our Allegiance, it is *Disloyaltie*, to give our teares any stop, any termination, any measure.

As this solitary and silent girl stood there in the moonlight, a straight slim figure, clothed in a plaitless gown, the contours of womanhood so undeveloped as to be scarcely perceptible, the marks of poverty and toil effaced by the misty hour, she touched sublimity at points, and looked almost like a being who had rejected with indifference the attribute of sex for the loftier quality of abstract humanism. She stooped down and cleared away the withered flowers that Grace and herself had laid there the previous week, and put her fresh ones in their place.

[148]

'Now, my own, own love,' she whispered, 'you are mine, and on'y mine; for she has forgot 'ee at last, although for her you died! But I—whenever I get up I'll think of 'ee, and whenever I lie down I'll think of 'ee. Whenever I plant the young larches I'll think that none can plant as you planted; and whenever I split a gad, and whenever I turn the cider wring, I'll say none could do it like you. If ever I forget your name let me forget home and heaven! . . . But no, no, my love, I never can forget 'ee; for you was a good man, and did good things!'

The first of these, Donne's requiem for James I,[1] makes a magnificent Funeral March. With its splendour of imagery, its sullen refrain of 'Dead' like the tolling of the bell of old Saint Paul's, it reveals in every line the practised orator, the master-organist; and yet—as those gaunt lips roll out the cadences of this *Dies Irae,* does not the ear perhaps catch something that rings as hollow as the dead king's vault? Donne should have known well enough that James Stuart's three kingdoms had plenty of matter for 'complaint';[2] that there were plenty of eyes from which that blundering hand had never 'wiped all tears'; that no honest man in that year 1625 could really feel in honour bound to weep for the dead king with the frantic desperation of a 'murmurer against God'. Donne was a priest, and therefore vowed to truth; he stood in the presence of death, which should check vanities. No doubt, dead Caesars must be praised; but few men cannot be honestly praised for something; and 'the wisest fool in

[1] *Fifty Sermons,* XXXIII.

[2] Cf., for instance, James I's ineffable defence, to his Council, of his expensive minions: 'I, James, am neither a god nor an angel, but a man like any other. Therefore I act like a man and confess to loving those dear to me more than other men. You may be sure I love the Earl of Buckingham more than anyone else, and more than you who are here assembled. . . . *Jesus Christ* did the same, and therefore I cannot be blamed. *Christ had his John and I have my George.'*

Christendom' had his genuine parts. But not these. Did Donne know he was lying? Or was he swept away? One cannot tell. But because of that underlying falsity some of his readers are not.[1]

In the second passage, at the close of *The Woodlanders*, Hardy is writing of a girl who never lived, grieving for a man who never died. Yet here, for me, is precisely that reality—that truth—which the other lacks. George Moore thought Hardy could not write prose; Robert Bridges thought he could not write verse. So capricious is the Muse of Criticism. One may grant that Hardy seems sometimes less sure when he speaks in his own person (I am not wholly happy here about 'touched sublimity at points' or 'abstract humanism') than when he speaks through the mouths of his simpler characters. But the grief of Marty South moves me far more than the genius of John Donne. Through her voice one catches the tones of one of the most lovable writers in English Literature. If aesthetic wiseacres find this a sentimental folly, I would wish them—were it not too uncharitable—friends like themselves. And it would, I think, be a strange person who would sooner have the last words spoken over himself by Donne, with all his gifts, than by the bleak, yet compassionate honesty of Hardy. Goodness, indeed, is in literature no substitute for genius; but neither is genius for goodness.

The conclusion seems that, if you would write well, you will be wise to flee falsity like the plague; that, if you would move your readers (and for worthier motives also), it is better not to palter for one moment with sincerity. That may not save you from accusations of insincerity: but you can at least avoid deserving them. One cannot

---

[1] Beside the Sermon on the Mount, Donne's Sermons seem like Solomon in his glory beside the lilies of the field. But whether Donne's ballets of skeletons in cloth of gold have really much in common with genuine Christianity is another question.

ask oneself too often, both in writing and in re-reading
what one has written, 'Do I really mean that? Have I
said it for effect, though I know it is exaggerated? Or
from cowardice, because otherwise I should be ill thought
of?'

Clough is hardly an outstanding writer; but here he
is better worth remembering than many, because he
possessed this kind of intellectual conscience to a rare
degree. Indeed he carried it to excess. For a conscience
should be robust as well as sensitive. Still, his remains a
rare kind of excess.

> I tremble for something factitious,
> Some malpractice of heart and illegitimate process.

After all, perhaps there was something factitious about it;
I have had pain it is true: I have wept, and so have the
actors.

> But play no tricks upon thy soul, O man;
> Let fact be fact, and life the thing it can.

The language is often wry, the rhythm clumsy; but I
would have every writer know those last two lines by
heart.

Some do not agree. I remember an argument with a
clever admirer of Yeats, who admitted that Yeats was
apt at times to pose; but pleaded that all the world's a
stage on which, if he wishes, a man must be allowed a
mask. I do not feel this. Reticence, by all means—but
not pretence. Veils—but not masks.

One should not, indeed, be pedantic about veracity.
The world would be the poorer if Johnson, despite his
great phrase about 'enormous and disgusting hyperboles',
had not allowed himself a good many of them in his
conversation—if he had talked as if on oath. But conversation is not writing; and even in books one can see
that there are many hyperboles which do not deceive,
and are not meant to deceive. But, for a writer, any

serious deception remains, I think, dangerous; above all, self-deception. Indeed one can often feel more respect for a man who deceives others than for one who deceives himself. For these reasons I prefer Byron's prose to most of his verse, in which he was prone to strike attitudes, sometimes rhetorical, sometimes cynical; and to most of Shelley's verse (with certain fine exceptions), because Shelley seems to me, though in some ways the soul of sincerity, to have plunged, with the highest intentions, from one quagmire of self-deception into another.

We hear a great deal of the 'artistic conscience' which commands a writer to make his work perfect to the final hair; but I find myself perpetually driven to beg my own pupils to acquire from our scientists here some also of that scientific conscience which demands that evidence be weighed to the last scruple. I remember the late Sir John Clapham saying to me: 'When we get your men coming over to History, the trouble is that they seem to think, if they have written a nice sentence, it must be true.' I had no answer; I knew it only too well. I have spent years saying: 'Your generalization is beautifully epigrammatic. I understand that you could not bear to leave it unwritten. But consider all these exceptions to it. You knew them. If you could not bear to kill your darling, why not introduce it with the words "It might be said that", and then yourself point out the fatal objections? Then you could serve Beauty and Truth at once. At the least you could have inserted "possibly" or "sometimes" into this sweeping pronouncement.' But this advice does not seem to produce much effect. The literary mind is too apt to spurn such petty prudences. Which is why so much of our criticism, from age to age, remains a shoddy, slovenly pseudo-science—the astrology of literary stars.

One great obstacle to steady vision is, of course, not weakness of sense, but strength of feeling. Artists, even more than most men, are confronted by the perpetual dilemma—*without* passion they are likely to do little that is worth doing; yet *with* it they are constantly duped into doing the wrong thing. The only answer is to combine strong passions with strong control; but that proves not so easy. Among the most distorting of such passions is the often generous one of enthusiasm. Consider these two examples from Chesterton and Belloc—excellent and now, I think, unduly forgotten writers. Both passages seem to me quite needlessly ruined by a falsity of exaggeration, due to lack of control.

The Battle of the Marne

The driven and defeated line stood at last almost under the walls of Paris; and the world waited for the doom of the city. The gates seemed to stand open; and the Prussian was to ride into it for the third and the last time: for the end of its long epic of liberty and equality was come. And still the very able and very French individual on whom rested the last hope of the seemingly hopeless Alliance stood unruffled as a rock, in every angle[1] of his sky-blue jacket and his bull-dog figure. He had called his bewildered soldiers back when they had broken the invasion at Guise; he had silently digested the responsibility of dragging on the retreat, as in despair, to the last desperate leagues before the capital; and he stood and watched. And even as he watched[2] the whole huge invasion swerved.

Out through Paris and out and round beyond Paris, other men in dim blue coats swung out in long lines upon the plain, slowly folding upon Von Kluck like blue wings. Von Kluck stood an instant; and then, flinging a few secondary forces to delay the wing[3] that was swinging round on him, dashed

[1] The reader may wonder if this round bull-dog figure can have had many 'angles'.

[2] A small point. But unless there is a comma after 'watched', the reader may be misled for a fraction of a second to read 'watched the whole huge invasion'. And I am against readers being misled, if it can be avoided, even for a fraction of a second.

[3] 'The wing.' A moment since, it was 'wings'. And not all ears may like the jingle of 'wing' and 'swinging'.

[153]

across the Allies' line at a desperate angle, to smash it at the centre as with a hammer.[1] It was less desperate than it seemed; for he counted, and might well count, on the moral and physical bankruptcy of the British line and the end of the French line immediately in front of him, which for six days and nights he had chased before him like autumn leaves before a whirlwind. Not unlike autumn leaves, red-stained, dust-hued, and tattered, they lay there as if swept into a corner. But even as their conquerors wheeled eastwards, their bugles blew the charge; and the English went forward through the wood that is called Creçy,[2] and stamped it with their seal for the second time, in the highest moment of all the secular history of man.

But it was not now the Creçy in which English and French knights had met in a more coloured age, in a battle that was rather a tournament. It was a league of all knights for the remains of all knighthood, of all brotherhood in arms or in arts, against that which is and has been radically unknightly and radically unbrotherly from the beginning. Much was to happen after—murder and flaming folly and madness in earth and sea and sky; but all men knew in their hearts that the third Prussian thrust had failed, and Christendom was delivered once more. The empire of blood and iron rolled slowly back towards the darkness of the northern forests; and the great nations of the West went forward; where side by side as after a long lover's quarrel, went the ensigns of St. Denys and St. George.

(G. K. CHESTERTON, *The Crimes of England*)

Now all this is vigorous enough till we come to 'the highest moment of all the secular history of man'. There my interest collapses. It is as if one had watched Mr.

[1] There seems some anticlimax in 'as with a hammer'—Von Kluck was provided with equipment a good deal more formidable than hammers.

[2] Why 'Creçy' for 'Crécy' (or, if you will, 'Cressy')? Further, it becomes horribly apparent here that the author has confused Crécy-en-Brie, E. of Paris, with Crécy-en-Ponthieu, N. of Abbeville, the scene of Edward III's victory, over 100 miles away.

Chesterton with puffed cheeks blowing larger and larger this beautiful, iridescent bubble, mirroring the world; but there it bursts, leaving only dank nothingness behind. When I am told that the Marne was the highest moment in human history, even with the proviso 'secular history', I can only answer—'How do you know? How can anyone know? How can one measure such things?' Even within twenty-six years, Dunkirk and the Battle of Britain were to dwarf the Marne.

From that point onwards the passage seems to me to run romantic-mad. When I am asked to believe that England and France were the repositories of all chivalry and brotherhood in the world, or that the English and French have been through the centuries in love with one another, I can only plead that my imagination is not equal to it.

In the Belloc passage, on the other hand, the fatal hyperbole comes at the outset.

The Normans

They have been written of enough today, but who has seen them from close by or understood that brilliant interlude of power?

The little bullet-headed men, vivacious, and splendidly brave, we know that they awoke all Europe, that they first provided settled financial systems and settled governments of land, and that everywhere, from the Grampians to Mesopotamia, they were like steel when all[1] other Christians were like wood or like lead.

We know that they were a flash. They were not formed or definable at all before the year 1000; by the year 1200 they were gone. Some odd transitory phenomenon of cross-breeding, a very lucky freak in the history of the European family, produced the only body of men who all were lords and who in their collective action showed continually nothing but genius.

[1] 'All'?

[155]

(At this point a reader might excusably mutiny. Yet it is worth going on.)

The Conquest was achieved in 1070. In that same year they pulled down the wooden shed at Bury St. Edmunds, 'Unworthy,' they said, 'of a great saint,' and began the great shrine of stone. Next year it was the castle at Oxford; in 1075 Monkswearmouth, Jarrow, and the church at Chester; in 1077 Rochester and St. Alban's; in 1079 Winchester. Ely, Worcester, Thorney, Hurley, Lincoln, followed with the next years; by 1089 they had tackled[1] Gloucester, by 1092 Carlisle, by 1093 Lindisfarne, Christchurch, tall Durham . . . And this is but a short and random list of some of their greatest works in the space of one boyhood.

(HILAIRE BELLOC, Hills and the Sea)

Might it not have been wiser to let these great stones of the Normans cry aloud for themselves, in this splendid catalogue, rather than daub them with hyperbolical pictures of men 'all lords', gifted with 'continual genius'? But this seems the constant weakness of Romantic minds —what Landor called 'the hot and uncontrolled harlotry of a flaunting and dishevelled enthusiasm'. The eighteenth century had often tended at its beginning to excess of restraint. We may recall Swift's warning to a young gentleman taking orders, to avoid a moving manner of preaching—'if you ever be so unfortunate as to think you have it'. 'Else I may probably have occasion to say of you as a great person said of another upon this very subject. A lady asked him coming out of church whether it were not a very moving discourse. "Yes," he said, "I was extremely sorry, for the man is my friend."' This seems impossibly bleak; but better even that than the total abandonment of restraint which this same eighteenth century sometimes saw at its close; when, for

---

[1] I am not much taken with the idea of 'tackling' Gloucester. It seems to me an example of writing that comes *too* close to colloquial speech; which is as bad as departing too far from it.

example, Barras could screech in public at Carnot: 'There is not a louse on your body but has the right to spit in your face.'

Even Burke did not wholly escape that contagion;[1] and yet, when he flung on the floor of the House a dagger like a carving-knife, you may remember how the spirit of classicism, speaking through the lips of Sheridan, is said to have reduced melodrama to farce by sardonically inquiring, 'Where's the fork?' Almost as devastating, though less brief, was Arthur Balfour's rejoinder, just over a century later, to a similar hysteria in that eminent Nonconformist, Dr. Clifford:

We may easily forgive loose logic and erratic history: strong language about political opponents is too common to excite anything but a passing regret. . . . But I have often wondered how a man of Dr. Clifford's high character and position can sink to methods like these, and I am disposed to find the explanation in the fact that he is the unconscious victim of his own rhetoric. Whatever may have been the case originally, he is now the slave, not the master, of his style: and his style is unfortunately one which admits neither of measure nor of accuracy. Distortion and exaggeration are of its very essence. If he has to speak of our pending differences, acute, no doubt, but not unprecedented, he must needs compare them to the great Civil War. If he has to describe a deputation of Non-

---

[1] For example, when he accused Pitt's Regency Bill of putting a crown of thorns on the King's head, and a reed in his hand, with the cry, 'Hail, King of the British!'; when he called Louis XVI 'a man with the best intentions that probably ever reigned'; and the French clergy of the Old Régime 'the most discreet, gentle, well tempered, conciliatory, and pious persons who in any order probably existed in the world'; and the bringing of Louis XVI from Versailles to Paris 'the most horrid, atrocious, and afflicting spectacle, that perhaps ever was exhibited to the pity and indignation of mankind'. At such moments Burke forgot the wise advice of Hamlet to the players: 'in the verie Torrent, Tempest, and (as I may say) the Whirlewinde of Passion, you must acquire and beget a Temperance that may give it Smoothnesse.'

conformist ministers presenting their case to the leader of the House of Commons, nothing less will serve him as a parallel than Luther's appearance before the Diet of Worms. If he has to indicate that, as sometimes happens in the case of a deputation, the gentlemen composing it firmly believed in the strength of their own case, this cannot be done at a smaller rhetorical cost than by describing them as 'earnest men speaking in the austerest tones of invincible conviction. . . .' It would be unkind to require moderation or accuracy from anyone to whom such modes of expression have evidently become a second nature. Nor do I wish to judge Dr. Clifford harshly. He must surely occasionally find his method embarrassing, even to himself.[1]

It would not be easy to produce anything more restrained, yet more deadly, than this passage of unruffled composure, and aristocratic disdain—what Tennyson in a satiric moment called

> That repose
> Which stamps the caste of Vere de Vere.

Aristocracy is now out of fashion; in politics this may be an advance; but I could sometimes wish for a little more of it in that wilderness of contemporary literature whose sacred calf, not wholly golden, is 'the common man'. And I have quoted this passage at length because the excesses of overstatement that it rebukes are, I find, one of the hardest faults to cure in the writing of those whom I have the pleasure to teach personally.

It is not in the least that one wishes, like Swift, to ban a style that is 'moving'. Where a writer feels strongly I would have him by all means speak strongly. The emotional prudery which besets some twentieth-century intellectuals is as disgusting as the physical prudery of their Victorian grandparents. I despise those who always praise hedgingly, or blame timidly. For that is, after all,

[1] A. J. Balfour, *Dr. Clifford on Religious Education*; quoted by Desmond MacCarthy in *Portraits*, pp. 21-2.

[158]

only another form of falsity. What I cannot forgive a style for lacking is sense and truth.

'Speaking in a perpetual hyperbole,' says Bacon, 'is comely in nothing but love.' Even in love it seems to me pretty tedious. I know that it is not uncommon for Romeo to assure Juliet that she is the most wonderful woman that ever has existed or will exist; and that, if she will accept him, he will make her the happiest. But if I were Juliet, I should prefer him to have wit enough to discover praises of me that, though more moderate, were also true. That excellent critic Mr. E. E. Kellett records a scientific acquaintance of his who objected to poetry on account of its total lack of accuracy. For it was perpetually asserting absurdities—such as that love was woman's 'whole existence'; whereas Venus herself could not possibly have devoted to it more than ten per cent of her time. 'Poets should study statistics.' Rather a simple scientist perhaps. Yet I must own to great sympathy with him.

But, be poetry as it may, my conclusion is this—that a prose-writer should not overstate, except when he carries overstatement to such outrageous lengths that he is obviously jesting. (As in Giles Earle's comment, reported by Walpole, on the Lord Mayor's address to the Commons: 'By God, I have heard an oyster speak as well twenty times.') For the rest, a prose-writer should state exactly what he feels; or else—and this is often more effective—deliberately understate. But how difficult to persuade young writers of this! So often their impulse is to assume that talking big is the same as talking vigorously. As well suppose that the best way to sing well is to sing loud. I have been told that when the late Sir Edward Marsh, composing his memoir of Rupert Brooke, wrote 'Rupert left Rugby in a blaze of glory', the poet's mother, a lady of firm character, changed 'a blaze of glory' to 'July'. I cannot guarantee that this is true; but it is worth remembering.

Here I am brought back to my Icelanders. Never, I think, were men and women more passionate than those of the Sagas; and yet at crises of their fate they are content with a sentence or two, perhaps of grim understatement, where a character in Attic or Elizabethan drama might howl or roar for pages together. 'Do not weep, mother,' is Grettir's last farewell to her. 'If they fall on us, it shall be said you bore sons, not daughters.' And (though I also laugh at him) I have a specially fond memory for a certain obscure Helgi in the *Helganna Saga*, who in some fray had his lower lip cut off. 'Then said Helgi, "I was never a handsome man, but thou hast not mended matters much." Then he put up his hand and thrust his beard into his mouth and bit it with his teeth.' After which the battle proceeded. Contrast and compare this with Lavater's description of the romantic Fuseli: 'His look is lightning, his word a storm, his jest death, his vengeance hell. At close quarters he is rather trying.' I cite this because its style illustrates the effectiveness both of humorous overstatement and of dry understatement at the same time.

In short, you may ironically overstate, or ironically understate; but I suggest that you should always flee from blind exaggeration as from the fiend.

Now among the various passions that tempt a writer to distort, one seems to me especially dangerous. And that is a passion for his own cleverness. Well for those who can be both wise, and good, and clever; but this third quality, though the least valuable of the three, has a horrid habit of playing cuckoo in the nest to the two others. A useful essay might be written on the ravages of cleverness in literature (and indeed in all the arts). In Greece I suppose this fault first appears with the rhetorical euphuism of Gorgias; but even Euripides is at times too clever to be true. At Rome cleverness corrupted the verse of Ovid and Lucan, the prose and verse of Seneca.

In our own literature this dangerous ingeniousness reappears in the euphuism of Lyly, the Metaphysical poetry of writers like Donne, Herbert, Vaughan, Crashaw, and Marvell, the Metaphysical prose of Browne and Fuller. If much of their work remains memorable, this is partly, I think, because, thank Heaven, these writers were not always conceited or Metaphysical—Donne can be as passionately direct as Catullus, Herbert as simple as Christina Rossetti. And partly because some of them, like Lyly, Marvell, and Fuller, had also a sense of humour. For it is when cleverness leads to falsity that it becomes hateful; but there is no deception in a jest. Thus Donne can cry to a mistress sick with fever:

> Oh doe not die, for I shall hate
> All women so, when thou art gone,
> That thee I shall not celebrate,
> When I remember, thou wast one.

I see no sign that this is meant to be taken humorously; yet I cannot take it seriously; accordingly I find it merely silly—a futile and heartless juggle with paradoxes. But with Marvell's *Coy Mistress*, since I see an ironic smile hovering round the poet's mouth ('The grave's a fine and private place'), its hyperboles become magnificent jesting, and the whole piece one of the best of all really Metaphysical poems. The weakness of writers of this school is that they so often ask one to accept mere mental antics as profound truth or sincere feeling. Most of us are familiar with Johnson's verdict, honest but incomplete, in his *Life of Cowley*; some may remember Housman's two-word summary—'intellectually frivolous'; but the best criticism I know of Metaphysical writing, and indeed of all writing which sacrifices truth to cleverness, comes from one of the Metaphysical poets themselves—George Herbert; who, I suppose, was too genuine a person not to grow tired of fooling, as he sometimes did,

[161]

with such quips and quibbles as 'Jesu'—'I ease you', or
the idea of Christ leaving us his grave-clothes to serve as
a handkerchief.

> When first my lines of heavenly joys made mention,
> Such was their lustre, they did so excel,
> That I sought out quaint words, and trim invention;
> My thought began to burnish, sprout, and swell,
> Curling with metaphors a plain intention,
> Decking the sense, as if it were to sell. . . .
>
> As flames do work and wind, when they ascend,
> So did I weave myself into the sense.
> But while I bustled, I might hear a friend
> Whisper, *How wide is all this long pretence!*
> *There is in love a sweetness ready penn'd:*
> *Copy out only that, and save expense.*

If ever we are tempted overmuch to seek, or overmuch
to admire, the tinsel of mere brilliance and ingenuity,
it is time, I think, to remember those moving lines.

Of course, I am aware that this attitude is today far
from orthodox. Our century has made a craze of Metaphysical poetry. But that does not alter my opinion. This
is a critical age; and critics very humanly prefer the kind
of writing where they can expound difficulties and
subtleties, as with the Metaphysicals; or, at need, invent
them, as with Greek Drama or Shakespeare. You can
talk for days about a stanza of Donne's, where with a
stanza of Christina Rossetti's there may be nothing to do
but feel it. But I am not convinced that this makes
Donne's the better kind of poetry. Indeed, I sometimes
wonder if there have not been two great disasters in the
history of modern letters: the first when literature began
to be a full-time profession, with writers like Dryden and
Lesage, instead of remaining a by-product of more sanely
active lives; the second, when the criticism of literature
became likewise a profession, and a livelihood for pro-

fessors. However, that pretty problem would take too long to pursue.

With the later seventeenth century, both in England and in France, good sense reasserted itself and an end was made to the reign of paradoxy. As has been admirably summarized by Boileau:

Jadis de nos auteurs les pointes ignorées
Furent de l'Italie en nos vers attirées.
Le vulgaire, ébloui de leur faux agrément,
A ce nouvel appât courut avidement.
La faveur du public excitant leur audace,
Leur nombre impétueux inonda le Parnasse:
Le Madrigal d'abord en fut enveloppé;
Le Sonnet orgueilleux lui-même en fut frappé;
La Tragédie en fit ses plus chères délices;
L'Elégie en orna ses douloureux caprices;
Un héros sur la scène eut soin de s'en parer,
Et sans pointe un amant n'osa plus soupirer;
On vit tous les bergers, dans leurs plaintes nouvelles,
Fidèles à la pointe encor plus qu'à leurs belles;
Chaque mot eut toujours deux visages divers:
La prose la reçut aussi bien que les vers;
L'avocat au palais en hérissa son style,
Et le docteur en chaire en séma l'évangile.
La raison outragée enfin ouvrit les yeux,
La chassa pour jamais[1] des discours sérieux. . . .
Ce n'est pas quelquefois qu'une muse un peu fine
Sur un mot, en passant, ne joue et ne badine,
Et d'un sens détourné n'abuse avec succès:
Mais fuyez sur ce point un ridicule excès.[2]

The last hundred years, however, have seen other creative writers succumb to this form of too ingenious falsity; which is less generous than the kind of enthusiastic exaggeration we have just seen in Belloc and Chesterton. For *they* were at least carried away by enthusiasm for their subject—for the Normans or the English; but the

[1] 'Pour jamais'! What optimism!   [2] *L'Art Poétique*, II.

falsity of the too clever is due to excessive enthusiasm for their own cleverness. Browning did not always escape that; nor Meredith; nor Henry James. With Wilde it mattered less, for he was the jester of his generation; though when he does touch serious subjects, as in his dictum that books cannot be moral or immoral, only well or badly written, one can see the symptoms of that self-deception which was to turn his jests at last into tragedy. But, among all English writers, I know no clearer example of the perils of cleverness than Bernard Shaw, who ended by selling himself to his own wit, as Faust sold his soul to Mephistopheles; until this onetime disciple of serious thinkers like Samuel Butler and Ibsen, this onetime reformer who had laboured generously for Fabian Socialism and fearlessly denounced British oppression in Ireland and in Egypt, became, I feel, a hoary mountebank with no passion left except for making men stare by representing every worse cause as the better, and assuming the permanent role of devil's advocate, whether for Mussolini in Ethiopia or for Stalin in the Kremlin. Voltaire too was often over-clever; he could at times behave ignobly towards personal opponents, fulsomely towards the great; but at least he devoted his later years to denouncing oppression, not to condoning it. I cannot tell how time will judge Shaw as compared with his old rival Wells; but justice, I think, must finally recognize that Wells, even if he died in disillusion and despair, was all his life a man of passionate good will towards mankind, where G.B.S. became in the end merely a kind of courtzany to the British public. Wellington was very sound in his rooted distrust and contempt for 'clever devils'.

I draw the conclusion that it is wiser to use one's mind as telescope, or microscope, or magic crystal, than as a looking-glass; and I would suggest that it is foolish to take singing-lessons from peacocks.

I will close with one precise example, from a mind more

[164]

civilized, I think, and more human than Shaw's, of the danger of falling in love with one's own epigrams. Lytton Strachey's reputation has suffered in recent years because it has become felt that he, too, preferred wit to truth; in my own opinion this reaction has gone too far, for his *Victoria*, his *Portraits in Miniature*, and some of his criticism seem to me likely to last. But consider this from his famous essay on *The Lives of the Poets*: 'Johnson's aesthetic judgments are almost invariably subtle, or solid, or bold; they have always some good quality to recommend them—except one:[1] they are never right.' An amusing paradox; it might well please the author when he hit on it; but it should not have pleased him so much as to blind him to its untruth and let him print it. Had he written 'they repeatedly seem to us wrong', his epigram would still have kept plenty of point; as it stands, it exaggerates. For I should not have thought it difficult to adduce judgements of Johnson's that are not only admirably put, but also admirably true: for instance, his argument that the Three Unities are, as dogmatic rules, a vain superstition; or his statements that 'words too familiar, or too remote, defeat the purpose of a poet', that Milton knew human nature 'only in the gross', that Gray is 'tall by walking on tiptoe', that Congreve's characters with their perpetual repartee are 'intellectual gladiators', that the philosophical parts of Pope are shallow. Even those who do not wholly accept these verdicts would be rash to pronounce them false. And how excellent are many of Johnson's notes on Shakespeare; to say nothing of his *Preface*!

'Johnson', continues Strachey, 'never inquired what poets were trying to do.' He inquired with the Metaphysicals; he inquired with Pope. 'He could see nothing', his critic proceeds, 'in the splendour and elevation of Gray, but "glittering accumulations of ungraceful orna-

[1] 'Some good quality except one' seems dubious English.

[165]

ments"'"; yet what of that noble tribute to the *Elegy* with which Johnson's *Life of Gray* concludes?

'Johnson', we are finally told, 'had no ear, and he had no imagination.' No ear?

> Yet hope not life from grief or danger free,
> Nor think the doom of man revers'd for thee.

> Loosen'd from the minor's tether,
> Free to mortgage or to sell,
> Wild as wind and light as feather,
> Bid the sons of thrift farewell.

No imagination? 'That man is little to be envied, whose patriotism would not gain force upon the plain of *Marathon*, or whose piety would not grow warmer among the ruins of *Iona*.' And were not Johnson's later years hag-ridden by the imagined terrors of the afterworld?

Strachey knew all this; but I imagine he forgot it, as Macaulay might have done, in the effort to make his own paradox as dazzling as possible. Where so cultured and gifted a writer could be temporarily blinded, we may well take warning.

The conclusion is simple, yet hard. A writer should remember that about his Muse there is a good deal of the Siren. He should view his mental offspring as relentlessly as a Spartan father—if it is not perfectly sound, let it be cast out. If he does not expose it, others will, in a different sense. No doubt such austerity is not easy. It may involve infanticide on the scale of Herod; and it was not his own children that Herod was killing. Yet better that, than falsity.

> But play no tricks upon thy soul, O man;
> Let fact be fact, and life the thing it can.

[166]

VIII

GOOD HEALTH AND VITALITY

HONESTY and veracity, it seems then, can be kept only by constant self-control. 'Know thyself'—'Nothing too much'. But our much-governed generation, at least, should have learnt that too many controls are dangerous. Beginning as necessities, they often end as abuses. Through the ages, indeed, men have swung uneasily backwards and forwards from indulgence to austerity, from austerity to indulgence; partly from force of circumstances, partly because the innate aggressiveness of human nature can easily turn from tyrannizing others to tyrannizing itself. The ascetic is often one who sacrifices healthier pleasures to that of playing dictator in his own soul.

There is the more danger of this because our conscious will-power finds it far easier to multiply checks and constraints on our vitality than to multiply that vitality itself. Bridles are sooner made than horses; but much less valuable. In literature at all events, energy without control is at least better than control without energy.

When Mlle. Dumesnil was being rehearsed by Voltaire, she ended by crying in protest: 'Il faudrait avoir le diable au corps pour arriver au ton que vous voulez me faire prendre.' But Voltaire caught up her phrase: 'Eh vraiment, oui, c'est le diable au corps qu'il faut avoir pour exceller dans tous les arts.' For once Blake would have emphatically agreed with him.

'Bother the *New Statesman*,' runs a letter of T. E. Lawrence, 'and the *Odyssey*, and all manufactured writing. Only the necessary, the inevitable, the *high-*

[167]

pressure stuff is worth having.' There is substance in his doctrine; though to decry the *Odyssey* as 'manufactured' seems mere perversity, due, I suppose, to his having exhausted and surfeited himself in translating it.

It is this energy that strikes the reader of Aeschylus or Aristophanes among the ancients (though the classical mind, with its insistence on control, sometimes criticized them both for that very reason); it is this zest that makes so vivid some medieval writers like Chaucer or Froissart.

> But it was joye for to seen hym swete!
> His forheed dropped as a stillatorie.

> But, Lord Crist! whan that it remembreth me
> Upon my yowthe, and on my jolitee,
> It tikleth me aboute myn herte roote.
> Unto this day it dooth myn herte boote
> That I have had my world as in my tyme.

Là se combattit le roi au dit Messire Eustache moult longue-ment, et Messire Eustache à lui, et tant qu'il les faisoit moult plaisant voir.

Sachez que l'oubliance du voir et la plaisance du considérer y étoit si grande,[1] que qui eût eu les fièvres ou le mal des dents, il eût perdu la maladie. . . .

Many a typical figure of Reformation and Renaissance shows the same vibrant vitality—Henry VIII and Rabelais, Tamburlaine and Falstaff. 'I pray better,' cries Luther, 'and I preach better when I am angry'; of the no less vehement Knox, the English Ambassador writes to Sir William Cecil, in a sentence that itself breathes the same magnificent energy: 'I assure you the voice of this man . . . is able in one hour to put more life in us than five hundred trumpets continually blustering in our ears'; while Melville describes how the old preacher, after

---

[1] He is describing the vast French preparations at l'Écluse for invading England.

painfully climbing the pulpit, was the next moment
'like to ding that pulpit in blads and flee out of it'.[1]

The pulses of the neo-classic age take a more measured
beat. Even the inner savagery of some of Racine's
characters goes satin-clad and silken-phrased. Yet at
moments, in the rustic Bunyan or the polished Saint-
Simon, the old fire blazes out again. Hatred and rage
are not endearing; when roused by childish trivialities
they become comic; and yet what verve in passages like
these!

(Saint-Simon to the Regent on the Duc de Noailles.)
'Je ne cache pas que le plus beau et le plus délicieux jour
de ma vie ne fût celui où il me serait donné par la justice
divine de l'écraser en marmelade et de lui marcher à deux
pieds sur le ventre.'

(Of the public humiliation of the Duc du Maine.) 'Je
mourois de joie; j'en étois à craindre la défaillance; mon
coeur, dilaté à l'excès, ne trouvoit plus d'espace à
s'étendre. La violence que je me faisois pour ne rien
laisser échapper étoit infinie, et néanmoins ce tourment
étoit délicieux. . . . Je triomphois, je me vengeois, je
nageois dans ma vengeance; je jouissois du plein accom-
plissement des désirs les plus continus de toute ma vie.'

(How many novelists could give us such a glimpse into
the realities of a human soul? But then I have long failed
to understand how readers can be content with the trivial
talk and shallow psychology of the ordinary novel.)

Art is of course sometimes produced by frail and delicate
personalities, as well as by those that are robustly intense
—by figures like Gray with his wistful 'leucocholy', or
Pater with his atmosphere of churchyard lilies, or Dowson
who died at thirty-two in the very last year of the nineteenth century, as if resolved, even in that, to be perfectly
fin-de-siècle. Yet the work of such weaker temperaments
(despite the splendid exception of Gray's *Elegy*) seems

[1] 'Smash that pulpit to fragments and fly out of it.'

seldom first-rate. Dowson, for instance, ends by becoming a complete Lydia Languish. *His* love is not 'a red, red rose'—roses, for him, must be pallid; and women, shadows.

> With pale, indifferent eyes, we sit and wait
> For the dropt curtain and the closing gate.
>
> I was not sorrowful, but only tired
> Of everything that ever I desired.

Such a world of anaemic spectres soon grows intolerable. I find myself turning back with longing and relief to the midnight laughter of Johnson, re-echoing from Fleet Ditch to Temple Bar; to the vigour of Scott or Hugo, Dickens or Dumas, Trollope or Balzac. Macaulay may be a Philistine; but he remains a Goliath, whose spear is as a weaver's beam, and whom no critical pebbles can kill. One understands (though one may also smile) the letter of Stendhal congratulating a friend on her son's falling in love—'Peu importe l'objet, c'est une passion'; one accepts the verdict of de Tocqueville (who was no Romantic)—'À mesure que je m'éloigne de la jeunesse je me trouve plus d'égards, je dirai presque de respect, pour les passions. Je les aime quand elles sont bonnes, et je ne suis pas bien sûr de les détester quand elles sont mauvaises. C'est de la force, et la force, partout où elle se rencontre, paraît à son avantage au milieu de la faiblesse universelle qui nous environne.'

In fact, there are things less worth remembering than Gladstone's view of sponges; at some weekend party the conversation turned on the bores of packing, particularly of packing wet sponges; and with his usual vehemence Gladstone interjected: 'The only way is to wrap your sponge in a towel, put it on the floor, and stamp on it!' Pleasing vision! Yet here stands revealed for a moment a glimpse of the character that made Gladstone's career. Better be Gladstone than the sponge.

Can such vitality be acquired? Hardly. One is born with it, or without. Yet at least one can avoid wasting it. When we read the lives of writers, it seems often as if they had squandered in one splendid conflagration the energy slowly accumulated, like a coal-measure, through a long, obscure ancestry of bourgeois or countryfolk. Sometimes, indeed, as with Scott or Trollope, the vigour of a writer seems merely one healthy outlet of his general robustness; but too often it is something artificially stimulated by excitements, mistresses, drink, or drugs. Probably the ideal life for the artist is an alternation of turbulence and tranquillity; as Wordsworth gained by the French Revolution and Annette Vallon, but lost in the end by too much Grasmere. Aeschylus at Marathon, Sophocles at the siege of Samos, Chaucer in his custom-house, Wyatt as marshal of Calais or ambassador, Cervantes at Lepanto, Milton as Latin Secretary of the Commonwealth, were all being diverted from their vocation as writers; yet they wrote enough; and their work might well have lost its vigour, had they been mere sitters by the fire.

In comparison with inborn character, then, technical precepts can do little to make a style vital. But something, I have suggested, may be gained by forcing oneself to be brief; and something further by forcing oneself to be concrete. As life becomes more complex, sophisticated, and scientific, language is constantly tending to fade from a gallery of pictures to a blackboard of mathematical symbols. But concrete terms are to abstract as living things to ghosts. And abstractions are often deceiving ghosts at that. They tend to acquire so many meanings that they have none. Defoe said that in his England there were a hundred thousand stout fellows ready to fight to the death against Popery, without knowing whether 'Popery' were a man or a horse; doubtless there are nearly as many million stout fellows in the U.S.S.R.

ready to fight to the death for 'democracy' without any idea that 'democracy', strictly speaking, is government not only for the people but *by* it. Yet in the language of the educated, and the half-educated, abstract terms constantly tend to encroach and multiply—partly from pretentiousness, partly from mere indolence. No doubt philosophers and scientists are compelled to live largely in a phantasmal world of general ideas; but the literary artist who too freely adopts their type of language may develop a sort of pernicious anaemia. Indeed, in the eighteenth century, with its worship of generalities, this disease became endemic.

Le tube, image du tonnerre.
(DELILLE, of a shot-gun)

Là de l'antique Hermès le minéral fluide
S'élève au gré de l'air plus sec ou plus humide;
Ici par la liqueur un tube coloré
De la température indique le degré.
(COLARDEAU, of barometer and thermometer)

When now with better skill and nicer care,
The dexterous youth renews the wooden war,
Beyond the rest his winding timber flies
And works insinuating and wins the prize.
(NICHOLAS AMHURST, *The Bowling Green*)

To the rocks,
Dire-clinging, gathers his ovarious food.
(THOMSON)

But these have at least unconscious humour; the prose of abstraction and periphrasis seldom offers even that consolation.

That system of manners which arose among the Gothic nations of Europe, and of which chivalry was more properly the effusion than the source, is without doubt one of the most peculiar and interesting appearances in human affairs. The moral causes which formed its character have not, perhaps, been hitherto investigated with the happiest success; but to confine ourselves to the subject before us, chivalry was certainly one of the most prominent of its features and most remarkable of its effects. Candour must confess, that this singular institution was not admirable only as the corrector of the ferocious ages in which it flourished; but that in contributing to polish and soften manners it paved the way for the diffusion of knowledge and the extension of commerce, which afterwards, in some measure, supplanted it. Society is inevitably progressive.[1] Commerce has overthrown the 'feudal and chivalrous system' under whose shade it first grew; while learning has subverted the superstition whose opulent endowments had first fostered it. Peculiar circumstances connected with the manners of chivalry favoured this admission of commerce and this growth of knowledge; while the sentiments peculiar to it, already enfeebled in the progress from ferocity and turbulence, were almost obliterated by tranquillity and refinement. Commerce and diffused knowledge have, in fact, so completely assumed the ascendent in polished nations, that it will be difficult to discover any relics of Gothic manners, but in a fantastic exterior, which has survived the generous illusions through which these manners once seemed splendid and seductive. Their direct influence has long ceased in Europe; but their indirect influence, through the medium of those causes which would not perhaps have existed but for the mildness which chivalry created in the midst of a barbarous age, still operates with increasing vigour. The manners of the middle age were, in the most singular sense, compulsory: enterprising benevolence was produced by general fierceness, gallant courtesy by ferocious rudeness; and artificial gentleness resisted the torrent of natural barbarism. But a less incongruous system has succeeded, in which commerce, which unites men's interests, and knowledge, which excludes those prejudices that tend to embroil them, present a broader basis for the stability of civilized and beneficent manners.

[1] At last a plain sentence. Unfortunately it is as plainly false. Yet happy age that could believe it!

Mackintosh was a good, clever, and learned man, honoured by Macaulay and adored by Mme. de Stael. His *Vindiciae Gallicae* (1791), from which this extraordinary passage comes, was translated by Louis Philippe and praised by Napoleon. Lord Abinger sat up all night to read it; and, with Paine's *Rights of Man*, it is still remembered, where other replies to Burke's *Reflections* are forgotten.

Again, Mackintosh was a painstaking writer. We hear of his spending four or five days considering whether 'utility' or 'usefulness' were the better word. Yet the style of this passage seems to me abominable. Mackintosh is replying to Burke's lament that chivalry is dead in an age when swords do not leap from their scabbards in defence of Marie Antoinette. About that famous purple patch I am not, I own, enthusiastic; I feel a certain sympathy with Sir Philip Francis's dismissal of it as 'pure foppery'; but Burke *is* at least alive. With Mackintosh, who can feel that he is discussing the real behaviour of real men who once really walked this solid earth, wearing uncomfortable clothes of real steel, living in uncomfortable walls of real stone; and still lie, some of them, under strangely real effigies in English cathedrals? Though dead six centuries, they seem to me far less dead than this fog-bank of abstract language, too vague for meaning and too sweeping for truth. Mackintosh is not without sonority, though his rhythm grows monotonous—too much like a pompous summing-up in a court of law. And he knows the use of alliteration. On the other hand there are too many whiches. But the real malady is, for me, his disastrous passion for abstract nouns—often three to a single line.

No doubt the influence of Johnson is here largely to blame. But Johnson, fortunately, tended to grow out of this way of writing, so that the best parts of his *Lives* are more like his robust talk. True, at times even his talk became too like his earlier books; the story is familiar of his saying about *The Rehearsal*, 'It has not wit enough to keep it sweet.' 'This', Boswell continues, 'was easy; he therefore caught himself, and pronounced a more round sentence; "It has not vitality enough to preserve it from putrefaction."' But, for us, Johnson lives by his other type of sentence which is not 'round', but hits straight; by images as concrete as the famous stone he kicked to confute Berkeley; by that homely realism which, like some boisterous cockcrow, scatters back to nothingness the 'extravagant and erring' phantoms of speculation. 'Who eats a slice of plum-pudding the less because a friend is hanged?'—'Five hours of the four-and-twenty unemployed are enough for a man to go mad in; so I would advise you, Sir, to study algebra. . . . Your head would get less muddy, and you will leave off tormenting your neighbours about paper and packthread, while we all live together in a world that is bursting with sin and sorrow.' —'Buckinger had no hands, and he wrote his name with his toes at Charing Cross, for half a crown apiece; that was a "new manner of writing!"'

The truthfulness of these pronouncements may sometimes be questioned; but not, at least, their vigour. Or again, to turn to less frequented paths, there is that vociferous style (so startling to encounter in the eighteenth-century *noblesse*) which marks the letters of Mirabeau's father and uncle as they discuss the young Mirabeau's wayward character, and what to do with it. 'C'est un embryon de matamore ébouriffé, qui veut avaler le monde avant d'avoir douze ans.'—'Je ne connais que l'impératrice de Russie avec laquelle cet homme peut être bon encore à marier.'—'Un brûlot, un fagot, une fusée, une ombre, un fou, du bruit, du vent, du pouffe et rien. C'est la pie des beaux-esprits et le geai des carrefours . . . ce n'est qu'un brouillard, c'est Ixion copulant dans la nue.'—'Je n'ai rien à changer dans tes plans; mais tu m'envoies ton fils, est-ce pour le faire bouillir ou rôtir?' Not a happy family (wife, son, daughter imprisoned by the tyrannical old Marquis, till even Maurepas complained, 'Voilà soixante lettres ou ordres pour la famille Mirabeau. Il faudrait un sécretaire d'état exprès pour eux.'); but a most enviable pungency of expression. Chesterfield might well have thought both brothers 'Hottentots'; but the over-artificial delicacy of eighteenth-century society was bound to bring a revulsion towards the noble Hottentot. And though, like most human revulsions it went too far, better sea-wind than hothouse; better a touch of nature untamed than fables like Florian's without a wolf, or histories, like Lamartine's of the Revolution, 'without the mud'.

For the same reason, still, one may turn back with relief to Defoe or Johnson or Macaulay from a rarefied atmosphere like that of the later Henry James whose characters, an enemy might say, find their main occupation in thought-reading ('It ended in fact by becoming quite beautiful, the number of things they had a manifest consciousness of not saying'), or in counting under the microscope the bruises inflicted on their hypersensitivity[1] by some pea beneath ten mattresses (where the simplest remedy might have been a decent day's work); while even their physical appetites are elusively satisfied on such ethereal fare as 'something fried and felicitous'. Even those who are grateful for all that James added to life's diversity, would perhaps do well to remember also the

[1] It is curious that this hypersensitivity does not always go with a very sensitive style. 'Waymarsh, who *had had* letters yesterday, *had had* them again today'; the use of personal pronouns is sometimes sluttish; and James, to some minds, can be overfond of that makeshift 'the latter', which Johnson so curtly (and rightly, I think) condemned. It is curious, too, how part of a writer's character can come out in a single epithet: 'The balconied inn stood on the very neck of the sweetest pass in the Oberland.' Would any other writer in history have called Alpine passes 'sweet'?

legend of Antaeus. When that giant son of Earth wrestled with Heracles, each time he was thrown to the ground he rose with strength renewed. For he had found fresh vigour in his immortal mother's lap; and Heracles only prevailed by crushing him in the air. Style too must renew its strength by recurrent contact with solid earth.

Therefore I would suggest, especially in prose, an inveterate distrust of all abstract words that are in the least vague; for the sake not only of vividness and life, but also of accuracy and truth. Sometimes such abstractions are indispensable; sometimes they gain brevity; but clarity usually matters more. When you say 'horse', anyone knows what you mean; but when you say 'democracy', half a dozen controversies bare their teeth in the shadows. Has not Professor Lovejoy catalogued over three-score different meanings in eighteenth-century use of that overworked word 'Nature'? A clear word is like a finger-post pointing straight at its object; but our abstract terms are too often like signposts with many arms, some broken, some twisted, some half-effaced, pointing into a fog.

But if concreteness is thus the backbone of style, there remain, as usual, limitations. For one thing, here too the law of variety overrules. No writer is more master of the concrete than Shakespeare.

> He that depends
> Upon your favours, swimmes with finnes of Leade,
> And hewes down Oakes with rushes.

> *King*, be thy thoughts Imperious, like thy name.
> Is the Sunne dim'd, that Gnats do flie in it?

> By Heaven, I had rather Coine my Heart,
> And drop my blood for Drachmaes.

> Th' expence of spirit in a waste of shame.

> To lie in cold obstruction, and to rot,
> This sensible warme motion, to become
> A kneaded clod . . .

> Th' expectansie and Rose of the faire State,
> The glasse of Fashion, and the mould of Forme.

But notice also that, with Shakespeare, even abstractions do not remain the impalpable wisps and waifs of mist that they too often are on ordinary lips. They grow solid; they take life; the 'cloud like a man's hand' grips like a hand indeed.

> Thou visible God,
> That souldrest close Impossibilities,
> And mak'st them kisse.

> And arte made tung-tide by authoritie,
> And Folly (Doctor-like) controuling skill,
> And simple-Truth miscalde Simplicitie,
> And captive-good attending Captaine ill.

> Adversity's sweet milke, Philosophie.

> Leane Famine, quartering Steele, and
> climbing Fire.

Personification, you say, is easy? But not personification so solid and tangible as this. Shakespeare's vividness even in abstraction seems the healthy offspring of a mind that disdained all vaporous vagueness; cared little for general theories; saw, heard, smelt, tasted, or touched even the most rarefied concepts; materialized and embraced even the most platonic ideas.

But the writer who seeks vitality in concrete details and vivid touches has still to beware of confounding his skill with covetousness. He can become nigglingly minute, oppressively multitudinous.

> Why has not Man a microscopic eye?
> For this plain reason, Man is not a fly.
> Say what the use, were finer optics giv'n,
> T' inspect a mite, not comprehend the heav'n?

How minute a description should be remains a fascinating problem; and I know no better starting-point for discussing it than Johnson on tulips.

You will remember, in Johnson's *Rasselas*, Imlac's theory of poetry: 'The business of a poet is to examine, not the individual, but the species; to remark general properties and large appearances; he does not number the streaks of the tulip, or describe the different shades in the verdure of the forest. He is to exhibit in his portraits of nature such prominent and striking features, as recall the original to every mind; and must neglect the minute discriminations, which one may have remarked, and another have neglected, for those characteristicks which are alike obvious to vigilance and carelessness.'

Art, thought Johnson, following Aristotle, is imitation; the artist's business is to remind us; and our pleasure is to recognize.[1] 'If the poet says a tulip has seventeen streaks of tawny-yellow, am I to run into the garden to count them? When tulips, anyway, are probably out of season? (A strange view. Johnson wisely says elsewhere that the writer makes *new* things familiar, as well as familiar things new. Why may he not tell us something new about tulips? If he seems trustworthy, we would take his word for it—as we take Shakespeare's when, flatly transgressing Johnson's rule, he describes on Imogen's breast 'a mole Cinque-spotted: Like the Crimson drops I' th' bottome of a Cowslippe'.)

Moreover Johnson held, again following Aristotle, that serious poetry should both generalize (for this is more philosophic) and idealize (for this is nobler). Now petty peculiarities are not general—the streaks of tulips may vary; and they are not noble. God may see with

[1] Cf. Johnson's *Preface to Shakespeare*: 'Nothing can please many and please long but just representations of general nature. Particular manners can be known to few, and therefore few only can judge how nearly they are copied.'

equal eye 'A hero perish or a sparrow fall': but we do not.

Similarly Johnson's friend, Reynolds, on painting: 'The whole beauty and grandeur of the art consists in my opinion in being able to get above all singular forms, local customs, particularities, and details of every kind.' (Just those details, in fact, that Romantics and Realists were lovingly to seek.) But Reynolds makes one vital admission which Johnson had not made: 'I am very ready to allow that some circumstances of minuteness and particularity frequently tend to give an air of truth to a piece, and to interest the spectator in an extraordinary manner'; this, however, needs 'peculiar nicety of discernment'. Reynolds, in short, might have allowed the warts in Cromwell's portrait; Johnson presumably not (unless to humiliate the Whig dog). Fortunately Boswell was to include plenty of warts in his portrait of Johnson.

Reynolds's view seems to me much more reasonable than Johnson's; how far is it borne out by the practice of literature?

The Greeks, I think, tend to keep, in this also, near to the happy mean. Homer (who surely cannot have been blind from birth) has the keenest vision for little, vivid things, especially in his similes—he sees the dog Argus wagging his tail and laying back both his ears as he recognizes, dying, his master returned after twenty years of war and wandering; or the sudden darkening of the sea as the west wind rises; or the way the inrolling wave washes off the falling snow upon a beach. 'Homère,' observes Voltaire, 'exprime tout ce qui frappe les yeux'; whereas 'les Français, qui n'ont guère commencé à perfectionner la grande poésie qu'au théâtre, n'ont pu et n'ont dû exprimer alors que ce qui peut toucher l'âme'. This does not seem to me quite true. Homer does not express *everything* that strikes the eye; he markedly avoids the ugly. He will, indeed, describe wounds in even excessive detail; but, by an extraordinary departure from realism, if his heroes survive, they are never permanently maimed or disfigured. No one-legged warrior hobbles across the Trojan plain.[1] The only human deformity I can recall among his characters is the loathed demagogue Thersites. None the less, Voltaire's distinction remains essentially just.

Similarly, Hesiod notices such details as the swollen foot nursed by the vagrant's hunger-wasted hand. Amid the giant figures of Aeschylus there is place also for the lice that torment the warriors under Troy, for the tiny whining gnat that could wake Clytemnestra, as she pretends, from slumbers tormented with anxiety for her husband oversea. Theocritus can paint the lizard in the old stone walls beneath the blaze of noon, or the reflection in the calm Sicilian sea of the dog that dashes barking along the beach. To be subtle without ceasing to be simple; to be realist, yet not crude; to be minute at the right moment, but not all the time; to add here and there the little concrete touch, but only here and there—this, at their best, the Greeks achieved.

Latin literature dwells perhaps less on such vivid details—except in its comedy; in didactic poetry like Virgil's *Georgics*; in familiar poetry like some of Horace; in satire like Juvenal; or in fiction like Petronius. (And such exceptions even eighteenth-century taste allowed.) But the Middle Ages, uncowed by criticism, went back to enjoying the tulip with all its streaks. 'Dante,' says Voltaire, 'accoutuma les Italiens à tout dire.' For example, as the Sodomites peer at him and Virgil through the dimness of Hell,

---

[1] Perhaps in the then state of medical science the loss of a limb would mean bleeding to death—as Aeschylus' brother died when his hands were cut off at Marathon, seizing a Persian ship. But even then not *all* mutilations could be fatal.

sì ver noi aguzzavan le ciglia
Come vecchio sartor fa nella cruna.[1]

Villon, again, sees the blackened faces of his comrades
aswing on the gallows, pecked and pitted by the crows,
'like thimbles'. Chaucer notes unerringly the hare-like
glare in his Pardoner's eyes; the hairs on the Miller's
wart,

Reed as the brustles of a sowes eryes;[2]

how the slack skin shakes on old January's neck, as he
trolls to his young May; how the friar in the Summoner's
Tale, kissing the goodwife, 'chirketh as a sparwe' and—
superb touch—shoos the cat from the bench where he
sits down (for cats cannot pay subscriptions). Chaucer,
indeed, seems to me a perfect master in the art of dealing
with tulips; he never becomes one of those writers with
whom one cannot see the tulip for the streaks.

But here, on the other hand, is the sort of thing that
can happen when the temptation of realistic detail is
indulged to excess. 'There came and stood at the foot of
my bed the shape of a mannikin (*homunculi*) most hideous
to behold. His stature, as far as I could discern, was
middling, his neck thin, his face emaciated, his eyes coal-
black, his brow knitted and wrinkled, his nostrils squat,
his mouth pouting, his lips blubber, his chin narrow and
receding, his beard goatish, his ears hairy and pointed, his
hair bristling and dishevelled, his teeth canine, the back
of his head tapering, his chest protruded, his back
humped, his haunches quivering, his raiment filthy, his
whole body vibrating with eagerness and impatience.
Seizing hold of the top of the bed on which I was lying,

---

[1] Towards us there they peered with sharpened glance,
  As an old tailor at his needle's eye.
[2] Cf., in Balzac, the wen on Grandet's nose which changes colour
as his anger rises.

he shook the whole bedstead in terrible fashion.'[1] Raoul
Glaber has here drawn a most conscientious devil; but
the reader's memory and imagination are so smothered
under this inventory, often illogical in its order, that the
vision, intended to be horrific, remains blurred and unconvincing. Far better are the devilkins which, says
Caesarius of Heisterbach, a priest saw at Mainz dancing
attendance on an overdressed lady, 'as gay as a peacock'.
'On the train that trailed far behind her he observed a
number of demons sitting. They were small as dormice[2]
and black as Ethiops, grinning and clapping their hands
and hopping hither and thither like fish caught in a net.'
These imps are much more vivid; partly because they
are less catalogued, partly because, as Lessing would have
noted with approval, they become a moving picture,
instead of being painted statically, like Raoul Glaber's
demon, item by item, feature by feature.

With the earlier Renaissance the 'General' has not yet
been hoisted into the saddle to become a tyrant; Montaigne or Ronsard or Shakespeare can still be realistically
precise without being thought 'low'. The sentry in
Hamlet can speak of 'Not a Mouse stirring', and the hero
stabs Polonius behind the arras with the cry 'How now,
a Rat?' But Voltaire found that mouse grotesque; Racine,
whose father and grandfather had been content to have,
for their punning arms, a rat and a swan (Rat-cygne),
bestirred himself to get rid of 'ce vilain rat'; and Grainger,
it will be recalled, in his *Sugar-cane* having first written
'Now, Muse, let's sing of mice', ennobled 'mice' to
'rats', and then 'rats' to 'the whisker'd vermin race'.
For 'race' is a glorious abstraction; no one has ever seen

[1] R. Glaber, *Historiae*, V, i, 2. (The original is, of course, in
Latin.)

[2] *I.e.* three to three and a half inches long, without the tail.
Note the beautiful precision. 'Small as mice' would be less definite,
and so less scientifically convincing.

a race. On similar principles, the technical sea-terms used in his *Annus Mirabilis* later gave Dryden pangs of artistic conscience incomprehensible to readers of Masefield.

Fortunately some less noble forms like fiction, satire, or burlesque had escaped these aristocratic taboos; hence the circumstantial detail which enlivens Defoe's novels, or *Gulliver*, or *The Rape of the Lock*. The Romantics restored this freedom to literature at large, realizing once more that even small things may become great by their associative, suggestive, or symbolic power—like the daisy or the mouse of Burns; or Coleridge's last red leaf dancing on its December bough; or Wordsworth's lesser celandine, or *his* daisy

> with its star-shaped shadow thrown
> On the smooth surface of the naked stone.

This realization is, indeed, summed up in the flower that Tennyson plucked from the wall:

> Flower in the crannied wall,
> I pluck you out of the crannies,
> I hold you here, root and all, in my hand,
> Little flower—but *if* I could understand
> What you are, root and all, and all in all,
> I should know what God and man is.

Our ignorance remains; but so, henceforward, does the nameless flower that symbolized it so well.[1]

The Pre-Raphaelites in their turn made the truthful counting of tulip-streaks one of their basic principles. Thus Rossetti records how the agonized grief that bowed a man's head to earth might leave him, unlike Coleridge's wedding-guest, no wiser—except for the vain, irrelevant vision that

> The woodspurge has a cup of three.

[1] Johnson might have retorted that here the poet uses the *general* term—'flower'; but I do not see that it would have done any harm, had he been as specific as Wordsworth with his lesser celandine.

That counting of the cups of woodspurges is not futile: it becomes an emblem of grief's tragic futility.

But in the modern world the danger of excess in minute realism has grown greater, perhaps, than ever before. The novel in particular, seeking verisimilitude, has often accumulated trivial observations and trumpery conversations (as if there were not bores enough in real life, without looking for them in books), till the reader often feels as if he were buried to the neck in an ants' nest of petty, laborious, irritating creatures. Rossetti might vividly put a mouse in the cell of his praying monk, as a sign of its rapt silence; but not hundreds of mice, as if it were the tower of the Bishop of Bingen. The later Tolstoy reacted strongly against the 'superfluous detail' of realistic fiction like Gogol's and his own. The common-sense conclusion still seems that one should love vivid details, but love them with discretion and with distrust. For without a fastidious, yet practical sense of values this sort of art can degenerate into a sedulous incatenation of fleas. One feather of the eagle will often suffice—and 'I forget the rest'.

There is, for example, a touch in Flaubert's *Madame Bovary* that by its subtle simplicity has left a lasting mark on my memory—his picture of his poor romance-besotted heroine in her drab, provincial home gazing nostalgically at the stain of yellow wax on her dancing-shoes, which recalls her momentary glimpse of her false paradise in the ball at the château. That yellow wax seals itself on the reader's mind.

Here, again, are four silences.

(Of lovers.)

> They tread on clouds, and though they sometimes fall,
> They fall like dew, but make no noise at all.
> So silently they one to th' other come,
> As colours steal into the Peare or Plum.

(HERRICK)

(Night in the American wilderness.) On dirait que des silences succèdent à des silences.

(CHATEAUBRIAND)

(After the speech of Hamilcar before the Ancients at Carthage.) Et le silence pendant quelques minutes fut tellement profond qu'on entendait au loin le bruit de la mer.

(FLAUBERT)[1]

He was sitting, motionless, on the bare ground—so motionless that as I came near a little bird rose from the dried mud, two paces from him, and passed across the pond, with little beats of its wings, whistling as it went.

(TURGENIEV)[1]

All four seem to me superb; but in different ways. Herrick, as a poet, is not so much concerned to intensify our impression as to enrich it with the similar beauty of other silences—the noiselessness of the summer orchard, of the clouds that sink along the hills. Chateaubriand heightens our sense of the hush of the virgin forest by making the concrete more abstract—'des silences succèdent à des silences'; and thus achieves a stillness yet completer than those lovely lines of La Fontaine:

O belles, évitez
Le fond des bois et leur profond silence.

(In both writers, naturally, the beauty of their verbal music helps.) Flaubert and Turgeniev, on the other hand, make us hear the stillness more vividly by adding one small concrete detail of circumstantial evidence—how utter the quiet must have been, if the distant sea could be heard, or a little bird grow so bold! Johnson, I suppose, might have approved the sentence of Flaubert—the sea is grand, and general, and appropriate here because on its shifting restlessness was built the dominion of Carthage herself; he might have questioned Turgeniev's little

[1] Quoted in A. Albalat, *L'Art d'Ecrire* (1899), pp. 242-3.

bird, the little beats of its wings, its whistling as it flew, as being too trivial—and yet how they too bring the scene to life!

It was this same sense of the need to make writing vividly alive that made Dostoievski demand of a writer who had described a man throwing money from the window to an organ-grinder, 'I want to hear that penny hop and chink.'[1] And so, more and more, Reynolds seems to me right, rather than his friend Johnson. 'Some circumstances of minuteness and particularity frequently tend to give an air of truth to a piece, and to interest the spectator in an extraordinary manner'; though Reynolds seems no less right in stressing the need for 'a peculiar nicety of discernment'.

All this, no doubt, applies particularly to descriptive writing; but there are, I think, few styles of any kind that do not gain new strength from a passionate hatred of unreality, of the woolly and the nebulous, the indefinite and the imprecise. Well for the writer who remembers always not only sense, but also the senses.

This seems to me one of the great excellences of Macaulay. Often his ideas may be somewhat shallow; but they are sharp. His mind was so richly furnished with vivid details from the past that he was never at a loss for illustration and analogy; and where so many historians or political thinkers have produced only valleys of dry bones, he could add living flesh and coloured raiment. He might deride the relic-mongering of Horace Walpole—'researches after Queen Mary's comb, Wolsey's red hat, the pipe which Van Tromp smoked during his last sea-fight, and the spur which King William struck into the flank of Sorrel'; but perhaps he was himself, in a way, less unlike Walpole than he supposed. For, mentally, he too was a tireless collector of precise antiquarian detail; and it is typical, not only that he should love thus to catalogue

[1] Quoted in J. M. Murry, *The Problem of Style* (1922), p. 78.

Walpole's treasures, but that he should add to them the name, even, of King William's horse.

What's in the name of Sorrel? Quite a lot, I think, for the vividness of the passage. How much duller, if he had said simply 'King William's spurs'! Indeed this magic of proper names exemplifies yet again the power of the concrete, the definite, the individual. And of that magic, like Marlowe and Milton, Macaulay was well aware. It is easy, for instance, to propound the general principle that men have repeatedly been fooled by hopes that a hostile nation will collapse economically; but from Macaulay's pen it comes with a very different energy: 'As if Alboin could not turn Italy into a desert till he had negotiated a loan at five per cent, as if the exchequer bills of Attila had been at par.'[1] Rhetoric? And why not? The

---

[1] Compare:

> Una ingens Amiterna cohors priscique Quirites,
> Ereti manus omnis oliviferaeque Mutuscae;
> Qui Nomentum urbem, qui Rosea rura Velini,
> Qui Tetricae horrentis rupes montemque Severum
> Casperiamque colunt Forulosque et flumen Himellae,
> Qui Tiberim Fabarimque bibunt, quos frigida misit
> Nursia, et Ortinae classes populique Latini,
> Quosque secans infaustum interluit Allia nomen.   (VIRGIL)

> Is it not brave to be a king, Techelles!—
> Usumcasane and Theridamas,
> Is it not passing brave to be a king,
> And ride in triumph through Persepolis?   (MARLOWE)

> Though all the Giant brood
> Of *Phlegra* with th' Heroic Race were joyn'd
> That fought at *Theb's* and *Ilium*, on each side
> Mixt with auxiliar Gods; and what resounds
> In Fable or *Romance* of *Uthers* Son
> Begirt with *British* and *Armoric* Knights;
> And all who since, Baptiz'd or Infidel,
> Jousted in *Aspramont* or *Montalban*,
> *Damasco*, or *Marocco*, or *Trebisond*,
> Or whom *Biserta* sent from *Afric* shore

[188]

English seem often curiously prim and prudish about rhetoric. There is good rhetoric and bad; and I see no cause why we should avert fastidious faces from what satisfied Pericles and Pitt, Burke and Abraham Lincoln.

Indeed, I suspect it was from the oratorical Burke that Macaulay may have got his idea about Alboin and Attila. If so, he vastly improved what he took, by being trenchantly brief where Burke grows long-winded: 'Would it be wise to estimate what the world of Europe, as well as the world of Asia, had to dread from Jinghiz Khan, upon a contemplation of the resources of the cold and barren spot in the remotest Tartary, from whence first issued that scourge of the human race? Ought we to judge from the excise and stamp duties of the rocks, or from the

> When *Charlemain* with all his Peerage fell
> By *Fontarabbia*. (MILTON)

Qui sont-ils ces nouveaux auteurs? Ce sont des gens bien habiles et bien célèbres, me dit-il. C'est Villalobos, Coninck, Llamas, Achokier, Dealkozer, Dellacrux, Veracruz, Ugolin, Tambourin, Fernandez, Martinez, Suarez, Henriquez, Vasquez, Lopez, Gomez, Sanchez, de Vechis, de Grassis, de Grassalis, de Pitigianis, de Graphaeis, Squilanti, Bizozeri, Barcola, de Bobadilla, Simancha, Perez de Lara, Aldretta, Lorca, de Scarcia, Quaranta, Scophra, Pedrezza, Cabrezza, Bisbe, Dias, de Clavasio, Villagut, Adam à Manden, Iribarne, Binsfeld, Volfangi à Vorberg, Vostbery, Strevesdorf. O mon père! lui dis-je tout effrayé, tous ces gens-là étoient-ils chrétiens? (PASCAL)

These barbarous names of Jesuit casuists, so cunningly arranged by the merciless art of Pascal to suggest, rather, a catalogue of names of devils, were probably more damaging by their ludicrous grotesqueness than pages of argued controversy. Who, indeed, could believe in the Christian orthodoxy of an Achokier, a Dealkozer, or a Volfangi à Vorberg?

> Les souffles de la nuit flottaient sur Galgala. . . .
> Tout reposait dans Ur et dans Jérimadeth. (HUGO)

What do we know of Galgala, Ur, or Jérimadeth? Yet they become words as blessed as the old lady's 'Mesopotamia'.

[189]

paper circulation of the sands of Arabia, the power by which Mahomet and his tribes laid hold at once on the two most powerful empires of the world . . .?'[1]

Again, Macaulay will make some generalization vivid by the lively particularity, not of proper names, but of trenchantly precise examples; as when he denounces the whimsical tyranny of some literary conventions. 'We do not see why we should not make a few more rules of the same kind; why we should not enact that the number of scenes in every act should be three or some multiple of three, that the number of lines in each scene should be an exact square, that the *dramatis personae* should never be more or fewer than sixteen, and that, in heroic rhymes, every thirty-sixth line should have twelve syllables.'

But of all methods of obtaining this essential concreteness, and the vitality that concreteness alone can give, none, I think, is so important as simile and metaphor. That, however, is so large a question as to demand a chapter to itself.

[1] *Letters on a Regicide Peace* (*Works* (1792), IV, p. 491).

IX

SIMILE AND METAPHOR

'AS prose is essentially the art of analytical description,[1] it would seem that metaphor is of no particular relevance to it; for poetry it is perhaps a more necessary mode of expression. . . . But whatever we may say of it, and however great and inclusive the function we assign to it, essentially it belongs to the sphere of poetry. Poetry alone is creative.[1] The art of prose is not creative, but constructive or logical.'[1]

Such is the austere view of Sir Herbert Read.[2] Aristotle, on the other hand, thought more highly of metaphor. After discussing the value of unusual and poetic words, he continues: 'But far the greatest thing is a gift for metaphor. For this alone cannot be learnt from others and is a sign of inborn power.' (*Poetics*, xxii.)

Sir Herbert, citing this passage, pleads that Aristotle is here writing only of poetry. But Aristotle—more wisely, I think—did not fix this gulf between poetry and prose; Isocrates, indeed, had done so; but Aristotle's *Rhetoric* (III, 2) explicitly stresses the value of metaphor for *prose* oratory as well: 'In conversation all of us use metaphors and ordinary, current words. Evidently by a proper combination of these one may attain a style that will remain clear, yet unobtrusively avoid the commonplace. . . . In prose there is all the *more* need to take pains with this because prose has fewer resources than verse.'

Here, then, are two flatly opposite views on the value of metaphor in prose. Which of them we adopt, remains

---

[1] Why?

[2] *English Prose Style* (1928), pp. 26, 34. In the second edition (1952) the last two sentences are omitted.

ultimately a matter of personal preference. Taste is relative. But you will soon see, if you read the enduring prose-works of the past, that most men, in many ages and nations, have felt with Aristotle. Childish of them, maybe, or meretricious; but, for myself, I will own at once that a style without metaphor and simile is to me like a day without sun, or a woodland without birds.

Living metaphor is a kind of two-headed Janus, looking two ways at once and making us see two things almost simultaneously.

Ah would that from earth and Heaven all strife were for
    ever flung,
And wrath, that makes even a wise man mad! Upon the
    tongue
Its taste is sweeter than honey, that drips from the comb—
    but *then*
Like a smother of blinding smoke it mounts in the hearts
    of men.

So cries Homer's Achilles in his remorse above Patroclus; and the likeness of wrath and honey is even more vividly concentrated in the metaphor than the likeness of blinding anger and blinding smoke in the simile. The simile sets two ideas side by side; in the metaphor they become superimposed. It would seem natural to think that simile, being simpler, is older. Indeed, it might be thought that this is why the prehistoric Homer, whose similes are so lovely, should be less remarkable for metaphor; whereas in Aeschylus and Pindar, some four or five centuries later, simile is overshadowed by a bold skill in metaphor such as poetry has never since surpassed.

But this explanation will hardly work. Of the not very numerous metaphors in Homer, many seem already old traditional formulae (such as 'wingéd words', 'paths of the fishes', and so on), not new inventions.[1] Similarly

[1] See Milman Parry, 'The Traditional Metaphor in Homer', *Classical Philology*, 1933; W. B. Stanford, *Greek Metaphor*, 1936.

Old English and Scandinavian poetry, more primitive
than *Iliad* or *Odyssey*, abounds in metaphorical kennings
already stereotyped.

The truth seems that metaphor too is older than any
literature—an immemorial human impulse perhaps as
much utilitarian as literary. For there appears little
ground for assigning poetic motives to the first man who
called the hole in a needle its 'eye', or the projections on
a saw its 'teeth'. In fine, metaphor is an inveterate
human tendency, as ancient perhaps as the days of the
mammoth, yet vigorous still in the days of the helicopter.[1]
Why then should it be banned from prose?

It is, indeed, astonishing how much ordinary language
is built of dead metaphors; as a coral-reef is formed of the
skeletons of dead madrepores and constantly increased by
those of their living brethren. In the words of Professor
Weekley,[2] 'Every expression that we employ, apart from
those that are connected with the most rudimentary
objects and actions, is a metaphor, though the original
meaning is dulled by constant use.' Consider the words of
that very sentence: an 'expression' is something squeezed
out; to 'employ' something is to wind it in (*implicare*);
to 'connect' is to tie together (*conectere*); 'rudimentary'
comes from the root RAD, 'root, sprout'; an 'object' is
something thrown in the way, an 'action' something
driven or conducted; 'original' means 'rising up', like
a plant or spring or heavenly body; 'constant' is 'standing
firm'. 'Metaphor' itself is a metaphor, meaning the
'carrying across' of a term or expression from its normal
usage to another.

Even in so humdrum a phrase as 'well off' there is said
to have lurked once the metaphor of a ship well away
from the perils of a lee shore. Even a seemingly simple
word like 'zest' has gained its meaning metaphorically;
from its literal sense of 'orange or lemon peel' (Fr.

---

[1] Lit. 'screw-wing'.   [2] *The Romance of Words* (1912), p. 97.

zeste) it came to be used for 'flavour, relish', and thence for 'a feeling of relish'. Even our most ideal terms are metaphors with material roots; an 'idea' is merely a 'shape'; 'πνεῦμα', 'anima', 'spirit' meant once no more than 'breath'.

If languages are so largely built of dead metaphors, this is no doubt partly for reasons of obvious convenience; picture-thinking is as natural at a primitive stage as picture-writing; but it shows also, I think, how deeply innate is the human pleasure in simile and metaphor themselves, quite apart from their utility. 'A good saying well spit out is a Christmas fire to my withered heart.'

Why? Partly, I suppose, because imagery pleases the simpler side of us, as pictures please children. And again it is a relief and a reassurance to descend from the clouds of the abstract to the solid world of things tangible, visible, or audible. Concepts are enlivened and illumined by percepts. But it is only the dream-interpretation of modern psychology that has fully revealed what a persistent and fundamental part is played in our less conscious thinking by symbols—how much our dream-life is devoted to disguise and masquerade; so that, for example, a man who is afraid of being carried away by some passion will dream, without ever having heard of the chariot of the soul in Plato's *Phaedrus*, that he is endangered by some uncontrollable horse. The visions of our sleep are often a fancy-dress ball of symbolic figures.

> Is it Murder whets his blade?
>   No!—a woodman, axe in hand.
> (*That*, for sure, 's an honest trade.)
>   What, Priapus? There you stand?
> Veil you in our masquerade
>   As a churchtower old and grey,
>   Primly pointing Heaven's way.
> Aphrodite brazen there,
>   Bare in beauty?—quickly mask it!

> Though Pandemos otherwhere,
> Seem you here a simple casket.
> Rhadamanthus, Minos, sleep!
> Blameless revels here we keep.

But whatever the reasons and origins, anyone who troubles to look will, I think, be surprised to find how often the power and pleasure of the most memorable passages of prose and verse spring mainly from a gift for metaphor. No doubt its use is often difficult, often dangerous. It is difficult because, after so many centuries, new metaphors are not so easy to find. And weary old metaphors, decrepit with long years of service, bring at each reappearance, not pleasure, but nausea. 'The long arm of coincidence' has become palsied with overwork; the non-existent 'snakes of Iceland' have long lost their bite; 'the jam that sweetens the powder', telling enough once in Lucretius, no longer sweetens the reader's temper; 'trump-cards' are dog-eared, 'burning questions' leave us cold, and 'the eleventh hour' no longer strikes.

There are also ways in which metaphor can prove dangerous. It does not do to adore *this* sort of image with one's eyes shut. The writer who informs us that 'there is no life in standing water', or that 'meaning is an arrow that reaches its mark when least encumbered with feathers', simply appears never to have seen a duckpond or shot an arrow. Or take the following sentences from Robert Byron's[1] *The Byzantine Achievement*.

'But not only are we poised on the footboard of the encyclopaedic civilisation now being launched; in addition, we are gathered to the brow of infinity by the initial achievement of the scientific revolution.'

(Of Constantinople.) 'It was here at this thwarted kiss of two continents, that the trade between the richest

---

[1] For Robert Byron, Gibbon was 'a pseudo-historian'. But at least Gibbon could write. Nor would he have spelt Cilicia 'Silicia'.

extremities of Europe, Asia and Africa, was sucked and spewed at the lips of the Golden Horn.'

Ships with footboards? Humanity as a swarm of midges deposited on the noble forehead of infinity? Asia and Europe trying to kiss like Hero and Leander, in the intervals of vomiting? Horns with lips? Imagery is not for those who cannot use, and control, their imaginations.

The mixed metaphor comes simply from failure to visualize. There seems no harm, whatever some may suppose, in a rapid succession of metaphors. These need not trouble any mind of ordinary quickness. And by this means Shakespeare has produced some of his most tumultuously brilliant passages. The objection is only to any coupling of ideas that breeds monstrous hybrids. The orator who cries 'we will burn our ships and . . . steer boldly out into the ocean of freedom', the journalist who urges the government to 'iron out vicious circles of bottlenecks', are ludicrous merely because they have not *seen* what they are talking about, and therefore amuse, or irritate, readers who do.

Yet such lapses are surprisingly common. One can only conclude that many imaginations are strangely blind. Sir Herbert Grierson cites an extraordinary instance from Mark Pattison: 'Even at this day a country squire or rector, on landing with his cub under his wing' (a sort of lion of St. Mark?) 'at Oxford, finds himself at sea.' Then there is that enthusiastic vision I once encountered in a book on the Oxford Group: 'the University atmosphere is stabbed with praying giants'. And here are two examples from Saintsbury:

But brevity has the Scylla and Charybdis of obscurity and baldness ever waiting for it; and balance those of monotonous clock-beat and tedious parallelism. The ship is safe through all these in such things as the exquisite symmetry of the Absolution.[1]

[1] *English Prose Rhythm*, p. 126.

[196]

(A truly strange voyage of vessels manned by Brevity and Balance through seas perilous with obscurity and baldness, clock-beats and parallels. Besides, Scylla and Charybdis were alternative dangers: whereas there is, unfortunately, nothing to prevent a writer from being *both* bald *and* obscure, *both* monotonous in rhythm *and* tedious in antithesis. On the contrary, such faults can easily be combined.)

Similarly Saintsbury writes of Ruskin:

Whether he shows any influence from the older prose harmonists who had begun to write, as it were, like fairy parents over his cradle, I must leave to some industrious person to expiscate or rummage out; for the haystack of Ruskinian autobiography is not only mighty in bulk but scattered rather forbiddingly.

(An equally odd vision of prose-musicians as fairy godparents scribbling, like a posse of reporters, above an infant's cradle; of angling; and of haystacks scattered before being built.)

When a man as clever as Saintsbury can produce such absurdities, all of us may well be on our guard. The trouble comes partly from employing hackneyed imagery like fairy godparents, or Scylla and Charybdis, which have done such long service that they might now be allowed a rest. Their very familiarity is apt to blur the image that a living metaphor should present; and the writer allows these half-dead metaphors to collide with other metaphors less dead.

It must, of course, be owned that very distinguished authors have written things as queer. There are plenty of examples in Shakespeare. There is that phrase of Milton's which, when pointed out by Rogers to Coleridge, is said to have given him a sleepless night:

Sight so deform what heart of rock could long
Dry-eyed behold?

[197]

There is Cromwell's—'God has kindled a seed in this nation.' There is De Quincey's—'The very recognition of these or any of these by the jurisprudence of a nation is a mortal wound to the very keystone upon which the whole vast arch of morality reposes.' But whoever may have written so, I still feel they would have done better not to. In any case they are hardly for imitation; especially in prose.

Really dead metaphors, like really dead nettles, cannot sting; but often the metaphors are only half dead; and these need careful handing. It may, of course, be argued that some mixed metaphors bother none but readers with too vivid imaginations. Yet I doubt if readers *can* have too vivid imaginations. At all events you will find, I think, that you lose esteem with many readers if they come to feel that you have a less vivid imagination than they have themselves. A main purpose of imagery is to make a style more concrete and definite; and it is interesting to note how much that imagery itself may gain by being made still more concrete and still more definite, as when Webster borrows images from Sidney or Montaigne.

She was like them that could not sleepe, when they were softly layd.

(SIDNEY, Arcadia)

You are like some, cannot sleepe *in feather-beds*,
But must have *blockes for their pillowes*.

(Duchess of Malfi)

See whether any cage can please a bird. Or whether a dogge grow not fiercer with tying.

(SIDNEY, Arcadia)

Like *English Mastiffes*, that grow fierce with tying.

(Duchess of Malfi)

The opinion of wisedome is the plague of man.

(MONTAIGNE)

[198]

Oh Sir, the opinion of wisedome is *a foule tettor*, that runs all over a mans body.

(Duchess of Malfi)

Never, it seems to me, was theft better justified—the plagiarist here is far more praiseworthy than his victims; simply because in each case the picture becomes much more precisely visualized. 'A dogge' is vague beside 'English Mastiffes'; a 'plague' is feeble compared to 'a foule tettor'. Here, as with other kinds of clarity, preferences may indeed differ according to taste and temperament; there are doubtless times when, here too, writing gains by half-lights, mists, and shadows; but I own that I love, particularly in prose, keen vision; sharp focus; and clearest air.

Imagery, however, is also exposed to other dangers. It can become too far-fetched. Aeschylus is magnificent when he speaks of

the jaw of Salmydessus,
Sour host to sailors, stepmother of ships;

but many of us smile when we come upon things so fantastic as 'the thirsty dust, twin-sister unto mud'. On this point, indeed, at least in prose, ancient taste tended to be far more cautious than ours. Thus Aristotle objects to the image of Alcidamas that 'the Odyssey is a lovely mirror of human life'; 'Longinus', to Plato's phrase in *The Laws* about allowing the walls of his ideal city to sleep beneath the earth (that is, to remain unbuilt). Yet it is not easy to see why these should be blamed; especially when Pericles is praised for calling hostile Aegina 'the eyesore of Peiraeus', or for saying over the young Athenians fallen in the Samian War that 'the spring had been taken out of the year'. Some, however, will agree that many Elizabethan conceits and much bad Metaphysical poetry are based on comparisons too hyperbolical. Similarly with some oriental imagery (for

[199]

'Metaphysical' poetry is far older than some of us realize).

> Night black as pitch[1] she bids bright day[2] bestride;
> Two sugar-plums[3] stars two-and-thirty[4] hide;
> O'er the red rose[5] a musky scorpion[6] strays,
> For which she keeps two antidotes[7] well-tried.
>
> (ABUL-QUASIM AL-BAKHARZI, *d.* A.D. 1075)

And here is a strange modern specimen of metaphors both mixed and forced.

> To the Giorgione in the Cathedral at Castel Franco a man must come should the dry biscuit of the desert have stuck in his throat or should the subtlety of life have bent his sleep. Here is the certain rejoinder to the intricacy of bitterness, here the sane assumption that is not keyed to mark the loaded hiss that whistles a drugging breath through the undergrowth of a Catholic dispensation.[8]
>
> (ADRIAN STOKES, *Sunrise in the West*)

Again, imagery may lapse into grossness and crudity, like Robert Byron's spewing Constantinople (p. 196), or the already quoted French-Revolutionary orator who cried to his adversary, 'There is not a louse on your body but has a right to spit in your face.' Or again imagery can become precious and affected as in *Euphues*: which also illustrates yet another danger—that metaphor and simile, instead of being used as a means to clearer meaning, may be abused as ends in themselves. When Sir Thomas Browne trots out his 'Bivious Theorems and Janus-faced Doctrines' and his negroes 'in the black Jaundice'; when he bids us not to look 'for *Whales* in the Euxine Sea, or expect great matters where they are not to be found'; then it becomes clear that he is more

[1] Her hair.   [2] Her face.   [3] Her lips.   [4] Her teeth.
[5] Her cheek.   [6] A lovelock.   [7] Her lips.
[8] Quoted in Sir Herbert Read, *English Prose Style* (1928 ed.), p. 31.

concerned with his art than with his matter, with
beauties and quaintnesses than with truth. In lesser men
such things became a fashion frivolous and futile; and
they were bound to provoke revolt in practical minds.
Even at the beginning of the seventeenth century, 'it
was', Aubrey records, 'a shrewd and severe animadver-
sion of a Scotish lord, who, when King James asked him
how he liked Bishop A's sermon, said that he was learned,
but he did play with his Text, as a Jack-an-apes does who
takes up a thing and tosses and playes with it, and then
he takes up another, and playes a little with it. Here's a
pretty thing, and there's a pretty thing.'[1]

Again, Bishop Samuel Parker (1640–88) would have
liked preachers prohibited by Act of Parliament from
using 'fulsome and lushious Metaphors'. And Hobbes,
no favourite of bishops, was at least in agreement here—
'metaphors . . . are like *ignes fatui*'.[2]

It is, too, familiar enough how, as the seventeenth
century drew towards its close, the men of the Royal
Society reacted still more drastically against this 'luxury
and redundance of speech'. But it is worth quoting a
little more fully from the tirades of their historian,
Sprat. 'Who can behold, without Indignation, how many
mists and uncertainties their specious *Tropes* and *Figures*
have brought in our Knowledge? . . . Of all the Studies
of men, nothing may be sooner obtain'd, than this vicious
abundance of *Phrase*, this trick of *Metaphors*, this volu-
bility of *Tongue* which makes so great a noise in the
World. . . . And indeed, in most other parts of Learning,
I look on it as a thing almost utterly desperate in its
cure; and I think, it may be plac'd among those *general
mischiefs*; such as the *dissention* of Christian Princes, the

---

[1] *Aubrey's Brief Lives*, ed. O. L. Dick (1950), 'Lancelot
Andrewes', p. 7.
[2] Cf. Locke's view that, in writings which aim at truth, all
figurative expressions are 'perfect cheats'.

want of practice in Religion, and the like; which have been so long spoken against, that men are become insensible about them.' Hence, he says, the Royal Society formed 'a constant Resolution to reject all amplifications, digressions, and swellings of style: to return back to the primitive purity, and shortness, when men deliver'd so many *things* almost in an equal number of *words*'.

Never, surely, was verbal imagery subjected to so tremendous an anathema. 'The *dissention* of Christian Princes'—'the *want of practice* in Religion'—one may wonder if the iconoclastic Sprat was himself being very scientific, or (for a future bishop) very religious.[1] Naturally no serious scientist could be expected to have much patience with minds still fancifully medieval like Sir Thomas Browne, who is capable of beginning a chapter on lampreys: 'Whether Lampries have nine eyes, we durst refer it unto *Polyphemus*, who had but one, to judge it. An error concerning eyes, occasioned by the error of eyes. . . .' But even the scientist who wishes to persuade the world may find metaphor and simile far from valueless. Montesquieu, I suppose, may claim to be called a political scientist. And not the least part of his greatness is that, as Sainte-Beuve has said (with an admirable metaphor), 'Dans la pensée de Montesquieu,

---

[1] Nor was he even very consistent in avoiding simile and metaphor himself. He begins the first passage quoted above with a metaphor. Of alchemists seeking the Philosopher's Stone he says: 'if an Experiment lye never so little out of their rode, it is free from their discovery: as I have heard of some violent creatures in Africk, which still going a violent pace straight on, and not being able to turn themselves, can never get any prey but what they meet just in their way.' And again: 'Now there is an universal *desire*, and *appetite* after *knowledge*, after the peaceable, the fruitful, the nourishing *knowledge*: and not after that of the antient Sects, which only yielded hard indigestible *arguments*, or sharp contentions instead of *food*: which when the minds of men requir'd *bread*, gave them only a *stone*, and for *fish* a *serpent*.'

au moment où l'on s'y attend le moins, tout d'un coup la cime se dore.'

For example:

Le peuple a toujours trop d'action ou trop peu. Quelquefois avec cent mille bras il renverse tout; quelquefois avec cent mille pieds il ne va que comme les insectes.

L'Espagne a fait comme ce roi insensé qui demanda que tout ce qu'il toucheroit se convertît en or.

L'Angleterre est agitée par des vents qui ne sont pas faits pour submerger, mais pour conduire au port.

(Of relativity.) Il est l'éponge de tous les préjugés.

And, to take one more scientific example among many, has not Einstein excellently said (though of course for a popular audiénce) that it is hard to split atoms because it is like shooting birds in the dark, in a country where there are few birds?

But our concern is not, after all, with science but with literature, and with ordinary writing (and speech). Here, great as are the dangers of imagery, its gifts can be greater still. Metaphor, above all, can give strength, clarity, and speed; it can add wit, humour, individuality, poetry. After all, the one unpardonable fault in an author—and perhaps the commonest—is tediousness. It is easy for a monologue in conversation to become a bore; easier still for a speech; easiest of all for a book. But against boredom there are no better antidotes than these qualities that vivid metaphor can often bring.

Consider, first, the gain in energy and clarity of impression. Hundreds of thousands have groaned in the bitterness of homeless banishment; but their lamentations have been stifled in the silence of the years, while we still remember that double metaphor in which Dante cried how bitterly salt was the bread of exile, and how

steep for him its stairs.[1] Many an actor or dramatist must
have suffered from the sense of prostituting his own soul
to amuse an audience; but could any direct form of
utterance have been as moving as Shakespeare's simile
'my nature is subdu'd, To what it workes in, like the
Dyers hand', or the metaphor of Hugo, telling how, as
the curtain rose for the first night of *Hernani*, 'Je voyais
se lever la jupe de mon âme'?

Many an observer of human life has groaned at the
fickle brevity of human grief. Abstractly, it could hardly
be put with finer eloquence than Chateaubriand's—
'Croyez-moi, mon fils, les douleurs ne sont point éter-
nelles; il faut tôt ou tard qu'elles finissent, parce que le
coeur de l'homme est fini; c'est une de nos grandes
misères; nous ne sommes pas même capables d'être longtemps malheureux.' But, for one who remembers this,
there are a thousand who never forget the more concrete
vision that Shakespeare has created with the homely aid
of a dish and a pair of shoes.

> Thrift, thrift, *Horatio*: the Funerall Bakt-meats
> Did coldly furnish forth the Marriage Tables.

> A little Month, or ere those shooes were old,
> With which she followed my poore Fathers body
> Like *Niobe*, all teares.

Without metaphor could misogyny have found such
barbed invectives against women as Pope's phrase about
'the moving toyshop of their heart', or Balzac's savage
'des poêles à dessus de marbre'? Metternich, I think, was

---

[1]   Tu proverai sì come sa di sale
        lo pane altrui, e com' è duro calle
        lo scendere e il salir per l'altrui scale.
                                Paradiso, XVII.

    Thou shalt make trial what salt and bitter fare
    The bread of others; and how hard a path
    Still to toil up and down another's stair.

right: 'In politics calm clarity is the only true eloquence;
but, to be sure, this clarity can at times be best gained by
an image.'[1]

Next, speed. I know no better example of the power of
metaphor to crowd the maximum of ideas into every
minute than Ulysses' famous speech in *Troilus and
Cressida*.

> Time hath (my Lord) a wallet at his backe,
> Wherein he puts almes for oblivion:
> A great-siz'd monster of ingratitudes:
> Those scraps are good deedes past,
> Which are devour'd as fast as they are made,
> Forgot as soone as done: perseverance, deere my Lord,
> Keepes honor bright, to have done, is to hang
> Quite out of fashion, like a rustie mail,
> In monumentall mockrie: take the instant way,
> For honour travels in a straight so narrow,
> Where one but goes abreast, keepe then the path:
> For Emulation hath a thousand Sonnes,
> That one by one pursue; if you give way,
> Or hedge aside from the direct forthright,
> Like to an entred Tyde, they all rush by,
> And leave you hindmost:
> Or like a gallant Horse falne in first ranke,
> Lye there for pavement to the abject rear,
> Ore-run and trampled on: then what they doe in present,
> Though lesse then yours in past, must ore-top yours:
> For Time is like a fashionable Hoste,
> That slightly shakes his parting Guest by th' hand;
> And with his armes out-stretcht, as he would flye,
> Graspes in the commer: the welcome ever smiles,
> And farewel goes out sighing: O let not vertue seeke
> Remuneration for the thing it was:
> For beautie, wit,
> High birth, vigor of bone, desert in service,
> Love, friendship, charity, are subjects all
> To envious and calumniating Time:

[1] Varnhagen von Ense, *Denkwürdigkeiten* (1843–59), VIII, p. 112.

One touch of nature makes the whole world kin:
That all with one consent praise new-borne gaudes,
Though they are made and moulded of things past,
And give to dust, that is a little gilt,
More laud then gilt oredusted.

'I use the metaphorical', said Meredith, 'to avoid the long-winded.' Often he did this effectively.

Slave is the open mouth beneath the closed.

Time leers between above his twiddling thumbs.

When the renewed for ever of a kiss
Whirls life within the shower of loosened hair.

A kiss is but a kiss now! And no wave
Of a great flood that whirls me to the sea.
But as you will! We'll sit contentedly
And eat our pot of honey on the grave.

Strain we the arms for Memory's hours,
We are the seized Persephone.

Thousand eyeballs under hoods
    Have you by the hair.
Enter these enchanted woods
    You who dare.

Unfortunately, I feel, Meredith lacked a Greek sense of restraint; as might be expected from one who held the somewhat simple faith that 'the core of style' is 'fervidness', and would even rebuke young ladies because their nostrils were not lively, nervous, and dilated. Vitality became for him, at times, a sort of St. Vitus' dance; and in the coils of his twisted ideas he would writhe and mouth like a new Laocoön. Thus sharing Browning's cult for mere violence, he shared also Browning's slightly vulgar itch to astonish; so that Morley could describe him at home, on the approach of a new visitor, 'forcing himself without provocation into a wrestle for violent effects'; and Stevenson lament the admixture with his finer qualities of 'the high intellectual humbug'. Hence a frequent abuse of metaphor in his later work, such as these lines from *The Empty Purse*.

> He cancelled the ravaging Plague
> With the roll of his fat off the cliff.
> Do thou with thy lean as the weapon of ink,
> Though they call thee an angler who fishes the vague
> And catches the not too pink.
> Attack one as murderous, knowing thy cause
> Is the cause of community. Iterate,
> Iterate, iterate, harp on the trite:
> Our preacher to win is the supple in stiff:
> Yet always in measure, with bearing polite.

Yet to Meredith there does belong the credit of seeing and stating the truth that metaphor need not be, as some suppose, an otiose and time-wasting ornament, like a maze in a country-house garden; but can provide at times a most trenchant short-cut.

As for the humour that imagery can give, I do not know who illustrates this better than dear Fuller. Naturally he got into trouble for it, then and since, with critical owls. Sometimes, indeed, it is not clear whether his humour is intended, or is just the quaintness of his wit—whether we are laughing with him or at him. But often there is no doubt; and, for me, passages like the following make him much more congenial than some Metaphysical minds before him, in the school of Donne, who display their quips with such peacock gravity, and seem too conceited about mere conceits.

Some serious books that dare flie abroad, are hooted at by a flock of Pamphlets.

There are some Birds (Sea-pies by name) who cannot rise except it be by flying against the winde, as some hope to achieve their advancement, by being contrary and paradoxical in judgement to all before them.

(Of tall men.) Ofttimes such who are built four stories high, are observed to have little in their cockloft.

(Of Sir Francis Drake.) In a word, should those that speak against him fast till they fetch their bread where he did his, they would have a good stomach to eat it.

Thus dyed Queen Elizabeth, whilest living, the first maid on earth, and when dead, the second in heaven.

They who count their calling a prison, shall at last make a prison their calling.

(Of a crippled saint.) God, who denied her legs, gave her wings.

Wherefore I presume my aunt Oxford will not be justly offended, if in this book I give my mother[1] the upper hand and first begin with her history. Thus desiring God to pour his blessing on both, that neither may want milk for their children, nor children for their milk, we proceed to the business.

(Of Cambridge Castle.) At this day the castle may seem to have run out of the gate-house, which only is standing and employed for a prison.

Take away Fuller's images, and you rob his humour of half its charm.

For wit in simile and metaphor, let us turn to Swift. His case is the more interesting in that he is sometimes supposed to have almost wholly disdained such imagery. But to say 'the Rogue never hazards a figure'[2] is absurd. He put one (a half-dead metaphor, it is true) even on his tomb—'ubi saeva indignatio ulterius *cor lacerare* nequit'.

---

[1] Cambridge.
[2] Joseph Warton (*Pope's Works* (1797 ed.), IX, p. 84) asserts that Johnson said this to him. Johnson, as he himself admitted, could talk at times very 'loosely'; but I feel some doubt whether he can really have uttered anything so inaccurate. (See G. B. Hill, *Johnson's Lives of the Poets* (1905), III, p. 51; and contrast p. 210 below.)

It would be special pleading to point out that *The Tale of a Tub* is a series of metaphors, or to recall the Big-endians and Little-endians, the high Heels and low, of *Gulliver*. But the comparative rarity of Swift's images is not more marked than their point, and often their deadliness, when they do occur. It was Swift that provided Matthew Arnold with a famous watchword in the allegory of the bee's 'sweetness and light', as contrasted with the dirt and poison of the spider (though Swift himself, unhappily, too often chose to be more spider than bee). And when Swift proclaims 'Surely man is a broomstick'; when he compares Dryden under Virgil's helmet to a mouse under a canopy of state; or poets preyed on by poets to fleas bit by lesser fleas; when he predicts 'like that tree, I shall die at top'; when he groans that he *is* dying 'in a rage, like a poisoned rat in a hole', could his rancour have found utterance half so telling without the images? And how bitter is the wit of these!

Old men and comets have been reverenced for the same reason; their long beards, and pretences to foretell events.

The reason why so few marriages are happy, is, because young ladies spend their time in making nets, not in making cages.

(Of lovers.) They seem a perfect moral to the story of that philosopher, who, while his thoughts and eyes were fixed upon the constellations, found himself seduced by his lower parts into a ditch.

If the quiet of the state can be bought by only flinging men a few ceremonies to devour, it is a purchase no wise man would refuse. Let the mastiffs amuse themselves about a sheepskin stuffed with hay, provided it will keep them from worrying the flock.

It remains true, however, that Swift is, in general, unusually sparing of simile and metaphor. (And the

[209]

images he does use are mainly meant not to charm, but to wound.) That is partly why, to me, he is on the whole an unattractive writer—bleak, monotonous, and depressing, though impressive, like a Pennine moorland—not like the Highlands. But Johnson has already said it. 'That he has in his works no metaphor, as has been said, is not true; but his few metaphors seem to be received rather by necessity than choice.'[1] 'This easy and safe conveyance,' Johnson continues, 'it was Swift's desire to attain, and for having attained he deserves praise. For purposes merely didactic, when something is to be told that was not known before, it is the best mode; but against that inattention by which known truths are suffered to lie neglected, it makes no provision; it instructs, but does not persuade.' This, I think, is just. That widening of sympathy which, for me, is so largely the true end of literature, in Swift's writing remains rare. He does not persuade.

It is idle to wish, as Swift trots like a lean grey wolf, with white fangs bared, across his desolate landscape, that he were more like a benevolent Saint Bernard; he would cease to be Swift. Being what he was, he made a striking addition to the infinite variety of the world; but one Swift seems to me quite enough. And his style is of interest as showing both what trenchancy the presence of imagery can give, and how much charm and colour its absence takes away.

We have so far seen how imagery can add strength and speed, wit and humour. But no less important is its power to stamp a work with the writer's particular individuality. This was clear long before psychologists began using the images of our dreams to reveal mental conflicts hidden even from ourselves. The light thrown on Shakespeare's mind by the imagery of his plays, and of one play as contrasted with another, has been abundantly—perhaps too

[1] This I do not feel.

abundantly—examined.[1] Writers, again, have used
imagery to mark the personality of their characters. It
is not least by his metaphors and similes that the tone of
impatient impetuousness in Hotspur is brought to life.

I had rather be a Kitten and cry mew.

Oh, he's as tedious
As a tyred Horse, a rayling Wife,
Worse than a smoakie House. I had rather live
With Cheese and Garlick in a Windmill farre,
Than feede on Cates, and have him talke to me,
In any Summer-House in Christendome.

You sweare like a Comfit-makers Wife . . .
Sweare me, *Kate*, like a Lady, as thou art,
A good mouth-filling Oath: and leave 'In sooth',
And such protest of Pepper Ginger-bread,
To Velvet-guards and Sunday-Citizens.

Or consider that pair of very different soldiers, Uncle
Toby and his corporal. ''Tis supposed, continued the
Benedictine, that St. Maxima has lain in this tomb four
hundred years, and two hundred before her canonization
—'Tis but a slow rise, Brother Toby, quoth my father, in
this selfsame army of Martyrs.[2]—A desperate slow one,

---

[1] See especially W. H. Clemen, *The Development of Shakespeare's Imagery*, 1951—an excellent study, though at times, I
think, a little apt to grow too microscopic in the search for hidden
significances; too forgetful that the stage is not the study. Not the
least interesting thing in Shakespeare's images is their advance
from being merely ornamental to become relevant, concentrated,
suggestive. In his prentice work he often uses them merely to
impress; but later to express what in no other way could have been
expressed so poignantly. They had been mere jewellery: they
become the life and feature of his characters.

[2] Compare Sterne's own remark: 'If ever the army of martyrs
was to be augmented or a new one raised—I would have no hand
in it, one way or t'other.'

an' please your Honour, said Trim, unless one could pur-
chase. I should rather sell out entirely, said my uncle
Toby.—I am pretty much of your opinion, Brother
Toby, said my father.—Poor St. Maxima, said my uncle
Toby low to himself.'[1]

But a more solid instance may be found in Johnson of
the way a man's images can make him still more himself.
'His mind', says Boswell, 'was so full of imagery, that he
might have been perpetually a poet; yet it is remarkable,
that, however rich his prose is in this respect, his poetical
pieces, in general, have not much of that splendour, but
are rather distinguished by strong sentiment and acute
observation.' Take away Johnson's figures, especially in
his talk, and you will weaken a good deal that impression
of snorting, militant energy which made Goldsmith say
of him, in another metaphor, that if his pistol missed
fire, he would knock you down with the butt; and Boswell,
no less vividly, that he used no vain flourishes with his
sword—'he was through your body in an instant'.
Typical, for example, are Johnson's troops of 'dogs'—not
only 'Whig dogs', or 'factious dogs', or (of Chesterfield)
'I have hurt the dog too much already'; but also (before
his own portrait) 'Ah ha! Sam Johnson, I see thee! And
an ugly dog thou art!'—'I had rather see the portrait of a
dog I know than all the allegorical pictures they can shew
me in the world'[2]—'If you call a dog Hervey, I shall love
him'—'What, is it you, you dogs! I'll have a frisk with
you.'

Then there are the bulls he launched at Hume and at
Rousseau.

Truth, sir, is a cow which will yield such people no more
milk, and so they are gone to milk the bull.

[1] Another example of this somewhat obvious form of humour is
the nautical Ben of Congreve's *Love for Love.*
[2] A little curious when one recalls Johnson's rather excessive
fondness for allegory in *The Rambler.*

If a bull could speak, he might as well exclaim: 'Here am I with this cow and this grass; what being can enjoy greater felicity?'

And again, of Edwards's attack on Warburton: 'Nay, he has given him some smart hits to be sure; but there is no proportion between the two men; they must not be named together. A fly, sir, may sting a stately horse and make him wince; but one is but an insect, and the other is a horse still.' Omit the second sentence, and how much less Johnsonian the whole becomes!

So with Johnson's criticisms. Today they may at times seem false, or old-fashioned; but often, by their gift of metaphor, they still outlive the more meticulous judgements of lesser men. 'He treads upon the brink of meaning'—'if their conceits were far-fetched, they were often worth the carriage'—'a quibble was to him the fatal Cleopatra for which he lost the world and was content to lose it'—'if blank verse be not tumid and gorgeous, it is crippled prose.' When he dismissed Gray's Odes as 'cucumbers', it was in the scornful heat of conversation; but the more considered judgement in the *Life of Gray*—'He has a kind of strutting dignity, and is tall by walking on tiptoe'—lives longer, I find, in the memory than whole chapters by lesser critics. Again what mockery of literary vanity can compare with Johnson on Richardson?—'that fellow Richardson, on the contrary, could not be contented to sail quietly down the stream of reputation, without longing to taste the froth from every stroke of the oar'—'that fellow died merely for want of change among his flatterers; he perished for want of more, like a man obliged to breathe the same air till it is exhausted'. And finally when Johnson is himself confronting critics, how typically and genially gigantic is the figure with which he ends! (He is writing to Thomas Warton about the *Dictionary*.) 'What reception I shall meet with upon the shore, I know not . . .

[213]

whether I shall find upon the coast a Calypso that will court, or a Polyphemus that will eat me. But if a Polyphemus comes to me, have at his eye!'[1]

Lastly, the poetry of metaphor. There are owls who want prose to be wholly prosaic. Some kinds of it, yes. Like Locke's.[2] But, whereas poetry is better without any prose in it, prose can often embody a great deal of poetry. Prose in poetry is a blemish like ink on a swan; but prose without poetry becomes too often as drab and lifeless as a Sunday in London. By 'poetry' in this sense I do not mean 'fine writing', such as De Quincey or Ruskin were sometimes tempted to overdo; I mean a feeling for the beauty, grace, or tragedy of life. It is thanks to this that some can find more essential poetry in Sir Thomas Browne than in Dryden; in Landor than in Byron; in some paragraphs of Yeats's prose than in twenty shelves of minor verse. And one of the things that reduce me to annual rage and despair in correcting examination papers is the spectacle of two or three hundred young men and women who have soaked in poetry for two or three years, yet seem, with rare exceptions, not to have absorbed one particle of it into their systems; so that even those who have acquired some knowledge yet think, too often, like pedants, and write like grocers.

To illustrate, then, the poetry that can be added by metaphor and simile let our instances be Chateaubriand and Flaubert—both masters of prose, who yet carried through their lives a tormenting mixture of poetry and irony, romance and bitter realism. There are moments when they make one think of Swift; but, for me, their poetic gift lifts them far above him, as above the long

---

[1] Johnson wrote 'eyes'; but this plural must surely be a slip of his pen.

[2] Cf. Locke, *Of Education*: 'If he have a poetic vein, it is to me the strangest thing in the world, that his father should desire or suffer it to be cherished or improved.' At least, admirably honest!

aridity of the Sahara stands up the range of Atlas. Obviously it is not by imagery alone that prose can become poetic—it plays no part in words like those of the old priest to Atala: 'L'habitant de la cabane et celui du palais, tout souffre, tout gémit ici-bas; les reines ont été vues pleurant comme de simples femmes, et l'on s'est étonné de la quantité de larmes que contiennent les yeux des rois.' Here are simply mingled memories of the Hebrew Scriptures and of the French Terror. Yet Chateaubriand's images do remain one of the most frequent channels by which poetry enters his prose.

(Of great writers and their commentators.) On croit voir les ruines de Palmyre, restes superbes du génie et du temps, au pied desquelles l'Arabe du désert a bâti sa misérable hutte.

(How crushing the scorn of that last wretched monosyllable!)

Quelquefois une haute colonne se montrait seule debout dans un désert, comme une grande pensée s'élève, par intervalles, dans une âme que le temps et le malheur ont dévastée.

La redingote'grise et le chapeau de Napoléon placés au bout d'un bâton sur la côte de Brest feraient courir l'Europe aux armes.

La jeunesse est une chose charmante; elle part au commencement de la vie, couronnée de fleurs, comme la flotte athénienne pour aller conquérir la Sicile.

Le coeur le plus serein en apparence ressemble au puits naturel de la savane Alachua; la surface en paraît calme et pure, mais quand vous regardez au fond du bassin, vous apercevez un large crocodile, que le puits nourrit dans ses eaux.

Je ne fais rien; je ne crois plus ni à la gloire ni à l'amour, ni au pouvoir ni à la liberté, ni aux rois ni aux peuples. . . . Je regarde passer à mes pieds ma dernière heure.

Personne ne se crée comme moi une société réelle en invoquant des ombres; c'est au point que la vie de mes souvenirs absorbe le sentiment de ma vie réelle. Des personnes mêmes dont je ne me suis jamais occupé, si elles meurent, envahissent ma mémoire: on dirait que nul ne peut devenir mon compagnon s'il n'a passé à travers la tombe, ce qui me porte à croire que je suis un mort. Où les autres trouveront une éternelle séparation, je trouve une réunion éternelle; qu'un de mes amis s'en aille de la terre, c'est comme s'il venait demeurer à mes foyers; il ne me quitte plus.... Si les générations actuelles dédaignent les générations vieillies, elles perdent les frais de leur mépris en ce qui me touche: je ne m'aperçois même pas de leur existence.

Je vais partout bâillant ma vie.

La vie est une peste permanente.

I do not much like Chateaubriand as a person; but I do not envy those who cannot enjoy the melancholy music of this arrogant and lonely Lucifer.

Flaubert is less of a posing egotist; more honest and more lovable. But his strength, too, stands rooted in bitterness; which is, I suppose, not quite the finest kind of strength. (In his correspondence with George Sand he seems at times almost like some fretful child of genius whom that wise old woman tries vainly to console.) Yet not even his character, nor his characters, live more vividly in my memory than the brilliant images whose marble seems to gleam out, now defiant, now mournfully resigned, through the green gloom of that Norman garden beside the seaward windings of the Seine.

Moi, je déteste la vie; je suis un catholique, j'ai au coeur quelque chose du suintement vert des cathédrales normandes.

(Of Emma Bovary's fading passion.) Cette lueur d'incendie qui empourprait son ciel pâle se couvrit de plus d'ombre et s'effaça par degrés.

Leur grand amour où elle vivait plongée, parut se diminuer sous elle comme l'eau d'un fleuve qui s'absorberait dans son lit, et elle aperçut la vase.

[216]

La parole humaine est comme un chaudron fêlé où nous battons des mélodies à faire danser des ours, quand on voudrait attendrir les étoiles.

Les plaisirs comme des écoliers dans la cour d'un collège avaient tellement piétiné sur son coeur, que rien de vert n'y poussait et ce qui passait par là, plus étourdi que les enfants, n'y laissait pas même, comme eux, son nom gravé sur la muraille.

Il ne faut pas toucher aux idoles: la dorure en reste aux mains.

Elle le corrompait par-delà le tombeau.

Les noeuds les plus solidement faits se dénouent d'eux-mêmes, parce que la corde s'use. Tout s'en va, tout passe; l'eau coule et le coeur oublie.

L'avocasserie se glisse partout, le rage de discourir, de pérorer, de plaider . . . O pauvre Olympe! ils seraient capables de faire sur ton sommet un plant de pommes de terre.[1]

J'ai eu tout jeune un pressentiment complet de la vie. C'était comme une odeur de cuisine nauséabonde qui s'échappe par un soupirail. On n'a pas besoin d'en avoir mangé pour savoir qu'elle est à faire vomir.

Fais-toi une cuirasse secrète composée de poésie et d'orgueil, comme on tressait les cottes de maille avec de l'or et du fer.

L'auteur, dans son oeuvre, doit être comme Dieu dans l'Univers, présent partout, et visible nulle part.

Le vrai poète pour moi est un prêtre. Dès qu'il passe la soutane, il doit quitter sa famille . . . il faut faire comme les amazons, se brûler tout un côté du coeur.

Je suis un homme-plume.

(Of his art.) C'est un ulcère que je gratte, voilà tout.

[1] It seems unlikely that Flaubert had ever read Macaulay's serious exultation (in his Essay on Southey's *Colloquies*) at the pleasing prospect of cultivation being carried hereafter to the very tops of Helvellyn and Ben Nevis.

Pourvu que mes manuscrits durent autant que moi, c'est tout ce que je veux. C'est dommage qu'il me faudrait un trop grand tombeau; je les ferais enterrer avec moi comme un sauvage fait de son cheval.

Je n'attends plus rien de la vie qu'une suite de feuilles de papier à barbouiller de noir. Il me semble que je traverse une solitude sans fin, pour aller je ne sais où. C'est moi qui suis tout à la fois, le désert, le voyageur, et le chameau.

(Of Leconte de Lisle.) Son encre est pâle.

On peut juger de la bonté d'un livre à la vigueur des coups de poing qu'il vous a donnés . . . je crois que le plus grand caractère du génie est, avant tout, la force.

Les illusions tombent, mais les âmes-cyprès sont toujours vertes.

One cannot say of Flaubert what he himself said of Voltaire: 'Qui a eu plus d'esprit que Voltaire et qui a été moins poète?'

These examples of strength and swiftness, wit and humour, personality and poetry may well be more than sufficient. Try to rewrite such things without metaphor or simile—you will sacrifice half their life and energy. In fine, Johnson, like Aristotle, seems to me right: 'And, Sir, as to metaphorical expression, that is a great excellence in style, when it is used with propriety, for it gives you two ideas for one; conveys the meaning more luminously, and generally with a perception of delight.'

To say, then, that 'metaphor is of no particular relevance' to prose, seems to me stupefying. My conclusion is that those who have no gift for metaphor and imagery are doubtless wise to keep clear of it; but that those who have it, whether in writing or in speech, will find few qualities that better repay cultivation.

X

THE HARMONY OF PROSE

THE music of prose is a difficult and even dangerous subject:[1] difficult, because it is intricate and obscure; dangerous, because the more delicate elements in literature can sometimes be damaged by too much critical dissection. Critics, I know, are often indignant at this suggestion—they are apt to feel that the words, and even the bread, are being taken out of their mouths. But it did not really need Freud to discover that our emotions can often be weakened by excessive introspection. The more they know about literature, the less some people—though, of course, by no means all—seem really to feel it.[2] There are some things in its enjoyment that need sharp wits and concentrated attention: but there are also others that are, I think, best left to the less conscious parts of the mind. Therefore I should be the last to claim overmuch from the analysis that follows. Apart from a few simple principles, the sound and rhythm of English prose seem to me matters where both writers and readers should trust not so much to rules as to their ears. Such principles as do emerge are on the whole more likely to serve our sense of curiosity than our sense of beauty; at most, they may suggest not so much what to do as what to avoid.

[1] The reader who wishes to pursue it further will find a summary of recent theories on prosody and prose-rhythm in R. Wellek and A. Warren, *Theory of Literature* (1949), ch. XIII and bibliography.

[2] I shall not soon forget the ineffable remark of a girl undergraduate who, being asked by her supervisor if she had enjoyed some book, replied: 'I don't read to "enjoy". I read to evaluate.' Far better be a healthy farm-wench on a milking-stool.

The first consideration is practical. Speech should not be made difficult to speak: but it may become so if it juxtaposes sounds difficult to articulate (as in Browning's unspeakable 'Nor soul helps flesh now more than flesh helps soul'); or, again, if its clauses grow so long as to run the speaker out of breath. In short, as Flaubert put it, a good style must meet the needs of the respiration. It therefore seems common sense that a writer should carefully read his manuscript aloud, or at least read it to his inward ear.

True, most modern literature is meant for the silent reader; even so, a sentence is unlikely to be very good if anyone who quotes it, or reads it aloud, is left breathless —for other reasons than admiration.

Besides, an author who would please or move his readers will often wish to do so by sound as well as sense. Here rhythm becomes important. Feeling tends to produce rhythm; and rhythm, feeling. Further, a strong rhythm may have a hypnotic effect, which holds the reader, as the Ancient Mariner held the Wedding Guest; prevents his attention from wandering; and also makes him more suggestible. This, indeed, is a main function of metre.

But in prose, since it is *not* poetry, nor even *vers libre*, a too metrical rhythm will probably move the sensitive reader, not to sympathy, but to mirth or irritation—as, for instance, when Dickens is swayed by his feelings into patches of blank verse. Prose needs a less obtrusive, more elusive, kind of music. On the other hand, the writer who has no ear, or no care, for rhythm of any kind, may produce a sort of prose that is over-prosaic, humdrum, or downright ugly.

All this, indeed, is ancient history. 'The form of style', says Aristotle of oratory,[1] 'must be neither metrical nor yet without rhythm. For if it is metrical, it becomes

---

[1] *Rhetoric*, III, 8.

[220]

THE HARMONY OF PROSE

unconvincing, because it seems artifice. Also it distracts the hearer, by making him listen for some cadence to recur.... On the other hand, the unrhythmical is formless. Prose style must have form, but not metre: for the formless is both unpleasing and ungraspable.' Similarly Isocrates: 'Prose should not be wholly prosaic; for that would be dry: nor metrical; for that would be too obvious. It should contain a mixture of metrical forms, especially iambic and trochaic.'[1]

In practice, many classical writers took elaborate pains with rhythm, particularly at sentence-ends (the 'clausula'). But they do not help us much; partly because of the great difference between the classical languages, where the main factor was quantity, and our own, where stress is supreme; and also because in their preferences they differ widely among themselves.[2] It seems more practical here to consider some specimens of English rhythmical prose—both as models and as warnings.[3]

---

[1] C. Walz, *Rhetores Graeci* (1834), VI, pp. 165-6 (quoted in Saintsbury, *English Prose Rhythm*, p. 2).

[2] See p. 225.

[3] Much as I admire Saintsbury's *History of English Prosody*, I can make little of his *History of English Prose Rhythm*. I do not believe the ordinary reader attaches the slightest importance (even if he knows what they are) to all these amphibrachs and molossi, dochmiacs and paeons. And, in practice, I am often baffled by Saintsbury's scansions. Why 'heārthstănĕ ăt Éllăngōwăn', but 'Laīrd ŏf Éllăngōwăn'? A misprint? Why on one page 'rĕcŏllēctiŏn', on another 'rēcŏllēctiŏn' (which seems to me impossible)? Why 'pūrplĕ | moūntaĭns | swēll | cĭrclĭng | roŭnd ĭt'? (Surely 'cīrclĭng'?) Why 'ăcclămătiŏns | ăt thĕ ĭnaūg|ŭrātiŏn'? (Surely 'ācclămātiŏns'?) Why turn the Latin *dĭēs* into *dĭĕs*, but the English 'dĭŭtūrnĭtў' into 'dĭŭtūrnĭtў'? And can one possibly scan the climax of Macaulay's description of Warren Hastings's trial— 'shōne | roŭnd Geōrgĭănă, | Dūchĕss | ŏf Dēvŏnshĭre'? 'Geōrgĭ-ănă', seems essential: and, to me, the rhythm is markedly trochaic-iambic: 'Shóne round | Geórgi|ána, || Dúchess | of Dév|on-shire' (in fact, a sort of trochaic Alexandrine).

Take one of the golden passages of the Authorized
Version, where Job curses the day that gave him birth:

Let the stárs | of the twí|light thereóf | be dárk;[1]
(iambic-anapaestic)

let it lóok | for líght, | but have nóne;
(iambic-anapaestic)

(P) *neíther | lèt it | seé the | dáwning | òf the | dáy.*
(trochaic)

Becaúse | it shút | not ùp || the doórs | of my móth|er's
wómb,
(Alexandrine)

nor hid sorrow from mine eyes.

Why diéd | I nót | from the wómb? (iambic-anapaestic)
whý did | I nót | give ùp | the ghóst || when I cáme |
oùt of | the bél|ly?
(fourteener)

Whý did | the knées | prevént | me? || or whý | the
breásts | that Ì | should súck?
(fourteener)

For now I should have lain still and been quiet,[2]
I shoúld | have slépt: | thén had | I beèn | at rést,
(blank verse)

(P) *With kíngs | and coún|sellors òf | the eárth,*
(4-foot, *Christabel*-metre)

(P) *which buílt | désolate | pláces | for themsélves;*
Or with prínc|es thàt | had góld, || who fílled | their
hoú|ses with síl|ver:
(Alexandrine)

ór as | an hídd|en untíme|ly bírth | I hàd|not
béen;
(Alexandrine)

as ín|fants which név|er saw líght.
(iambic-anapaestic)

Thére the | wícked | ceáse from | troúbling;
(4-foot trochaic)

and thére | the weár|y bè | at rést.   (4-foot iambic)

Here, and in the extracts which follow, I have italicized
passages that scan as they stand; and put a (P) (meaning
'potential verse') against others that *would* scan quite

---

[1] Throughout this chapter a main stress is indicated by ´; a
secondary, minor stress by ˋ.

[2] Even this is a perfectly possible Elizabethan blank verse.

easily if they occurred in a stretch of verse, where the
metrical pattern already runs in the reader's head.[1] No
doubt other arrangements and scansions are possible;
but this seems enough to show what a large proportion of
metrical fragments can be imbedded in this kind of prose
—a perhaps surprising amount to those who have been

[1] I do not wish to plunge into the morasses of metrical theory,
buzzed over by so many fretful and stinging creatures; but, as I
speak of metrical elements in prose, I should perhaps briefly
explain my views of metre in verse.

Some prosodists seem to me too lawless; to find as many as seven
stresses in some decasyllabic lines, and as few as three in others,
brings mere anarchy. Others seem too rigid; it is clearly ridiculous
to scan in mechanical sing-song—

While SMOOTH AdONis FROM his NATive ROCK
Ran PURple TO the SEA.

For 'from' and 'to' are syllables less prominent, or stressed, than
the unstressed 'While' or 'Ran'. But the fallacy lies in taking *all*
the stressed syllables in a verse line to be more strongly stressed
than *all* its unstressed syllables. Stress is only *relative*, not absolute
—relative to the syllable before and the syllable after. ('From',
helped by the metrical *pattern*, is more strongly stressed than
'-is' before it, or 'his' after it; 'to' than '-ple' or 'the'.)

In short, an iambic or trochaic line undulates like a telegraph-
wire—not like a telegraph-wire on a dead level, but like a telegraph-
wire on a rolling plain, where the crests of some undulations are
actually lower than the troughs of others; but, none the less, the
undulations remain. Apart from this principle of the *relativity* of
stress, I am in general agreement with the views of Saintsbury in
his *History of English Prosody*.

Stress itself seems partly vocal (corresponding, it is said, to
increased pressure of breath in the speech-canal), partly mental.
For the mind needs to keep hold of the rhythmical pattern; since,
although some verse-lines will continue to scan themselves even if
embedded in a prose-passage, in others the metre is murdered if
they are read as prose.

I would add that when musicians apply themselves to metre, the
results seem to me usually unhappy. Music and metre are further
apart than they suppose; even a metrical magician like Swinburne
could be totally unmusical.

brought up to believe that it is for some reason wicked
to include in a prose passage a single line of potential
verse.

You may reply that such a passage from the Bible is
no fair example of prose, being itself half poetry. Then
look at this piece of Ruskin on Venice.

It lay | along | the face | of the wat|ers, no larg|er,
(blank verse)

(P) as its capt|ains saw | it from | their masts | at
even|ing,
(blank verse)

than a bar | of sun|set that could | not pass | away;
(blank verse)

but, for | its power, | it must | have seemed | to them
(blank verse)

(P) as if | they were sail|ing in | the expanse | of
heav|en,
(blank verse)

and this | a great plan|et, whose or|ient edge
(4-foot, *Christabel*-metre)

widened | through eth|er. A world | from which
(4-foot, *Christabel*-metre)

*all ignob|le care | and pett|y thoughts | were
ban|ished,*
(blank verse)

(P) with all | the com|mon and poor | elements | of life.
(blank verse)

(P) No foul|ness, nor tum|ult in | those trem|ulous
streets,
(blank verse)

that filled, | or fell, | beneath | the moon;
(4-foot iambic)

(P) but rip pled mus|ic of | majest|ic change,
(blank verse)

or thrill|ing sil|ence.
No weak | walls could | rise ab|ove them;   (trochaics)
no low-|roofed cott|age, nor straw-|built shed.
(*Christabel*-metre)

*Only | the strength | as of rock, | and the fin|ished
sett|ing of stones | most prec|ious.*   (fourteener)
And around | them, far | as the eye | could reach,
(*Christabel*-metre)

Still the | soft mov|ing of stain|less wat|ers,
    proud|ly pure;   (Alexandrine)
as not | the flower, | so neith|er the thorn | nor the
    thist|le,   (blank verse)
could grow | in the glanc|ing fields.

(P)   Ether|eal strength | of Alps, | dreamlike, | vanishing
                           (blank verse)
in high | process|ion beyond | the Torcell|an shore:
                           (blank verse)
blue is|lands of Pad|uan hills, || poised in | the
    gold|en west.   (Alexandrine)

Some of this is not only metre, but fine metre. No writer of blank verse need be ashamed of 'In high procession beyond the Torcellan shore'. Yet it does seem perilously metrical for prose. Indeed, many of Ruskin's verbal landscapes are so full of poetic imagination and poetic rhythm, that one may wonder whether they would not have been better if written as poetry, rather than in a hybrid form that divides the reader between admiration and a certain discomfort.

Let us look at Landor (whom George Moore put even above Shakespeare—though that seems going rather far). If this passage I quote has grown hackneyed, why has it grown hackneyed? Because of its power to please. And I refuse to be put off great passages just because a lot of people have liked them.

(P)   Aᴇsop. Lao|damei|a died; | Hel|en died;
        Leda, | the beloved | of Jup|iter, went | before.

(P)   It is bett|er to repose | in the earth | betimes | than
    to sit | up late;[1]
better, than to cling pertinaciously to what we feel crumbling
    under us,

(P)   and to | protract | an inev|itab|le fall.

We may enjoy the present, while we are insensible of

---

[1] The quadrisyllabic second foot would not deter some modern writers of blank verse; nor, I think, need it.

infirmity and decay; but the present, like a note in music,
is nothing but as it appertains

to what | is past | and what | is to come.

There are no fields of amaranth on this side of the grave;
there are no voices, O Rhodope,

that are not | soon mute, | howev|er tune|ful;

there is no name, with whatever emphasis of passionate
love repeated,

of which | the ech|o is | not faint | at last.

RHODOPE. O Aes|op! let | me rest | my head | on yours;
it throbs | and pains | me.

AESOP. Whát are | thése id|eás to | thée?

RHODOPE. Sad, | sórrow|fùl.   (trochaics)

AESOP. Harrows | that break | the soil, || prepar|ing
it | for wis|dom.   (Alexandrine)

Many | flowers must | perish || ere a grain | of
corn | be rip|ened.[1]

And now | remove | thy head: || the cheek | is
cool | enough   (Alexandrine)

after | its litt|le shower | of tears.

Here, too, is a good deal of metre; but also passages
which resist scansion, mainly by their high proportion of
unstressed syllables; often occurring in long, Latin-
derived words like 'pertinaciously', 'insensible of infirmity', 'emphasis of passionate love'.

Let us go further back—to Gibbon.

While Julian struggled with the almost insuperable difficulties of his situation,

the sil|ent hours | of the night | were still | devot|ed
to stud|y and con|templat|ion.

Whenev|er he closed | his eyes || in short | and int|er-
rupt|ed slumb|ers, his mind was agitated with painful
anxiety; nor can it be thought surprising that the Genius of
the Empire should once more appear before him, covering
with a funereal veil his head and his horn of abundance,

[1] Cf. Meredith's *Love in the Valley*: 'Knees and tresses folded
to slip and ripple idly.'

(P)   and slow|ly retir|ing from | the Imper|ial tent.

The monarch started from his couch, and stepping forth to refresh his spirits with the coolness of the midnight air, he beheld a fiery meteor,

> *which shot | athwart | the sky | and sud|denly van|ished.*

Julian was convinced that he had seen the menacing countenance of the god of war; the council which he summoned, of Tuscan Haruspices, unanimously pronounced that he should abstain from action; but on this occasion necessity and reason were more prevalent than superstition;

(P)   and the trump|ets sound|ed at | the break | of day.

Naturally, here as in other passages, different readers will read differently. They will disagree as to what is metrical and what not, and how what is metrical should be scanned. But the passage illustrates, I think, a tendency not uncommon in prose to become more metrical as a sentence *ends*. 'And slowly retiring from the Imperial tent'—'which shot athwart the sky and suddenly vanished'—'and the trumpets sounded at the break of day'.

The next specimen is not only prose, but prose deliberately used to contrast with verse; yet Hamlet's prose has metrical patches.

I will tell you why; so shall my anticipation prevent your discovery and your secricie to the King and Queene moult no feather.

> *I have | of late, | but where|fore I know | not,*
> *lost all | my mirth,*
> *forgone | all cust|ome of ex|ercise;*

and indeed, it goes so heavily with my disposition, that this goodly frame, the Earth, seemes to me a sterrill Promontory; this most excellent Canopy the Ayre, look you,

> *this brave | ore-hang|ing Firm|ament,*
> *this Majest|icall Roofe, | fretted | with gold|en fire:*

[227]

why, it | appeares | no oth|er thing | to mee,
then a foule | and pest|ilent con|gregat|ion of
vap|ours.
What a piece | of worke | is a man! | how Nob|le in
Reas|on!
how in|finite | in fac|ulty!
in forme | and mov|ing how | expresse | and
ad|mirable!
in Act|ion, how like | an Ang|el! || in
ap|prehens|ion how like | a God!
the beauty of the world, the Parragon of Animals;
and yet, | to me, | what is | this Quintess|ence of Dust?
(P)　Man delights | not me; | no, nor Wom|an neith|er;
though by | your smil|ing you seeme | to say | so.

But at this rate, you may say, there is no English prose
from which you cannot torture whole series of metrical
fragments. But I do not think that is true. Consider
this, from Meredith.

Now men | whose in|comes have been | restrict|ed to
the extent that they must live on their capital, soon grow
relieved of the forethoughtful anguish wasting them by the
hilarious comforts of the lap on which they have sunk back,
insomuch that they are apt to solace themselves for their
intolerable anticipations of famine in the household by giving
loose to one fit or more of reckless lavishness. Lovers in like
manner live on their capital from failure of income: *they, too |*
for the sake | of stifl|ing ap|prehens|ion | [1] and pip|ing
to | the pres|ent hour, | are lav|ish of | their stock, | so as
rapidly to attenuate it: they have their fits of intoxication in
view of coming famine: they force memory into play, love
retrospectively, enter the old house of the past and ravage the
larder, and would gladly, even resolutely, continue in illusion
if it were possible for the broadest honey-store of reminiscences
to hold out for a length of time against a mortal appetite: which
in good sooth stands on the alternative of a consumption of the

[1] Throughout, a *thick* line indicates the beginning or end of a
verse.

hive or of the creature it is for nourishing.   Hére do | lóvers | shów that | thèy are | pérish|àble.[1]

I have marked some just conceivable scansions, in order to play fair. But, amid a passage whose general run is so prosaic, the reader's ear seems most unlikely to note them; besides, he is probably too preoccupied with making out the meaning. But I must add that, personally, I find both style and rhythm repellent, with a sort of bustling, boisterous pretentiousness.[2]

But that is not the point. Meredith's prose had, indeed, another, poetic manner, which may even be thought, on the contrary, *too* metrical: 'Golden | lie the | meadows; || golden | run the | streams. . . .'[3] But his more ordinary style, with its long, helter-skelter clauses and its jostling, jolting polysyllables, is usually at a very safe distance from verse. No one is likely to accuse you of misplaced fondness for metre, if you write such sentences as: 'Yet, if you looked on Clara as a délicàtelý inímitàblè pórcèlain[4] beauty, the suspicion of a délicàtelý inímitàblè ripple over her features touched a thought of innocent roguery, wild-wood roguery'. Though some may be dubious whether *this* remedy is better than the disease.[5]

But such doses of polysyllables are not the only antidote; metrical patches are less likely to occur in a style that is near in tone to conversation—like much prose of the earlier eighteenth century, before the return to sonority with Johnson, Gibbon, and Burke. The more

[1] *The Egoist*, ch. VII.
[2] Two equally unrhythmical and, to me, unpleasant specimens of Meredith's prose will be found in Saintsbury, *English Prose Rhythm*, pp. 438–9.
[3] *Richard Feverel*, ch. XIX. Cf. the metre of *Love in the Valley*: 'Tying up her laces, looping up her hair.'
[4] Dots indicate unstressed syllables.
[5] And yet even here a sort of blank verse persists in breaking in at the end of the paragraph: 'He detested but was haunted by the phrase.'

[229]

prosaic and unemotional a writer's general manner, the less likely is the reader to beat it unconsciously into regular rhythm.

He must have been a man of a most wonderful comprehensive nature, because, as it has been truly observed of him, | he has tak|en in|to the com|pass || of his Cant|erbur|y Tales | the various manners and humours (as we now call them) of the whole English nation, in his age. Not a single character has escaped him. All his pilgrims are severally distinguished from each other; and not only in their inclinations, but in their very physiognomies and persons.

(DRYDEN)

As Sir Roger is landlord to the whole Congregation, he keeps them in very good Order, and will suffer no Body to sleep in it besides himself; for if by Chance he has been surprized into a short Nap at Sermon, upon recovering out of it he stands up and looks about him, and if he sees any Body else nodding, either wakes | them himself, | or sends | his Serv|ants to | them. Several other of the old Knight's Particularities break out upon these Occasions: Sometimes he will be lengthening out a Verse in the Singing-Psalms, half a Minute after the rest of the Congregation have done with it; sometimes, when he | is pleased | with the matt|er of his | Devot|ion, he pronounces *Amen* three or four times to the same Prayer; and sometimes stands up when every Body else is upon their Knees, to count the Congregation, or see if any of his Tenants are missing. (ADDISON)

And as his lordship, for want of principle, often sacrificed his character to his interest, so by these means he as often, for want of prudence, sacrificed his interest to his vanity. With a person as disagreeable as it was possible for a human figure to be without being deformed, he affected following many women of the first beauty and the most in fashion, and, if you would have taken his word for it, not without success; whilst in fact and in truth he never gained anyone above the venal rank of those whom an Adonis or a Vulcan might be equally well with, for an equal sum of money. He was very short, disproportioned, thick and clumsily made; had a broad, rough-featured, ugly face, with black teeth and a head big enough for Polyphemus. Ben Ashurst, who said few good things, told Lord Chesterfield once that he was like a stunted giant, which was a humorous idea and really apposite.

(JOHN, LORD HERVEY, on Chesterfield)

Mr. *Allworthy* had been absent a full Quarter of a Year in *London,* | on some ver|y partic|ular Bus|iness, || though I know | not what | it was; | but judge of its Importance, by its having detained him so long from home, whence he had not been absent a Month at a Time during the Space of many Years. He came | to his House | very late | in the Even|ing, and after a short Supper with his Sister, retired much fatigued to his Chamber. Here, having spent some Minutes on his Knees, a Custom which he never broke through on any Account, he was preparing to step into Bed, when, upon opening the Cloaths, to his great Surprize, he beheld an Infant, wrapt up in some coarse Linnen, in a sweet and profound Sleep, between his Sheets.   (FIELDING)

So far as routine and authority tend to embarrass energy and inventive genius, academies may be said to be obstructive to energy and inventive genius, and, to this extent, to the human spirit's general advance. But then this evil is so much compensated by the propagation, on a large scale, of the mental aptitudes and demands which an open mind and a flexible intelligence naturally engender, genius itself, in the long run, so greatly finds its account in this propagation, and bodies like the French Academy have such power for promoting it, that the general advance of the human spirit is perhaps, on the whole, rather furthered than impeded by their existence.

(MATTHEW ARNOLD)

This is the academic, schoolmasterly Arnold, preaching with conscientious iterations to the Philistines of England, though without, one feels, any high hopes of them. It is not a style I much like. But what a change of rhythm, when he turns to Oxford, and begins once more to feel!

Ador|able dream|er, whose heart | has been | so
romant|ic!
(P) who hast giv|en thyself | so prod|igally,
given | thyself | to sides | and to her|oes not mine,
only never to the Philistines!
(P) home of | lost caus|es, and | forsak|en beliefs,
and unpop|ular names, | and imposs|ible loy|alties!

I find it hard to believe that such contrasts are merely
chance. No doubt chance plays its part. Even in Greek
prose, iambic trimeters can occur, apparently by pure accident; the *Annals* of Tacitus open with a bad hexameter
—*ūrbēm | Rōmam ā | prīncĭpĭ|ō rēg | ēs hăbŭ|ērĕ*
—and his *Germania* contains a better one—*aūgŭrĭ|īs*
pātrum | ēt prīsc|ā fōrm|ĭdĭnĕ | sācrām; and though
the hexameter is not a natural form for English speech,
the Bible offers examples like, 'Hów art thou | fállen
from | heáven, || O | Lúcifer, | són of the | mórning!'[1]
Further, in English, chance fragments of iambic,
trochaic, or anapaestic metre are likelier than in classical
languages because our prosody is so much simpler and
looser. In particular, while Greek and Latin have comparatively few syllables that can be long or short at will,
whichever suits the metre (*e.g. tĕnĕbrāe*), English simply
teems with syllables that can be stressed or unstressed,
according to position, at the poet's convenience. None
the less the extraordinary abundance of metrical passages
in some English writers as compared with others cannot
be explained by accident alone. But neither can I believe
it to be, as a rule, conscious and deliberate. Sometimes
it may be a mere bad habit. But in general, as at a certain
temperature a kettle begins to sing, so, when prose
becomes passionate, it has a spontaneous tendency to
begin to chant. And, within limits, why not?

In conclusion and confirmation, since there is no space
to quote further long passages, here are a few briefer

[1] *Isaiah* XIV, 12.

specimens of prose sentences that seem to me all the finer
for a touch of metre.

And thou were the godelyest persone that ever cam emonge
prees of knyghtes, and thou was the mekest man and the
jentyllest that ever ete in halle emonge ladyes, | and thou |
were the stern|est knyght | to thy mort|al foo | that ev|er
put spere | in the reeste. (MALORY)

O el|oquent, just, | and might|y Death!
whom none | could advise, | thou hast | persuad|ed;
what none | hath dared, | thou | hast done;
and whom | all the world | has flatt|ered,
thou on|ly hast cast | out of | the world | and despised.
Thou hast drawn | togeth|er all | the far-|stretched
    great|ness,
(P) all the | pride, cru|elty, and | ambit|ion of man,
and cov|ered it | all ov|er || with these | two
    narr|ow words,
Hic jacet. (RALEIGH)

Life is | a journ|ey in a dust|y way,
the furth|est rest | is death;
in this | some go | more heav|ily burth|ened than
    oth | ers;
swift and | active | pilgrims || come to | the end | of it
in the morn|ing or | at noon, | which tort|oise-
    paced wretch | es,
clogged with | the frag|mentary rubb|ish of | this
    world,
scarce with | great trav|ail crawl | unto | at
    mid|night. (DRUMMOND of Hawthornden)

For so | have I seen | a lark
rísing | fròm his | béd of | grass,
soaring | upwards | and sing|ing as | he ris|es
and hopes | to get | to Heav|en || and climb | above |
    the clouds;
but the | poor bird | was beat|en back
with the | loud sigh|ings of | an east|ern wind

[233]

and his mot|ion made | irreg|ular and | inconst|ant,
descend|ing more | at ev|ery breath | of the
    temp|est
than it could recover by the vibration and frequent weighing
of his wings;
    till the litt|le creat|ure was forced | to sit down |
        and pant
    and stay | till the storm | was ov|er;
    and then | it made | a prosp|erous flight
    and did rise | and sing
    as if | it had learned | music || and mot|ion from | an
        ang|el
    as he passed | sometimes | through the air || about |
        his min|istries here | below.   (JEREMY TAYLOR)

Now sìnce | these deád | bònes[1] have | alreád|y
    outlást|ed
the liv|ing ones | of Methus|elah,
ànd in | a yard | under ground, | and thin | walls of
    clay,
outworn | all the strong | and spec|ious build|ings
    above | it;
and quiet|ly rest|ed
under | the drums | and trampl|ings of | three
    con|quests;
what Prince | can prom|ise such | diuturn|ity
unto | his rel|iques, or might | not glad|ly say,
Sic ego componi versus in ossa velim?
                (SIR THOMAS BROWNE)

Nor will | the sweet|est delight | of gard|ens ||
    afford | much com|fort in sleep;
wherein | the dul|ness of | that sense
shakes hands | with delect|able od|ours;

---

[1] Saintsbury (*English Prose Rhythm*, p. 184) scans: 'Nōw :
sīnce : thēse : deād : bōnes'—that is, with five heavy stresses. But
surely, since '*dead* bones' is contrasted with the '*living* ones' of
Methuselah, 'dead' must be *more* stressed than its neighbours?

and though | in the bed | of Cle|opatr|a,
can hard|ly with an|y delight || raise up | the
    ghost | of a rose.   (SIR THOMAS BROWNE)

When all | is done, | human | life is, || at the
    great est and | the best,
but like | a frow|ard child | that must | be played | with
and hum|oured a litt|le
to keep | it qui|et till | it falls | asleep;
and then | the care | is ov|er.   (SIR WILLIAM TEMPLE)

. . . our dign|ity? That | is gone. || I shall say | no
    more | about | it.
Light lie | the earth | on the ash|es of Eng|lish
    pride!   (BURKE)[1]

She droops | not; and | her eyes,
rising | so high, | might be hidd|en by dist|ance.
But be|ing what | they are, | they can|not be
    hidd|en;
through the treb|le veil | of crape | that she wears,
the fierce | light | of a blaz|ing mis|ery
that rests | not for mat|ins or vesp|ers,
for noon | of day | or noon | of night,
for ebb|ing or | for flow|ing tide,
may be read | from the ver|y ground.
She is | the def|ier of God.
She al|so is | the moth|er of lun|acies,
and the | suggestr|ess of su|icides.
Deep lie | the roots | of her power;
but narr|ow is | the nat|ion that | she rules.
                (DE QUINCEY)

The pres|ence that | thus rose || so strang|ely beside | the
    waters,
is express|ive of what | in the ways | of a thous|and years
men had come | to desire.

    [1] I must add, however, that in general Burke does not seem to
me very metrical.

Hers is | the head | upon which ‖ all 'the ends | of the
world | are come . . .'   (PATER)[1]

> Let me | now raise | my song | of glor|y.
> Heaven | be praised | for sol|itude.
> Let me be | alone.
> Let me cast | and throw | away | this veil | of be|ing,
> this cloud | that chang|es with | the least breath,
> níght and | dáy, and | áll night | and áll | day.
> While I | sat here | I have | been chang|ing.
> I have watched | the sky change.
> I have seen | clouds cov|er the stars, | then free |
>   the stars,
> then cov|er the stars | again.
> Now I look | at their chang|ing no more.
> Now no | one sees | me and I | change no more.
> Heaven | be praised | for sol|itude
> that has | removed | the press|ure of | the eye,
> the solic|itat|ion of | the bod|y,
> and all need | of lies | and phras|es.   (VIRGINIA WOOLF)

In fine, English prose of a poetic kind contains, I think,
far more hidden metre than, so far as I know, has ever
been recognized. But this is a dangerous secret, to be
breathed only with discretion.[2] *Ars est celare artem.* It
may be added that this is another beauty of which
English literature would be robbed by those who would
apply to prose the Wordsworthian heresy about verse,
that the writer 'to excite rational sympathy must express

---

[1] Pater too, however, seems as a rule one of the less scannable of
poetic prose-writers.

[2] Similarly, of course, Alexandrines occur in good French prose-
writers. Renan, for example, has: 'Les dieux passent comme les
hommes . . . *il ne | serait | pas bon ‖ qu'ils fuss|ent ét|ernels.* La
foi qu'on a eue ne doit jamais être une chaine. On est quitte envers
elle quand on l'a soigneusement roulée *dans le | linceul | de
pourpre ‖ où dorm|ent les | dieux morts.*' (See J. Marouzeau,
Précis de Stylistique Français (2nd ed., 1946), p. 182.)

himself as other men express themselves'. Prose that comes *too* near to conversation must forfeit that rhythmical intensity which is rare in English talk (whatever may be true of Ireland).

There is, of course, another variety of rhythm which depends on the symmetrical arrangement of ideas as well as of syllables—antithesis. After its excessive use by prose-writers like Lyly and Johnson, by poets like Pope and his school, it might have been thought that antithesis would have become an exhausted and hackneyed thing. Yet it has not. Few modern writers, indeed, would dare abuse it as the eighteenth century did; yet antithesis keeps an eternal youth because it corresponds to an eternal need of human thinking. The mind is perpetually balancing and seeking balance; perpetually truth lies between opposed extremes, and wisdom between opposite excesses. So it is that when European literature begins, Homer is already full of μέν and δέ. Heaven knows the hoary antiquity of those two adversative particles. And there seems nothing more to say of antitheses but that a style which has too many of them will seem artificial, and a style which has too few will lack point.

There is another matter which concerns both rhythm and clarity alike—word-order. Just as the art of war largely consists in deploying the strongest forces at the most important points, so the art of writing depends a good deal on putting the strongest words in the most important places. In English, as I have said, the most emphatic part of a sentence is to be found at its end; the next most emphatic at its beginning; though, naturally, words or phrases that would normally come towards the end, gain emphasis by being put at the beginning, from the very fact that this *is* abnormal. '*This Jesus* hath God raised up.' '*The atrocious crime of being a young man,* which the honourable gentleman has with such spirit and decency charged upon me, I shall neither attempt to palliate nor deny.' (Written by Johnson in a speech attributed to Pitt.)[1]

Needless to say, this principle of keeping emphatic words for the end, and the end for emphatic words, is by no means inflexible. Emphasis may be important: but more important still is variety. To end sentence after sentence with a thump would lead to maddening monotony. Besides, a writer like Pater may develop a particular fondness for sentences that end, not strongly, but with a diminishing cadence and a dying fall. Again and again, hearing a sentence of his read aloud, you would think it had reached its end; but instead of a full-stop there comes only a semicolon; followed by some afterthought, often in the shape of a participial or subordinate clause. 'That flawless serenity, better than the most pleasurable excitement,[2] yet so easily ruffled by chance collision even with the things and persons he had come to value as the greatest treasure in life, was to be wholly his today, | he thought, | as he rode | towards Tib|ur, || und|er the ear|ly sun|shine; | the marb|le of | its vill|as || glist|ening all | the way | before | him on | the hill|side.' 'And the true cause of his trouble is that he has based his hope on what he has seen in a dream, or his own fancy has put together; without previous thought whether what he desires is in itself attainable and within the compass of human nature.' It all seems to me very characteristic of the man, with his air of languorous precision—Pater the Epicurean arranging with a slightly affected delicacy the folds of what seems sometimes a Stoic mantle, sometimes an Anglican sur-

[1] Quoted by A. Bain, *Rhetoric and Composition* (1887), Part I, p. 16. It seems to me far less effective if rewritten: 'The honourable gentleman has with much spirit and decency charged upon me the atrocious crime of being a young man: this I shall neither attempt to palliate nor deny' (though logic might prefer 'attempt neither to palliate nor to deny').

[2] How typical of Pater to think so!

plice. Still it is one way of ending sentences; and a useful variation.

In general, however, there seems to me much to be said for closes that are sharp and clean. Take this passage from Strachey's *Queen Victoria*.

The English Constitution—that indescribable entity—is a living thing, growing with the growth of men, and assuming ever-varying forms in accordance with | the sub|tle and com|plex laws | of *hum|an char|acter.* | It is the child of wisdom and *chance.* | The wise | men of 16|88 | moulded | it in|to the shape | we know; | but the chance | that George | I | could not | speak Eng|lish | gave it one of its essential peculiarities—the system of a Cabinet independent of the Crown and subordinate to the *Prime Minister.* The wisdom of Lord Grey saved it from petrifaction and destruction, and set it upon the path of *Democracy.* Then chance intervened once more; | a fem|ale sov|ereign happ|ened to marr|y | an ab|le and per|tinac|ious man; | and it seemed likely that an element which had been quiescent in it for years—the element of irresponsible administrative power—was about to become its predominant characteristic and to change completely the direction of its growth. | But what | chance gave, | chance *took* | *away.* | The Con|sort per|ished in | his *prime;* | and the English Constitution, dropping the dead limb with hardly a tremor, | contin|ued its | myster|ious life || *as if* | *he had nev|er been.*

Try ending these sentences with words less emphatic. Replace 'the subtle and complex laws of human character' by 'subtle and complex psychological laws'; 'It is the child of wisdom and chance' by 'Wisdom and chance were its parents'; 'subordinate to the Prime Minister' by 'which the Prime Minister controlled'; 'the path of Democracy' by 'a democratic path'. You will, I think, lose much of the energy.

Consider, again, the words of the angel in *Revelation*: 'Babylon is fallen, is fallen, that great city, because she made all nations drink of the wine of the wrath of her fornication.'[1] 'Q' in his *Art of Writing* suggests that our first impulse is to emend for emphasis: 'Babylon, that great city, is fallen, is fallen'[2] (though he defends the Authorized Version, as keeping the fading close of the Vulgate, 'cecidit, cecidit, Babylonia illa magna').[3] But I doubt this impulse to alter it. The emphasis seems to me to lie quite naturally on the city's *greatness*; which yet could not avert the retribution for her still greater crimes. The Revisers contrived to stress *both* the greatness *and* the fall, by putting one at the end of the clause, the other at its beginning: 'Fallen, fallen is Babylon the great.' And this seems best of all.

Take another example. Bain criticizes the word-order of Bacon's fine sentence, 'A crowd is not company, and faces are but a gallery of pictures, and talk but a tinkling cymbal, where there is no love.' For Bain argues that the reader mistakes the first three statements for universal truths, and is disconcerted by finding at the end the condition: 'where there is no love'. He would therefore move 'where there is no love' to the beginning. This appears to me a disastrous improvement. The stress is on the emptiness of life without love; therefore this absence of love can be rightly kept till the end. No doubt the reader is taken by surprise when he comes to it; but did not Bacon mean him to be?

Contrast the following sentences by Bain himself, where the interest seems to me to flag before the end. 'The Humour of Shakespeare has the richness of his genius, and follows his peculiarities. He did not lay himself out for pure Comedy, like Aristophanes; he was more nearly allied to the great tragedians of the classical

---

[1] *Rev.* XIV, 8. The *A.V.* has none of Flaubert's fear of successive 'of's.

[2] Cf. *Rev.* XVIII, 2: 'Babylon the great is fallen, is fallen'; and Tennyson, *Princess*: 'Our enemies have fall'n, have fall'n.'

[3] Similarly in the Greek: ἔπεσεν, ἔπεσεν Βαβυλὼν ἡ μεγάλη.

world. . . . The genius of Rabelais supplies extravagant vituperation and ridicule in the wildest profusion; a moral purpose underlying. Coarse and brutal fun runs riot. . . . For Vituperation and Ridicule, Swift has few equals, and no superior. On rare occcasion, he exemplifies Humour and, had his disposition been less savage and malignant, he would have done so much oftener.' It is rash work rewriting the style of others; Bain on Bacon has just illustrated that; but I cannot help thinking that here the result would at least have been clearer and crisper, had Bain paid more attention to his own sentence-endings. 'The Humour of. Shakespeare has the richness of his *genius*. He did not, like Aristophanes, lay himself out for *pure Comedy*; he was more nearly allied to the classic *Tragedians*. . . . The genius of Rabelais shows a wild extravagance of satire and ridicule, underlaid by *moral purpose*. His work is a riot of *coarse and brutal fun*. . . . In vituperation and ridicule none have surpassed and few have equalled *Swift*. But he rarely shows humour; he might indeed have done so oftener, had his temper been less *savage and malignant*.'

Or take a more recent example from a work on the Napoleonic period. Of the negotiations with Russia about the Emperor's second marriage, it says: 'A few days later, however—on the 5th of February—despatches which made it sufficiently clear that Alexander, embarrassed by his mother's dislike of Napoleon as a son-in-law, was countenancing delay to cover evasion, arrived from Petersburg.' It does not make for ease to put twenty-three words between subject and verb. Nor is it important that the despatches originated in St. Petersburg—the obvious place. The important thing is the evasion. I should therefore myself prefer, 'A few days later, however, on February 5th, despatches from Petersburg made it sufficiently clear that Alexander, embarrassed by his mother's dislike of Napoleon as a son-

[241]

in-law, was countenancing delay only to cover *evasion*.'
I suggest that anyone who goes through the next thing
he writes, seeing to it that most of his sentences end with
words that really matter, may be surprised to find how
the style gains, like a soggy biscuit dried in the oven.[1]
Though so simple (once it has been seen), this remains, I
think, one of the most effective tricks of the trade; being
based on a sound psychological reason. A similar principle applies to the endings of paragraphs.
Then there is the further art of suiting sound to sense,
rhythm to meaning. Here, I think, critical analysis is
mainly a matter of curiosity; it will not much help the
writer, who here too will probably do better to rely on
ear and intuition; and it may pervert the reader, either
by distracting his attention from more serious matters to
effects comparatively trivial, or by encouraging him to
find fanciful significances where none exist. However,
in verse (where sound is often relatively more important
than in prose) it is not hard to find examples of sound that
is clearly imitative.

πολλὰ δ' ἄναντα κάταντα πάραντά τε δόχμιά τ'ἦλθον.
(HOMER—mules on a rough mountain-track)

αὖθις ἔπειτα πέδονδε κυλίνδετο λᾶας ἀναιδής.
(HOMER—the stone of Sisyphus bounds downhill again)

ἔσωσά σ', ὡς ἴσασιν Ἑλλήνων ὅσοι ...
(EURIPIDES—the hissing scorn of Medea)

Quādrŭpĕd|āntĕ pŭtr|ēm || sŏnĭt|ū quătĭt | ūngŭla |
cāmpūm.   (VIRGIL—galloping cavalry)

Tūm cōrn|ĭx plēn|ā || plŭvĭ|ām vŏcăt | īmprŏbă | vōcĕ
Ēt sōla | ĭn sīcc|ā || sē|cūm spătĭ|ātŭr ăr|ēnā.
(VIRGIL—crow croaking and stalking on the sand)

[1] Cf. pp. 39–41.

[242]

    Heaven opened wide
Her ever-during gates, harmonious sound
On golden hinges moving.   (MILTON)

    On a sudden open fly,
With impetuous recoil and *jarring* sound,
The infernal doors, and on their hinges *grate*
Harsh thunder that the lowest bottom shook
Of Erebus.   (MILTON)

'Tis not enough no harshness gives offence,
The sound must seem an Echo to the sense.
Soft is the strain when Zephyr gently blows,
And the smooth stream in smoother numbers flows;
But when loud surges lash the sounding shore,
The hoarse rough verse should like the torrent roar.
    (POPE)

By the long wash of Australasian seas.

    (TENNYSON)

Dry clash'd his harness in the icy *caves*
And *barren chasms*, and all to left and right
The bare black cliff clang'd round him as he based
His feet on *juts* of slippery crag that *rang*
Sharp-smitten with the dint of armed heels—
And on a sudden, lo! the level lake
And the long glories of the winter moon. (TENNYSON)

The mellow ouzel fluted in the elm.[1] (TENNYSON)

The moan of doves in immemorial elms,
And murmuring of innumerable bees. (TENNYSON)

But such tricks soon find their limitations. And when fanciful modern critics try to persuade me that, in such-and-such a line, the broad 'a's suggest, say, the sound of

---

[1] Perhaps influenced (though Tennyson hated his style 'like poison') by James Thomson's:
  The blackbird whistles from the thorny brake,
  The mellow bullfinch answers from the grove.
But if Tennyson borrowed, he bettered what he took.

a peach growing, I remember regretfully the sturdy good sense of Johnson on these matters:

> This notion of representative metre, and the desire of discovering frequent adaptations of the sound to the sense, have produced, in my opinion, many wild conceits and imaginary beauties. All that can furnish this representation are[1] the sounds of the words considered singly, and the time in which they are pronounced. Every language has some words framed to exhibit the noises which they express, as *thump, rattle, growl, hiss.* These, however, are but few, and the poet cannot make them more, nor can they be of any use but when sound is to be mentioned. The time of pronunciation was in the dactyllic measures of the learned languages[2] capable of considerable variety; but that variety could be accommodated only to motion or duration, and different degrees of motion were perhaps expressed by verses rapid or slow, without much attention of the writer, when the image had full possession of his fancy: but our language having little flexibility, our verses can differ very little in their cadence.[3] The fancied resemblances, I fear, arise sometimes merely from the ambiguity of words; there is supposed to be some relation between a *soft* line and a *soft* couch, or between *hard* syllables and *hard* fortune.

> Motion, however, may be in some sort exemplified; and yet it may be suspected that even in such resemblances the mind often governs the ear, and the sounds are estimated by their meaning. One of their most successful attempts has been to describe the labour of Sisyphus:

> With many a weary step, and many a groan,
> Up a high hill he heaves a huge round stone;

[1] A precise grammarian might prefer 'is'.

[2] Johnson ignores the use of anapaests mixed with iambics in English, as in the Christabel-metre, or in lyrics like those of Swinburne's *Atalanta*. These he could not know. But the same thing can already be seen in Jacobean blank verse.

[3] Johnson, dominated by the heroic couplet, seems to me here again to underestimate the powers of English verse.

> The huge round stone, resulting with a bound,
> Thunders impetuous down, and smokes along the
>   ground.[1]

Who does not perceive the stone to move slowly upward, and roll violently back? But set the same numbers to another sense:

> While many a merry tale, and many a song,
> Cheer'd the rough road, we wish'd the rough road long.
> The rough road then, returning in a round,
> Mock'd our impatient steps, for all was fairy ground.[2]

We have now surely lost much of the delay, and much of the rapidity.[3] But to show how little the greatest master of numbers can fix the principles of representative harmony, it will be sufficient to remark that the poet who tells us that

> When Ajax strives some rock's vast weight to throw,
> The line too labours, and the words move slow:
> Not so, when swift Camilla scours the plain,
> Flies o'er th' unbending corn, and skims along the
>   main;

when he had enjoyed for about thirty years the praise of Camilla's lightness of foot, tried[4] another experiment upon

---

[1] Pope, *Odyssey*, XI.

[2] Cf. the admirable letter in which, by similar parodies, Tennyson annihilates the absurd theory of Patmore that the six-syllabled iambic is fundamentally gloomy, the octosyllable fundamentally joyous and gay (H. Tennyson, *Memoir* (1897), I, pp. 469–70).

[3] Here, I am afraid, Johnson cheats a little. He has not really provided equivalents for the long syllables 'weary', 'groan', and 'heaves'; 'merry', 'song', 'wish'd' seem to me to have much shorter vowels. On the other hand 'impatient steps' (in effect, four syllables) is no exact counterpart to 'impetuous down' (five syllables). The resulting anapaest ($\cup \cup -$) is important for the speed.

[4] Some texts read 'he tried'. It seems possible that Johnson forgot that he had already a subject for his verb in 'the poet'. It is always dangerous to embed longish quotations in the middle of sentences; the reader is apt to grow confused and lose the construction, even if the writer does not. Besides, if the quotation is

sound and *time*, and produced this memorable triplet:

> Waller was smooth; but Dryden taught to join
> The varying verse, the full resounding line,
> The long majestic march, and energy divine.

Here are the swiftness of the rapid race, and the march of slow-paced majesty, exhibited by the same poet in the same sequence of syllables, except that the exact prosodist will find the line of *swiftness* by one time longer than the line of *tardiness*.[1] Beauties of this kind are commonly fancied; and, when real, are technical and nugatory, not to be rejected, and not to be solicited.[2]

Though one may differ on details, in essentials Johnson seems to me right. Both in verse and prose there are occasions when the rhythm may be made to suit the sense. But such artifices, even when really intended, have only a limited scope, like noises off in the theatre. The sounds of galloping hoofs, rolling thunder, whistling winds or locomotives, so beloved by the B.B.C., are well enough, but they make a very minor part of the drama. There are critics who adore to analyse such minutiae of style, often because they like to admire artistic work for different reasons from those of the ordinary person, and

a good one, the part of the sentence that follows it tends to seem anticlimax.

[1] It is interesting, and to me pleasing, to find Johnson not afraid of italics. But I doubt if 'the exact prosodist' is here quite exact enough. 'Flies o'er th' unbending corn' does indeed provide an extra syllable or 'time', compared with 'The long majestic march'; but, by producing a rapid anapaest, it *does* make the line move faster. And it is the *speed* that matters, not the number of syllables. (Incidentally it is interesting that Johnson, unlike some earless persons, read 'th' unbending' without wholly eliding its 'the'— not 'thunbending'.)

It *might* also be urged that the 'sc' and 'sk' of 'scours' and 'skims' add to the sense of scurry.

[2] Johnson, *Life of Pope*. Cf. *Rambler* 94, *Idler* 60.

[246]

would rather dwell microscopically on the beauty of the blades of grass in Botticelli's *Primavera* than feel the tragic beauty of the whole. But such aesthetes do not seem to me very large-minded. It is too easy to become a kind of critical beauty-doctor more interested in make-up than in humanity.

Imitative passages exist. They can give pleasure. But it remains, I think, pleasure of a minor kind. A good example (whether or no it is a good passage) may be found in Kingsley's *Yeast* (ch. III).

He tried | to think, | but the riv|er would | not let | him. | It thund|ered and spout|ed out || behind | him from | the hatch|es, | and leapt madly past him, and caught his eyes in spite of him, | and swept | them away | down its danc|ing waves | , and let them go again only to sweep them down again and again,[1] till his brain felt a delicious dizziness | from the ev|erlast|ing rush || and the ev|erlast|ing roar. | And then below, how it spread, and writhed, and whirled into transparent fans, hissing and twining snakes, polished glass wreaths, huge crystal bells, which boiled up from the bottom, | and dived | again | beneath | long threads | of cream|y foam, | and swung | round posts | and roots, | and rushed blackening under dark weed-fringed boughs, and gnawed at the marly banks, | and shook | the ev|er-rest|less bul|rushes, | till it was swept away and down over the white pebbles and olive weeds, | in one | broad ripp|ling sheet | of molt|en sil|ver, | towards | the dist|ant sea. | Downwards | it fleet|ed ev|er, | and bore | his thoughts float|ing on | its oil|y stream; | and the | great trout, | with their yell|ow sides | and pea|cock backs, | lounged among the eddies, and the silver grayling dimpled and wandered upon the shallows, and the May-flies flickered and rustled round him like water-

[1] Three 'again's seem rather much in one line.

fairies, with their green gauzy wings; the coot clanked musically among the reeds; the frogs hummed[1] their ceaseless vesper-monotone; | the king|fisher dart|ed from | his hole | in the bank | like a | blue spark | of electr|ic light; | the swall|ows' bills snapped | as they twined | and hawked | above | the pool; | the swifts' wings whirred like musket balls,[2] as they rushed screaming past his head; | and ev|er the riv|er fleet|ed by, | bearing his eyes away down the current, till its wild eddies | began | to glow | with crim|son || beneath | the sett|ing sun.[3]

No doubt all this foams down as tumultuously as the river; yet I do not feel wholly happy about it. It seems to strain after effect too much to be effective. It froths a little.

But, apart from rhythm, there is also the wider question of beauty or fitness in the sound of words themselves. But here too there is a need for scepticism; for here too the ear is often duped. Logan Pearsall Smith, for example, asserted it was 'obvious' that 'long vowels suggest a slower movement than the shorter vowels'. Now it is true that 'crawl', 'creep', 'dawdle' have long vowels and connote slow movement; while 'skip', 'run', 'hop' have short vowels and suggest speed. But 'leap', 'dart', 'speed' are also long—and yet rapid; while 'drag', 'shilly-shally', 'hesitate', 'dilatory', despite all their short vowels, indicate slowness.

No doubt, again, there are some intrinsically ugly words in English, especially pompous polysyllabic words; and others that are intrinsically beautiful; but far fewer of both than we think. E. E. Kellett somewhere tells of some aesthetic body debating which was the most

---

[1] Do frogs 'hum'?
[2] This I doubt.
[3] Quoted in Saintsbury, *English Prose Rhythm*, p. 401.

beautiful word in the language; they had almost decided on 'swallow', when some ill-intentioned person asked 'Bird or gulp?' After that, no more was heard of 'swallow'. 'Greece' may be thought a beautiful word:

The Isles of Greece, the Isles of Greece!

The glory that was Greece.

But 'grease'? 'The glory that was grease'? Yet the sound is indistinguishable.[1] 'Grace' may seem lovely to the ear, as to the eye; but the French 'graisse'? 'Scavenger', on the other hand, so far as sound goes, might be a noble word; but the sense kills the sound. If 'forlorn' meant a kind of potato, would it still ring like 'a bell'? Would it please us any better than 'Cominform'? Would 'Mesopotamia' rejoice the ear, if it were the name of a disease? 'Mary Stuart' is etymologically 'Mary Styward', that is, 'Pig-keeper'; but fortunately for the dignity of that royal name which Alan Breck was proud to bear, most of us forget its derivation. One understands the small boy who said, shuddering, 'Death! I wish it wasn't called that. I don't think I should mind so much if it were called "Hig".' But I suspect that in a short time 'Hig' would come to sound as sombre and as sinister. 'Death' may seem a breathless, mysterious word; but, when it is a question of boiling a picnic-kettle, who finds anything terrible in the sound of 'meth'? It was this amazing power of *association* that Wordsworth forgot when he theorized about common words being best. English has hundreds of musical lines about the sea:

The unplum'd salt, estranging sea.

The sad, sea-sounding wastes of Lyonesse.

Yet surely FitzGerald was not unreasonable in complaining that English has nothing better than 'the miserable

---

[1] Cf. the not very happy title of a book of Greek travel (if it is not apocryphal): 'Hallowed Spots of Greece.'

word "sea"' to express that thing of beauty and terror
which for the Greeks was '*thalassa*'—in whose very
syllables one seems to hear the *dashing* of the surges on
some Aegean shore? Why, 'sea' is hardly even a word;
being identical in sound with a mere letter of the alpha-
bet. It seems inferior even to 'mer', 'Meer', 'mare'.
And yet our poets manage.

The point may perhaps be illustrated by analogy.
Think of the meanings (*and* associations) of a group of
words as an electric current; of their sounds as the con-
ductor. Some conduct better than others; some offer
marked resistance. A savage touching an electrified
copper-wire may suppose the magic to lie in the wire
itself; and similarly we are apt sometimes to attribute to
verbal sounds a beauty to which indeed they may lend
themselves, but which is not always intrinsically theirs.
The letter may borrow glories from the spirit. The ear
is enormously suggestible. Provided, in short, that a
sentence is fine in sense, and fine in rhythm, and easy to
articulate—not congested with consonants nor disfigured
by jingles, I doubt if it will gain quite so much further
beauty or effectiveness from the actual sounds of its
syllables—from vowel-play and dentals and labials and
the rest of it—as precious persons who revel in this sort
of subtlety sometimes suppose. The whole business is
liable to degenerate into mere foppery and frippery.[1]

I am not denying that play on consonants and vowels
can be found; as in this passage from Swift:

There is a *p*ortion of enthusiasm assigned to e*v*ery nation,
which if it hath not *p*roper objects to work on, will burst out
and set all into a *f*lame. If the quiet of the state can be bought

[1] It has been suggested by Mr. T. S. Eliot that, in Tennyson's
Mariana, 'The blue fly *sung* in the pane' is much better than
'The blue fly *sang* in the pane' would have been. 'Sung' is, I
think, nearer to the noise of a fly (cf. 'hum', 'buzz'); but even here
I remain a little dubious.

by only *f*linging men a *f*ew ceremonies to de*v*our, it is a *p*urchase no wise man would *r*e*f*use. Let the mastif*f*s amu*s*e themsel*v*es about a *s*heep*s*kin stu*ff*ed with hay, pro*v*ided it will kee*p* them *f*rom worrying the *f*lock.

Those who like this kind of analysis can point to the scornfully hissing sibilants at the end, to the snarling 'r's ('litera canina'), to that recurrence of 'p', 'v', and 'f' which Stevenson thought particularly potent.

So with this passage of Burke, likewise concerned with stuffed illusions:

We have not been drawn and tru*s*sed, in order that we may be *f*illed, like *s*tu*ff*ed birds in a museum, with cha*ff* and *r*ags, and *p*alt*r*y blur*r*ed *s*h*r*eds of *p*aper about the *r*ights of man. We *p*re*s*er*v*e the whole of our *f*eelings, nati*v*e and enti*r*e, un*s*op*h*i*s*ti*c*ated by *p*edant*r*y and in*f*idelity.

Here again are the scornful sibilants, the growling 'r's, the 'p's, 'v's, and 'f's.

How far such effects were consciously intended, I do not know. Whether they matter much, I am doubtful. It is dangerously easy to grow fanciful about them. After all, there is only a limited number of vowels available, and a rather less limited number of consonants. One must therefore allow a good deal for coincidence. As a colonel of mine used philosophically to remark, when German shells grouped themselves uncomfortably close, 'They *have* to burst somewhere.' Further, even where effects of this kind seem certainly intended, as in some of the lines quoted earlier from Tennyson, there may still be wide disagreement as to what sounds are pleasing. Tennyson, for example, had what seems to me something like a mania about 'kicking the geese out of the boat'; that is, avoiding the juxtaposition of a word ending with 's' and a following word beginning with it. Yet other poets like Pope, whose ear was no less punctilious, appear to find nothing so terrible about this, and would as

soon have written 'Freedom broadens slowly down' as
'Freedom slowly broadens down' (which is, in fact, apt to
be misquoted in the first form).[1] Similarly Dryden got
a bee in his bonnet about hiatus; but who minds it?[2]

There is, however, one sound-device whose importance
is less dubious. Let us return a moment to

The sad, sea-sounding wastes of Lyonesse.

There is nothing fanciful about the effects, here, of
alliteration. This ancient device was already potent in
classical poetry; it was the basis of the versification used
by our Teutonic forefathers; it has formed countless
stock-phrases in proverbial or daily speech, like 'naked
as a needle', 'common as the cartway', 'by might and
main', 'by fair means or foul', 'in for a penny, in for a
pound'. Apart from the pleasure alliteration appears to
produce, it does also, I think, act as a kind of lubricant to
language, making it easier to articulate.

No doubt, it is also a dangerous device. This 'hunting
the letter' grows monotonous in Langland, affected in
Lyly, tiresome in Swinburne; who indeed confessed the
faults of his style, while continuing to indulge them in the
very confession, when he wrote of his Gautier ode, 'the
danger of such metres is diffuseness and flaccidity. I
perceive this one to have a tendency to the dulcet and
luscious form of verbosity which has to be guarded
against lest the poem lose its foothold and be swept off its
legs, sense and all, down a flood of effeminate and
monotonous music, or be lost and spilt in a maze of
draggle-tailed melody.' Perhaps a still stranger example
is that quoted by Stevenson[3] from Macaulay:

[1] So with Housman's:
    Though the girl he loves the best
    Rouses from another's side.
[2] E.g. Meredith: 'The army of unalterable law.'
[3] The Art of Writing, 'Elements of Style'.

[252]

Meanwhile the disorders of Kannon's Kamp went on in-Kreasing. He Kalled a Kouncil of war to Konsider what Kourse it would be advisable to taKe. But as soon as the Kouncil had met, a preliminary Kuestion was raised. The army was almost eKsKlusively a Highland army. The recent viKtory had been won eKsKlusively by Highland warriors. Great chie*f*s who had brought siKs or seven hundred *f*ighting men into the *f*ield did not think it *f*air that they should be out*v*oted by gentlemen *f*rom Ireland, and *f*rom the Low Kountries, who bore indeed King James's Kommission, and were Kalled Kolonels and Kaptains, but who were Kolonels without regiments and Kaptains without Kompanies.

I confess that I find this rather shattering; indeed, difficult though that might be, I think it might have rather shattered Macaulay himself. Alliteration can be an excellent tool: but there are few that need more discretion in their use.

To recapitulate, then, I am driven to the following heretical conclusions about sound and rhythm.

(1) The reader of prose generally dislikes *obvious* patches of verse. Yet unobvious patches of verse often lurk in our finest pieces of impassioned prose. Therefore it appears that they please us, provided we do not notice exactly how we are being pleased.

(2) This disguise of metrical rhythms can be effected partly by moderation in their use; partly by wide variation of the rhythms employed—iambic, trochaic, anapaestic, even dactylic; partly by wide variation in their length, from two or three feet to six or seven. Blank verse, as particularly recognizable, is particularly dangerous. Safety lies in variety.

(3) Metrical fragments are specially common (and often specially effective), as a sentence nears its close.

(4) A tendency to metre can be counteracted by abundance of consecutive unstressed syllables. One way of obtaining this abundance is to employ plenty of poly-

[253]

syllables. But this easily becomes pompous or ugly, as in the passages quoted from Meredith.[1] (Indeed, Demosthenes is said to avoid any series of three or more short syllables.) It may also help to use rather short[2] or rather long clauses (for the metrical effect becomes most conspicuous when a clause is exactly the length of a verse). In general, prose of a rather flat, semi-conversational tone, remote from poetry, seems less apt to run to metre; or to be detected, if occasionally it does.

(5) But those who are *too* frightened of verse-rhythms are liable to produce a prosaic kind of prose, lacking rhythm of any kind.

(6) I cannot make it too clear that the effectiveness of verse-rhythms in prose depends on their remaining unobserved. To read them aloud *stressing* their metre would be as perverse as the contrary efforts of inferior actors to speak Shakespearian metre as if it were blank prose.

(7) Both in verse and in prose the sound and rhythm can sometimes be made echoes of the sense. But such things are limited in scope and importance. They are apt to seem trivial tricks. And critics who dwell too much on them, tend themselves to produce more sound than sense.

(8) Fewer words than is generally supposed are intrinsically beautiful or (apart from certain types of galumphing polysyllables) intrinsically ugly. The main thing is that sentences should meet the needs of the respiration, and that combinations of words should come easily off the tongue.

(9) Alliteration is valuable; but perilous.

A Note on Final Cadences

Ancient Greek and Latin writers of rhythmic prose developed certain favourite cadences (*clausulae*) for the

---

[1] Pp. 228–9.   [2] Cf. the Burton passage, p. 103.

ends of sentences, and even of clauses—to precede, in short, the places where the speaker paused to breathe. Indeed it becomes clear that ancient audiences had more delicate ears than ours; partly perhaps because ancient literature was far more largely spoken or read aloud.[1]

It is true that different writers or orators varied widely in their tastes (for example, Isocrates, Cicero, Plutarch liked – ᴗ ᴗ ᴗ –×; but Lysias, Aeschines, Brutus, Sallust, Livy, and Tacitus shunned it).[2] Again Cicero carefully eschewed in his own practice some *clausulae* that in theory he praised.

Since Cicero, however, was the one surviving classic eminent both in theory and in practice, medieval Latin adopted some of his favourite cadences (though, of course, with stress replacing quantity). These favourite cadences consisted of a cretic (– ᴗ –) followed by from one to two and a half trochees; and their three main varieties were called *cursus planus*, *cursus tardus*, and *cursus velox*.

Classical Quantitative Form	Later Accentual Form
1. *Planus.* – ᴗ – | – ×	′ . . | ′ .[3]
Voce testatur.	*Voces testantur.*
	Mércy and píty.
	(*I.e.* the ending of an accentual hexameter.)
(Also – ᴗ ᴗ ᴗ | – ×	′ . . . | ′ .)

[1] Yet any attentive ear can notice that B.B.C. News Bulletins, although spoken, are curiously insensitive to repetitions or jingles of words or syllables—*e.g.* 'it is re*por*ted that the *port* is blocked'.

[2] There is a good summary in the *Oxford Classical Dictionary*, *s.v.* 'Prose-Rhythm'.

[3] A dot indicates an unaccented syllable.

<table>
<tr><th></th><th>Classical Quantitative Form</th><th>Later Accentual Form</th></tr>
<tr><td>2. Tardus.</td><td>– ⏑ – | – ⏑ | ×
Nostra curatio.</td><td>´ . . | ´ . .
Posse subsistere.
Thém that be |
pénitent.</td></tr>
<tr><td></td><td>(Also – ⏑ ⏑ ⏑ | – ⏑ | ×</td><td>´ . . . | ´ . .)[1]</td></tr>
<tr><td>3. Velox.</td><td>– ⏑ – | – ⏑ | – ×
Gaudium pervenire.</td><td>´ . . | ` . | ´ .
Saecula saeculorum.
Lóse not the thìngs
etérnal.</td></tr>
<tr><td></td><td>(Also – ⏑ ⏑ ⏑ | – ⏑ | – ×</td><td>´ . . . | ` . | ´ .)[1]</td></tr>
<tr><td>4.</td><td>– ⏑ – | – ⏑ | – ⏑ | ×
Spiritum pertimescere.</td><td>´ . . | ` . | ´ . .
(Amari) tudinem
penitentiae.</td></tr>
</table>

Such accentual Latin cadences flourished from the fourth to the sixth century; they revived in the tenth, and were taken up by the Roman Curia; and they occur in the Latin of Dante and Petrarch. Renaissance scholarship, however, naturally dropped them as barbarous.

At the Reformation the writers of the English Prayer Book appear to have adopted, consciously or unconsciously, rhythms of this kind from the Roman Missal and Breviary. (They also occur in the English Bible.)

So far there seems general agreement. But it has further been argued that final cadences of this kind play an important part throughout artistic English prose.

This is asking a good deal. One can believe that English ecclesiastics at the Reformation, familiar with ecclesiastical Latin, might reproduce its cadences in their English; one could believe that later religious-minded writers, familiar with the Prayer Book, might reproduce its cadences in secular prose. But it remains a little hard

[1] Said not to occur in accentual Latin theory or practice, but found in English.

to believe that ordinary English writers who had never heard of *clausula* or *cursus* should reinvent their English equivalents.

Besides, when I open my daily paper, I encounter, in the first leading article I look at, the sentence-ending 'prévioús àd | mìnistr | átiòns'—a variety of *cursus velox*. I turn to the financial page and read: 'Dulness renewed in N. British Loco. at 12/6 was due to competítiòn còn | sìdèr | átiòns' (another *velox*!). These seem strange elegances (if they *are* elegant) for Fleet Street to hit upon accidentally. Now I have done it myself! 'Hít úpòn | àccid | éntàllý' (*cursus* 4).

Besides, it will be noted that all these cadences end with an unaccented syllable. But the finest English sentences often end with accented syllables (thirteen sentences out of eighteen, for example, in the Landor passage quoted on p. 225). 'Oh,' say the *cursus*-worshippers, 'but there are "native" cadences as well (such as ′. ′, ′. . ′, ′. . . ′).' Indeed, it might be urged that the second and third of these are shortened forms of ′. . ′. (*planus*) or ′. . . ′. (variation of *planus*), just as the English decasyllable corresponds to the Italian eleven-syllable line.

But at this point my scepticism begins to suspect that all these supposed graces are not the product of some secret apostolic succession from Cicero to Stevenson, but simply the spontaneous result, first, of the nature of English speech-rhythm; secondly of the problem of writing English prose that shall be neither too rhythmical nor yet too unrhythmical.

The following factors seem to me explanation enough:

(1) In English, rhythm tends to become trochaic or iambic.

(2) Yet a too trochaic or iambic rhythm grows obvious and artificial. A natural remedy is to disguise its regularity by inserting here and there extra unaccented syllables.

[257]

(3) But it is usually difficult, in English, to have more than three unaccented syllables in succession. For then a secondary accent tends to insert itself. (*E.g.* we tend to say 'intólerably' and 'impecúnious'; but 'intólerably impecúnious'.) Accordingly we get such variations as the following:

Regular trochaic rhythms	*Variations*
´ . ´ .	´ . . ´ . or ´ . . . ´ .
´ . ´ . ´	´ . . ´ . ´ , ´ . . ´ . . ,[1] ´ . . . ´ . ´ ,
	´ . . . ´ . .[1]
´ . ´ . ´ .	´ . . ´ . ´ .

These variations turn out to be our old friends *cursus planus*, *tardus*, and *velox*.
Consider two lines of Tennyson:

Cámelot a cíty of shádowy pálaces.

Príck'd with incrédible pínnacles ìnto heáven.

Tennyson has achieved in 'shádowy pálaces' a perfect *tardus* (´ . . ´ . .); in 'pínnacles ìnto heáven' a perfect *velox* (´ . . ` . ´ .); in 'Cámelot a cíty' a variety of *planus*. Who can suppose he intended it? He was merely trying to avoid the monotony of strict iambic rhythm by playing variations. The prose-writer often does the same.

At all events in practice I think the prose-writer should snap his fingers at these medieval relics, and trust his own ear. He will merely take care to avoid too metrical rhythms; and observe variety by mingling sentences that end on a stressed syllable with others that end on an unstressed. 'Cicero', says Lord Chesterfield in Landor, 'was himself a trifler in cadences, and whoever thinks much about them will become so, if indeed the very thought when it enters is not trifling.'

[1] As the last syllable is followed by the pause of the sentence-end, the amount of stress on the final syllable in cases like these becomes not very material.

Landor had little to learn about prose-rhythm from any man; the more honour to him that he kept his sense of proportion about such forms of ornament.[1]

[1] Those who wish to pursue the problem may consult the following:

John Shelley, 'Rhythmical Prose in Latin and English', in *Church Quarterly Review*, 1912.

A. C. Clark, *Prose Rhythm in English*, 1913.

P. Fijn van Draat, 'Voluptas Aurium', in *Englische Studien*, XLVIII, 1914.

M. W. Croll, *Cadence of English Prose* (University of N. Carolina Studies in Philology, XVI, 1919).

O. Elton, *A Sheaf of Papers*, 1922.

Of these van Draat seems to me the best (doubtless because he is as sceptical as I am); though misled by strange ideas of English stresses, such as 'áccommodátion', 'imaginátion', 'écclesiástic'.

XI

METHODS OF WRITING

TEMPERAMENTS are so various that there may be even more than 'nine-and-sixty ways' of writing books. Rousseau, for example, could not compose with pen in hand: but then Chateaubriand could not compose without. Wordsworth did it while walking, riding, or in bed; but Southey, only at his desk. Shakespeare, we are told, never blotted a line; Scott could toss first drafts unread to the printer; Trollope drilled himself, watch on desk, to produce two hundred and fifty words every quarter of an hour; Hilaire Belloc, so Desmond Mac-Carthy once told me, claimed to have written twenty thousand of them in a day; and in ten days Balzac could turn out sixty thousand.[1] On the other hand Ronsard and Montaigne, FitzGerald and George Moore, went on sedulously repolishing even their published works. One need not believe too literally in Oscar Wilde's account of how he spent the morning putting in a comma, and the afternoon in taking it out again; but Flaubert could really toil for three days to grind out eight lines—'qu'il faut pourtant raturer encore'.

None the less, varieties of method are usually interesting, sometimes instructive; and though every writer has to work out his own by trial and error, certain ways of writing seem intrinsically more promising.

Clearly the main problem is, again, one of practical psychology. When a writer thinks of brilliant ideas or

[1] Cf. his boast to Mme. Hanska in 1835: 'Il fallait dix ans à un auteur, dans le XVIIIme siècle, pour faire dix volumes. J'en aurai fait quatorze cette année.' Perhaps the eighteenth-century method, however, had more advantages than Balzac supposed.

phrases, such that neither he nor others can think how he thought of them, men used to call it 'inspiration'. 'Hé bien, Monsieur,' King Murat of Naples would cry to Samuel Rogers (of all people), when he met him out riding, 'êtes-vous inspiré aujourd'hui?' When Dickens was asked where he got Mr. Pickwick, he could only reply that he had *thought* of Mr. Pickwick. Such sudden illuminations the Hebrew prophet attributed to the spirit of the Lord; the Greek poet assigned them to the gracious hands of a Muse (etymologically akin to *mania*, 'madness', and *mantis*, 'seer'); but we appear to owe them rather to that amorphous and sinister monster, the Unconscious.[1]

That things go on in our heads without our knowing is, of course, no new idea. From time immemorial men perplexed by some problem have found it wise to sleep on it. Medieval poets repeatedly pretended to fall asleep and dream their poems. The ancient Persians, according to Herodotus, gave scope to their less conscious thinking by deliberating on important matters twice—first drunk, then sober; or first sober, then drunk. Dryden speaks vividly in the dedication of *The Rival Ladies* of 'a confused mass of Thoughts, tumbling over one another in the dark', and of the Fancy (what we should call 'Imagination') 'moving the sleeping images of things towards the light'. Similarly Johnson refers to 'the lucky moments of animated imagination'; to 'those felicities which cannot be produced at will by wit and labour, but must arise unexpectedly in some hour propitious to poetry'; to the influence exerted 'by causes wholly out of the performer's power, by hints of which he perceives not the origin, by sudden elevations of mind which he cannot produce in himself, and which sometimes rise when he expects them least'. Stevenson had his nocturnal

[1] Further details in the chapters on 'Wit' and on 'Creation and Criticism' in my *Literature and Psychology*.

Brownies. Ibsen, again, writes of putting his characters 'out to grass', in the hope that they will fatten. And the mathematician Henri Poincaré noted three phases in his own thinking—conscious effort; unconscious fermentation; and a final conscious analysis of the new combinations thus formed. But to Freud, whatever else may be questioned in his work, belongs the great discovery, not that unconscious mental processes exist, but that they are much more extensive and important than anyone had dreamed. Men know far less than they think; but they also think far more than they know.[1]

A great part of the writer's problem, then, is how to catch the ideas that creep forth in the stillness, like magic mice, from their holes. Here I suspect that the dog's method is less effective than the cat's. 'Wise passiveness' may succeed better than impatient rush and pounce. No doubt the artist or the thinker may carry his day-dreaming to excess, so that it becomes a vice—Balzac called it 'smoking enchanted cigars'. But it pays, I think, to meditate a good deal, both before beginning to write, and at intervals while writing. The processes of creation may refuse to be bustled. The writer's reverie with a cigarette by the fire may not be as wasteful as Balzac suggests. It may not only turn paper into smoke; it may also turn smoke into paper.

But besides the Unconscious there is a second important master to be served—the conscious, critical Reason. Otherwise one wanders into the bedlam of the Surrealist.

[1] Cf. Proust: 'Il y a plus d'analogie entre la vie instinctive du public et le talent d'un grand écrivain qui n'est qu'un instinct réligieusement écouté, au milieu du silence imposé à tout le reste, un instinct perfectionné et compris, qu'avec le verbiage superficiel et les critères changeants des juges attitrés.' (Le Temps Retrouvé (1927), II, p. 46.) 'Instinct' seems hardly the right word. But it remains true, I think, that many critics live to excess in conscientious consciousness; thinking too much, feeling and dreaming too little, blinded by inability to shut their peering eyes.

And it is important that neither conscious mind nor unconscious should usurp on the domain of the other. 'Render unto Caesar. . . .'

On the one hand, the Unconscious may breed happy ideas in incubation. Therefore it needs time to incubate. Therefore it is usually undesirable that a writer should be hurried or worried, hectically overworked or hectically dissipated. But this incubation need not always involve indolence—change of occupation may do better. Thus Scott found that it suited him to have a dozen irons in the fire at once. Metternich told Varnhagen von Ense that he could not concentrate on a problem day after day; he left it to work in him by itself, and got his best ideas in the middle of other occupations—eating, driving, ordinary talk. Others have gained their most illuminating thoughts on a subject while reading about another subject quite irrelevant; or again an inspiration for Chapter Ten may present itself as the writer toils at Chapter Two. It is often as if the Unconscious were a wayward child, playing truant when it is called, then offering help unasked. In other words, Muses are often coquettes.

But the suggestions of the Unconscious should be seized as soon as offered—or, as Samuel Butler phrased it, one must 'put salt on their tails'. For what the Unconscious thus unaccountably gives, it can as unaccountably take away again—often beyond recall. It will be remembered how Pope could mercilessly drag a poor domestic four times from bed on a freezing night to note inspirations that rose like apparitions from the dark. Similarly the eccentric Duchess of Newcastle kept a servant ready to take down her nocturnal inspirations: 'John,' she would cry, 'I conceive!' The soberer Bentham, again, would write with a green curtain beside him, where he pinned his stray notions on scraps of paper, like butterflies.

But luckily not all good ideas insist on arriving at the

[263]

wrong moment. They may also, when a writer is in the vein, be called forth by the rush and excitement of composition; just as the excitement of conversation may stimulate a talker to wit or wisdom that he would never have hit on in hours of solitary thought.[1] It follows that the process of composition should, if possible, have some rush and excitement about it—not remain too slow, cold, calculated, and self-critical. For this is not only chilling; it may lead the more conscious side of the mind to cramping interference. In tennis, to play with gritted teeth and tense concentration may merely stiffen the muscles: once the necessary reflexes have been formed by practice, it may work far better to use one's head to think where to put the ball, but leave it to one's body how to put it there. And so some have found (again like Scott) that their swiftest compositions were their best; and have gained inspiration from printers' devils rapping at their doors. This may arise partly from the challenge of working against time; partly from the stimulus of feeling that their words would be before the world within a few days, instead of after a year or more; but partly also from the lack of leisure to be hypercritical. For by taking too much thought a man may, not add, but even subtract a cubit from his literary stature.

Such tense self-consciousness was one of the weaknesses of our eighteenth-century poets—even Gray. They tended too much, while they wrote, to let their other, critical selves gaze with freezing eyes over their shoulders. What would Society say? Similarly in her later writing Fanny Burney seemed, paradoxically, to know less of

[1] Cf. Montesquieu's idea that one can give one's thoughts order and logic in one's study; but 'dans le monde, au contraire, on apprend à imaginer; on heurte tant de choses dans les conversations que l'on imagine des choses; on y voit les hommes comme agréables et comme gais; on y est pensant par la raison qu'on ne pense pas, c'est à dire que l'on a les idées de hasard, qui sont souvent les bonnes.' Happy age, when such conversation was to be found!

life as an experienced woman, than she had known as a spontaneous girl; while her style degenerated into a false and lumbering Johnsonese.

For the orator, again, self-criticism may prove more crippling still. De Tocqueville attributed his failure in speaking to his habit of listening to himself, instead of being carried away. Other speakers have been known to do best on some occasion when they happened to have lost their carefully composed manuscripts: for *now* they had no time to think too much. In Parliament, above all as a debater, Charles James Fox seems to have been, in the phrase of his opponent Pitt, 'a magician'; yet he never prepared a speech; but his *James II*, written 'drop by drop', with a purism that carefully restricted itself to the vocabulary of Dryden, remains today only a name. 'Tom Birch', said Johnson, 'is brisk as a bee in conversation; but no sooner does he take a pen in his hand, than it becomes a torpedo to him, and benumbs all his faculties.' And of his own most successful work, *The Lives of the Poets*, Johnson records that he wrote them 'in my usual way, dilatorily and hastily, unwilling to work and working with vigour and haste'.[1]

Therefore it seems that a writer may often gain by writing at high speed. It is rash to do so for long at a time; but he should perhaps often write in spurts. Flaubert's method was, on the contrary, a slow elaboration, like Gray's. For writers with their temperament no other way may have been possible. None the less Flaubert's letters, which must have been written faster and more freely, often seem to me better, even as style, than some of his more laboured work. (And, more important, I have heard a Frenchman say the same.)

---

[1] It seems to me not impossible that the superior ease of the *Lives* owes something to the incessant conversation, often with minds above the average, of Johnson's later years, when he had become a lion.

Therefore I suspect that in general it may answer better to follow the practice of Virgil who, we are told, would write a number of lines rapidly in the morning, then lick them into shape, as a few perfect verses, in the course of the day.

There are, indeed, limits to this. It may not answer at all well to write a first draft so quickly and carelessly that it needs to be not merely polished, but totally recast. For this not only wastes time; it is sometimes curiously difficult, once a piece of writing has been started on the wrong lines, to obliterate the memory of it, and begin afresh. Once the metal has cooled in the wrong shape, it may prove unexpectedly hard to remelt and remould. Gray, himself a slow writer, warned Mason against this danger of too rapid first drafts.[1]

On the whole, however, I think Johnson was probably wiser in urging that one should learn to write well by writing fast than Quintilian in advising, on the contrary, that one should learn to write fast by writing well. A Chinese connoisseur of painting put it more tersely still: 'Thinkee long. Work chop-chop.'

This does not of course mean that one should paint a whole picture, or write a whole book, at express speed. It is usually wiser to leave intervals for meditation and incubation; as a chick emerging from its egg alternately struggles and rests, struggles and rests. It merely means

---

[1] Cf. Quintilian, X, 3, 17–8: 'manet in rebus temere congestis quae fuit levitas. Protinus ergo adhibere curam rectius erit atque ab initio sic opus ducere ut caelandum, non ex integro fabricandum sit. Aliquando tamen adfectus sequemur, in quibus fere plus calor quam diligentia valet.' 'Things hastily thrown together keep their original flimsiness. Accordingly it will answer better to take more care, and conduct one's work from the start in such a way that it will need merely to be chiselled, not wholly recast. Still, at times we shall be wise to follow the moods of the moment, where warmth of feeling commonly provides more force than any laboured effort.'

that a given passage is often better written fast and not one word at a time, with pauses to seek inspiration from the ceiling, or sustenance from gnawing one's pen. Further, where hard thinking is needed it may often be better done *before* a man sits down to his desk. The students in the Bardic Schools of medieval Ireland (eleventh to fifteenth centuries), who—unlike some more modern poets—underwent six or seven years' hard training in their art, lay all day abed in darkened cubicles to compose; in the evening, lights were brought and then they wrote down their poems. Similarly, in a very different world, James Brindley, the canal-engineer (1716–72), when grappling with some difficult problem, would retire to bed to find ideas. For the mind may meditate best when the body is relaxed and the outer world shut off. 'Thinkee long. Work chop-chop.'

To sum up what I have said so far, a good many of these principles are embodied in the practice of Kant. He let his imagination work on a subject beforehand, but read works on quite different topics, such as stories or travel-books. He set a high value on sudden ideas ('dasjenige, worauf man sich am wenigsten präpariert, ist das naïvste') and carefully noted them down. Then he would read his notes, sketch his scheme in short sentences, and write ahead. If new ideas occurred during this process, he quickly left a space with a note of them, then pressed forward.[1]

---

[1] Coleridge's much-discussed distinction between Fancy and Imagination seems not irrelevant here. These terms do not strike me as happy, for in older English Fancy and Imagination are the same thing; and if one wishes to make scientific distinctions of this kind, it may be wiser, as scientists do, to coin new words, free from muddling associations. And the distinction itself seems to have occasioned a lot of false profundity. In general, what Coleridge would call 'imaginative' appears to differ from what he would call 'fanciful' merely by being more serious, more deeply felt, more an expression of real emotion than an exhibition of cleverness. But

But if I suggest the need for giving the less conscious levels of the mind their chance by long incubation and rapid writing, it is not that I wish to minimize the share of the conscious reason. On the contrary, with Jane Austen, I feel that 'to be rational in anything is great praise'. Our century has produced only too much tipsy literature. I much prefer Rossetti's 'fundamental brainwork'—first of all, before incubation begins (for the unconscious mind may fail to work seriously unless the conscious mind has worked seriously first); and again during actual composition. Unless he indulges in free association and automatic writing, or is carried away by 'poetic fury', or is drugged like Coleridge over *Kubla Khan*, the writer needs to keep his head as well as use it. For instance, it sometimes proves easier to write freely at night; but the results are apt, like fairy gold, to reveal themselves as withered leaves in the cold light of morning. For though at night the invention is sometimes more fertile, that may be only because the judgement is then drowsier. Just as alcohol does not really stimulate the brain, but merely drugs the part of it that acts as censor.

But it is, above all, in the final stage of revision that the conscious, critical reason can play its most dominant part. A work may have been composed with happy ease, or with intoxicated ardour; but now comes the time—for writers that can do it—to view the result with cold detachment.[1]

it may also be true that 'imaginative' ideas often gain their finer quality from having been brooded in the Unconscious, like the materials of *The Ancient Mariner*; not superficially juggled together by the fully conscious intellect. It would follow (as seems likely anyway) that no sharp line can be drawn between the 'fanciful' and the 'imaginative'—one fades into the other, like colours in the spectrum.

[1] The neo-Classic age already knew this. Cf. Roscommon—

And write with fury, but correct with phlegm;

and Walsh's notion that, ideally, one should be in love to write love-poems, and out of love to correct them.

After Sainte-Beuve had drafted each of his *Lundis*, he would hand it to his secretary and say, 'Lisez-moi en ennemi.'

The vital importance of this last stage, especially for style, is seldom realized by the general public. But it is here that some truth emerges from Buffon's paradox: 'Le génie n'est qu'une grande aptitude à la patience.' No doubt there are writers who revolt at revision—such as Shakespeare, or Dryden (in this, the reverse of Pope), or Byron who, if he missed his first spring, went growling back to his jungle.[1] But those who refuse to revise may pay dearly—though, of course, they may be rich enough to afford it. Even in Shakespeare there is plenty of 'sad stuff'; Scott's style is uneven; Trollope's,[2] undistinguished. Indeed, I can think of no constantly perfect stylist who has not laboured like an emmet.

Here I am not thinking so much of the toilsome apprenticeship needed to acquire a style—of Demosthenes five times copying out all Thucydides, or of Stevenson composing careful pastiches of older authors; of Buffon saying at seventy, 'J'apprends tous les jours à écrire', or of Goethe's, 'At length after forty years I have learnt to write German.'[3] I am thinking rather of the endless rewriting done, even by established writers, to an extent

---

[1] 'I can't correct, I can't and I won't. Nobody ever succeeds in it, great or small.' But Byron should have been content to speak for himself. And at times even he would revise, and discuss alternative revisions, with considerable care. (See R. E. Prothero, *Byron's Works* (*Letters and Journals*), II, pp. 145–161.)

[2] I find myself gasping at Trollope's advice, in his admirable *Autobiography*, to young writers: 'That their work should be read after it has been written is a matter of course—that it should be read twice at least before it goes to the printers, I take to be a matter of course.' Twice!

[3] Similarly Rodin at sixty observed that he was beginning to understand his art; Hokusaï (1760–1849) made a like remark at seventy-three.

that the public little guesses—of Plato's variant versions of the first words of *The Republic*, or Ariosto's of the first line of *Orlando*.

In fine, there is much to be said for the principle 'Write in haste; and revise at leisure.' And revision is usually best when one has had time to forget what has been written, and comes back to it with fresh eyes.

La Bruyère took ten years to write his *Caractères*; and nearly ten more to revise them. La Fontaine, seemingly so simple and so idle, revised indefatigably.

Pascal, it is said, composed his eighteenth *Provinciale* thirteen times;[1] Buffon made eighteen drafts of his *Époqües de la Nature*, and Xavier de Maistre seventeen of his *Lépreux*. Chateaubriand polished and repolished his *Mémoires* over a period of thirty years. Tolstoy's long-suffering countess copied out for him seven times the vast bulk of *War and Peace*; and he would send telegrams to change a word. No wonder his great works left him in a state of collapse. Virginia Woolf wrote parts of *The Waves* twenty times. Anatole France liked eight proofs. Balzac, for all his feverish haste, might go as far as twenty-seven. Indeed, he boasted that, if there were a million lines in his *Comédie Humaine*, they must have cost him two francs apiece in corrections (say £80,000, when the pound itself had a very different value from today). Obviously this passion for perfection can degenerate into a mania. Rousseau would run from his attic to recapture a note and revise it; Paul-Louis Courier would make seventeen drafts of a letter.[2] But, in general, the lesson is clear—good writing is often far harder work than most people suppose.

---

[1] His sixteenth *Provinciale* had to be produced in haste: 'cette lettre est donc plus *longue* qu'il ne souhaitoit'. As usual, brevity needed time.

[2] A. Albalat, *Le Travail du Style* (1903), p. 150. (A highly instructive book.)

Yet I notice that most of my pupils feel it a hardship if I suggest that they should make even one rough draft of their essays. Clearly they cannot, as Horace advises, keep them nine years before bringing them out; but it is optimistic to think one can write well without a tenth of the pains that it has cost even the masters. After all, no less labour is often needed to excel in other arts. Giardini, when asked how long it took to learn the fiddle, replied, 'Twelve hours a day for twenty years.' Paganini would practise the same passage for ten hours running. Leonardo would walk the length of Milan to change a single tint in his *Last Supper*. Monet painted a haystack eighty-three times. On many subjects an easy style may be one of the very hardest things to produce. 'Naturalness', says Anatole France, 'is what is added last.' Or in the words of Michael Angelo: 'What one takes most pains to do, should look as if it had been thrown off quickly, almost without effort—nay, despite the truth, as if it had cost no trouble. Take infinite pains to make something that looks effortless.'[1]

[1] The reader may like to be reminded by some examples of the vast improvements sometimes made by revision.

> (1) Since then at an uncertain hour,
>   Now ofttimes and now fewer,
>   That anguish comes and makes me tell
>   My ghastly aventure.

> (2) Since then at an uncertain hour
>   That agony returns:
>   And till my ghastly tale is told,
>   My heart within me burns.
>   COLERIDGE, *Ancient Mariner*

> (1) Underneath the bearded barley,
>   The reaper, reaping late and early,
>   Hears her ever chanting cheerly,
>   Like an angel, singing clearly,
>   O'er the stream of Camelot.

One has also to remember that revision is a means not only of polishing, but also of compressing. For perfect brevity—I need not repeat my praises of it—can seldom be had without long filing and cutting. Quintilian spoke the truth: 'A pen may be just as usefully employed in crossing out as in writing.' Kipling, who kept some of his short stories from three to five years, shortening them annually, had a special method for this, which he called 'the Higher Editing'. 'Take of well-ground Indian Ink as much as suffices and a camel-hair brush proportionate to the interspaces of your lines. In an auspicious hour, read your final draft and consider faithfully every paragraph, sentence and word, blacking out where requisite. Let it lie by to drain as long as possible. At the end of that time, re-read and you should find it will bear a second shortening. Finally, read it aloud alone and at leisure. Maybe a shade more brushwork will then indicate or impose itself. If not, praise Allah and let it go, and "when thou hast done, repent not".'[1]

> Piling the sheaves in furrows airy,
> Beneath the moon, the reaper weary
> Listening whispers, ''tis the fairy
>   Lady of Shalott.'

(2) Only reapers, reaping early
>   In among the bearded barley,
>   Hear a song that echoes cheerly
>   From the river winding clearly,
>   Down to tower'd Camelot:
>   And by the moon the reaper weary,
>   Piling sheaves in uplands airy,
>   Listening, whispers ''Tis the fairy
>   Lady of Shalott.'

TENNYSON, *Lady of Shalott.*

Compare the development of Housman's '*coloured* counties' from 'sunny', through 'pleasant', 'checkered', 'patterned', 'painted' (in a dream), to its final form.

[1] Quoted in R. Lynd, *Books and Writers* (1952), p. 93.

'In principle this seems to me most sound; but in method, too elaborate. Kipling may have felt a natural partiality for *Indian* ink and the hair of camels; but why delete the first version so irrevocably? One may wish, in places, to restore it after all. Therefore I would suggest that it would be more practical, though less poetical, to revise with humble pencil and rubber, and leave all this painting to pictorial artists.

It is only honest, however, to add that all such heroic efforts may in the end be worse than wasted. One's second thoughts—or one's twenty-second—are not always best; and too much revision may only sacrifice happy spontaneity for a tired correctness. Isocrates polished his *Panegyric* for ten or fifteen years; but Isocrates remains a minor writer. Cardinal Bembo made his manuscripts migrate through sixteen portfolios in turn, revising them at each migration from one to the next; it sounds a marvellous system; yet, somehow, it seems not to have brought the diligent cardinal much immortality. Again, the final versions of Wordsworth's *Prelude*, for instance, or FitzGerald's *Omar* please many readers less than the earlier versions they replaced.[1] Whether truly or not, it

[1] Examples of second thoughts that do *not* seem better.

(1) She took me to her elfin grot,
  And there she wept and sigh'd full sore,
  And there I shut her wild wild eyes
    With kisses four.

(2) She took me to her elfin grot,
  And there she gaz'd and sighed deep,
  And there I shut her wild sad eyes—
    So kiss'd to sleep.
          KEATS, *La Belle Dame Sans Merci.*
(The 'Knight at arms' also declines into a 'wretched wight'.)

(1) Awake! for Morning in the Bowl of Night
  Has flung the Stone that puts the Stars to Flight:
  And lo! the Hunter of the East has caught
  The Sultán's Turret in a Noose of Light.

[273]

was said of the excellence of Sainte-Beuve's *Lundis*, 'il
n'a pas le temps de les gâter'. And Pope made a similar
comment on Addison, who was a great corrector, except
in his *Spectators*.

Therefore it is important, not only to revise, but to
know when to stop revising. Personally, I take it as a
warning-signal when I find myself deleting what stands
in the last revision, and reinstating what stood there in
the last but one; then one had better give over.

So far I have been thinking mainly of creative literature
and, in that literature, of the element of style. But there
is another problem that seems worth briefly considering,
since bad management here can have disastrous effects
on style as well. I mean documentation. A critic or
scholar, for example, even a novelist or poet, may need
to master a large body of facts. In practice, I come across
this particular problem most in advising research
students; but it is of far more general application.

Now the first impulse of the conscientious writer may
be to assume that he should pore through everything
written on his subject, before he puts pen to paper. Thus
Flaubert relates on 25 January 1880, that he has devoured
over one thousand five hundred books for his *Bouvard et
Pécuchet*. (In the end he was to read some two thousand.) 'Cette surabondance de documents m'a permis de
n'être pas pédant.' I doubt it.

So apparently, sooner or later, did Flaubert himself.
Elsewhere he groans that he would gladly give up all the
ninety-eight volumes he has so far read, and the half-

(2) Wake! for the Sun, who scatter'd into flight
    The Stars before him from the Field of Night,
      Drives Night along with them from Heav'n, and
      strikes
    The Sultán's Turret with a Shaft of Light.
                 FITZGERALD, *Omar Khayyam*.

(The desert Arabs flung a stone into a cup as signal for striking
camp. In the later version this vivid local colour fades away.)

ream of notes he has compiled, if only for three seconds
he could feel really moved by the passions of his characters. And his niece records that he came to feel he had
spent too long on such preliminary researches, and wanted
to give the rest of his life to pure art.

Of course, different minds vary enormously in their
power to amass information without growing gorged and
surfeited. Nothing in Gibbon's vast history is more
astounding than the calm enjoyment with which he seems
to have produced it. He talks of it in the tone other men
use of their hobbies. 'This work', he writes, '*amused* and
exercised nearly twenty years.' And again: 'Some fame,
some profit, and the assurance of daily *amusement* encourage me to persist.' Whereas his great contemporary
Montesquieu, toiling through Visigothic statutes, compared himself wearily to Saturn swallowing stones; and
the completion of *L'Esprit des Lois* was reported to have
left him too exhausted to read anything profounder than
fairy-tales. All the more honour to him that his work yet
remains so readable and so alive.

But since for most of us the accumulation of facts does
often prove highly exhausting, the vital point is to avoid
getting stale. Often, indeed, the ideal of reading everything ever written on a subject seems to me a vain idol.
Five centuries ago such an ambition was often feasible;[1]
today it is often fantastic; tomorrow it will become still
more so. Therefore it is important to develop a quick
eye for fools whose books are not worth reading; and a
quick power of disembowelling other books less foolish,
but still of minor importance.[2] Otherwise, before the

[1] Still more, nine centuries ago, when the happy Benedict of
Clusa could boast in 1028 (whether or not one believes him): 'I
have two large houses filled with books..... There is not in the
whole earth a book that I have not.'

[2] 'Sir,' said Johnson, 'do you read books through?' There are
many, no doubt, that it is a pity not to; but many more where he
that runs and skips, reads quite enough.

author puts pen to his own paper, he may easily have become a stuffed owl, with nothing new to say and with no energy for saying it.

The second point, I think, is not to delay writing till too late. If one is going to read a hundred books on a given subject, it may often be better to start writing as soon as one has read, say, fifty of them. The rest can be taken in the intervals of writing, or after the first draft is written. In this way the writer will feel less like one of those Alpine peasants one sees scaling hillsides with hay-stacks on their heads. He will have more chance to produce original ideas of his own; and his style will be less likely to lose all life and lightness of touch.

Later on, when the stage of revision arrives, he can complete his reading of what really must be read; then he can add what he has omitted, and rectify what he has forgotten or failed to grasp, with a memory refreshed, and with spirits raised by a sense that the body of his work is already created and it now remains only to make it better and better.

No doubt there is a danger that such additions may overload or distort his original structure; but it proves, as a rule, far easier to lengthen a book than to shorten it. No doubt, too, one can be overtimid about losing inspiration while mastering material. I think Matthew Arnold sometimes was. He would write a poem like *Sohrab and Rustum*, based merely on some stray article in a French journal, without bothering to read further, either then or afterwards.

However, the essential point is that good writing can seldom come from a jaded body or a bloated mind. Indeed, I am constantly astonished that scholars and men of letters should overstrain and overburden their own irreplaceable minds and bodies as no prudent general would ever do with his troops, no prudent rider with his horse, no prudent driver with his car. For a time, indeed,

slavery may be made to pay—as with Balzac, writing
eighteen hours a day on black coffee. But not only was
the end of all that a total collapse; it is hard not to feel that
Balzac's output, had it been less in quantity, might have
gained in quality and in style.[1] One who would be a
stylist, I believe, should be a careful steward of his own
vitality.

To recapitulate, the method of writing I have suggested, though there are doubtless many others, falls
roughly into these stages.

1. (a) Meditation and documentation.
   (b) Incubation.
2. Periods of alternate thought, quick writing, and
partial revision, till the first draft is complete.
3. Revision; further documentation, correction, cur-
tailment, and amplification. This can be repeated indefinitely, subject to the danger of the book's growing
unwieldy, overloaded, or stale.

There are also various minor questions of method.
Gibbon got a paragraph perfect in his head before
writing it down; so did Pascal; it is probably far commoner
to write, and to revise, sentence by sentence, clause by
clause. Gibbon's way may have advantages; but it
requires an exceptional memory. Besides, I never know
whether a sentence will seem right till I have *seen* it with
my eyes in print. As one cannot afford in these times
to have Balzac's twenty-seven proofs (and even in that

---

[1] Cf. Browning's remark to Gosse, according to Mr. Harold
Nicolson (quoted by Miss B. Patch, *Thirty Years with G. B. S.*,
p. 243). Gosse had congratulated the poet on having nothing to
regret. But Browning replied that he regretted not having been a
civil servant: 'Had I been a civil servant, I should have been at my
office all day and only written in the evening. I have written too
much, my dear Mr. Gosse; I have over-written; I have written
myself out. If I had been a civil servant, I should have written
better and much less.' Of how many other professional writers
might the same be said!

period of sweated compositors these lavish habits of his helped to drown him in debt), one has to be content with typescript. But see it one must. Even then, there are faults that only reveal themselves when one reads it aloud. Lytton Strachey, who followed Gibbon's method, once argued to me that one cannot alter a word here and a word there, because each alteration of a word upsets other words which would have in their turn to be altered—and so *ad infinitum*. My only answer is, 'In that case the impossible perpetually happens. Look at a manuscript-page of *Madame Bovary*.' To some minds, however, I admit that this method of piecemeal alteration seems repugnant. Morris, for example, if dissatisfied with a piece of work, would write the whole thing afresh from the start.

None the less, when I read of authors rewriting whole volumes a dozen times (if they really mean what they say), I cannot help wondering whether it might not have been better to revise more and rewrite less. The mere mechanical labour of a dozen rewritings is enormous; and unless there is careful collation, good things may get scrapped along with the bad; suppose what one wrote at some point in the second draft was, after all, better than what has replaced it in the sixth, what labour to unearth it! And what a risk that it may get forgotten! Whereas if one writes the first draft on only a third or a quarter of each page, with plenty of space between lines, the rest of the page can be used for rewritings and additions. Then, all the variants remain under the writer's eye; and he continues free to change his choice, and revert if necessary to his first ideas. Finally, if a whole page grows too congested, it can then be retyped, in its revised version, with minimum waste of time, since any page contains only a few lines. Further, the less matter there is on each page, the easier it is to alter the order of passages, or to insert new. In this way it is possible to do an equal

[278]

amount of revising with far fewer rewritings of the whole.
But I should not dare to suggest anything so obvious if
writers did not often seem in practice to do the opposite,
and so crowd their manuscripts as to leave themselves no
room to turn. Paper may have grown costly; but it
remains less precious than time, life, and energy.

There is also a slight problem in the mechanical means
employed for writing. I have known authors compose
with a pencil in an armchair; but I think *that* process,
if carried on for any length of time, can prove curiously
demoralizing, and lead to slovenly style. Some can compose on a typewriter; but it needs considerable familiarity
for that clicking, mechanical contraption to become second
nature, whereas a pen soon grows a mere extension of
one's own forefinger. Lastly, there are those who, like
Stendhal or the later Henry James, dictate.[1] This does
well enough for business documents; but even antiquity
saw its dangers for a writer. Habit, I suppose, may
triumph even over these; but I feel that a serious writer
should create in solitude; and the stylistic results of
dictation can easily become abominable—facile, verbose,
and sluttish. I have suggested that, in general, prose style
should be neither too unlike talk, nor yet too like it; with
dictation it may grow too like loose chatter.

However, the main point in methods of composition
remains, I think, this—to hold the balance between the
more and the less conscious parts of the mind. Otherwise
one may become either too coldly correct or too wildly
eccentric. But naturally men will always disagree what
the right balance is, or perhaps whether there should be
any balance at all. Blake would deny the importance I
have given to the criticizing reason. Flaubert, on the
contrary, might claim a higher value for cold detachment. 'Il faut écrire froidement. Tout doit se faire à

[1] The blind Milton had to. But then he had presumably composed his verses first, and memorized them before dictating.

froid, posément.' Quand Louvel a voulu tuer le duc de
Berri, il a pris une carafe d'orgeat, et n'a pas manqué son
coup.' He might indeed have quoted Diderot's paradox
on the self-possession of great actors. For it seems likely
that, whereas the passionate player may be marvellous
on Monday, but mediocre on Tuesday, only his calmer
colleagues can be trusted to maintain a steady excellence.

However, from the beginning of recorded time some
temperaments seem born to prefer Dionysus, others
Apollo. Men have never long agreed how drunk they
liked art or literature to be. Most critical quarrels are
really about nothing else. For myself, I have come
passionately to prefer sense to sensibility, and even
cynics (if one must have either) to rhapsodists and
rapturists. To argue which gives more artistic pleasure
is futile (though nothing seems able to stop men arguing
about it). I can only suggest that humanity seems
throughout its history to have suffered far worse from
mental intoxications and fanaticisms than from any
rare excess of sober reason. Both the Apolline and the
Dionysiac types have produced memorable writers; but
the bad writer of the Apolline type can seldom become
anything worse than a bore, whereas the bad writer in the
Dionysiac style may prove a mere maniac, disseminating
mania. In short, though the pleasure-values of literature
are outside argument, its influence-values seem to me
in favour of balance and restraint. One cannot destroy
Dionysus (as Pentheus found to his cost). And Dionysus
has his gifts. But there are other powers better to trust
than he.

I There remains another respect in which I think it is
important for a writer not to let himself be tyrannized
over by the less conscious portions of his mind. He
should not wait passively for 'inspiration.' Ronsard,
Herrick, Gray averred that they could not write except
when the mood took them; Shelley denied that any man

could will to produce a poem; Macaulay attributed his
own success to never writing except when he felt in the
humour, and his ideas flowed fast. But about inspiration
there is a temptation to talk cant. Inevitably Gray's view
irritated Johnson who had lived on fourpence-halfpenny
a day, and learned that 'a man can always write if he
sets himself doggedly to it'; though what he called
'fantastick foppery' in Gray was rather lack of resolution, or of compulsion. Poetry, indeed, may be harder
to force than prose; but if Shelley's adage were true,
how could any long poem ever be written? Crabbe could
set himself his steady thirty lines a day. You may not
admire Crabbe. But Milton's *Paradise Lost*, or the
hundred and twenty dramas of Sophocles, could hardly
have been composed by waiting on the whimsies of an
imaginary Muse.[1] As for Macaulay, who appears to have
expressed himself at dinner-tables like a cloudburst, one
doubts if there were ever many days when *he* was disin-
clined to express himself on paper. There seems more
sense in honest Trollope's scornful comment that a
tallow-chandler might as well await 'the divine moment
of melting'. Certainly Trollope lived up to his principles,
and wrote even at sea, in the intervals of running out to
be sick. Probably most writers have to drag themselves to
their desks. There are minds that, like motor-cars, are
hard to start from cold; but if one's self-starter fails, the
remedy is not to go for a walk, but to swing the engine.
A man can make himself put down what comes, even if
it seems nauseating nonsense; tomorrow some of it may
not seem wholly nonsense after all. 'Not a day without
a line!'—or, as Swiss guides say, 'doucement, mais
toujours'—seems to me in general a wiser policy than an
alternating diet of lotus and midnight oil. For often, as

[1] Milton preferred to compose between the autumn and spring
equinoxes; but if he was thus limited to six months in the year, he
could all the less afford to be capricious while they lasted.

Gautier put it, 'L'inspiration consiste à s'asseoir à son bureau et à prendre la plume.'

It may be said, however, 'Granted that good writing turns out to depend less on inspiration, and more on hard grind, than most people suppose, is there any real need for all this rewriting and repolishing?' As Shelley is supposed to have said of Ariosto's traditional fifty-six versions,[1] 'is it worth so much trouble?'

I agree that, like most things, the passion for perfection can be overdone. It is part of that good sense which is so valuable to style itself, to remember that fine phrases are not, after all, the summit of human achievement. Few of us will shed tears over the Italian author who, spying a textual error in the volume he was going to present to the Pope, died of heart-failure in the carriage; or even feel much sympathy with Alfred de Musset passing three sleepless nights over a misprinted comma. Even Flaubert's distress at having written a double 'de' in 'un bouquet *de* fleurs *d*'oranger' may seem a little excessive.[2]

Again, it is a truism that art should not be obtrusive; and ages more interested than ours in the conception of 'the gentleman', or 'l'honnête homme', have included among his qualities, not without reason, a certain grace of negligence. Some readers are irritated by the too careful polish of Stevenson; the accomplished diction and rhythm of Tennyson's *Idylls* works less well for narrative than the less jewelled style of Chaucer or of Morris. For narrative generally gains by a rapidity like Homer's; whereas verbal felicities may have a delaying effect, as the golden apples on Atalanta.

There is also something irritating to robuster minds in a delicacy like Pater's, who would not read Stevenson or Kipling for fear their stronger style might infect his own.

[1] See note on p. 13.
[2] On the other hand Thackeray seems a little too slipshod with his 'wife *of* a clergyman *of* the Church *of* England'. But cf. p. 240.

Better, some may feel, if it had; better a muscular Philistine like Macaulay than such finicky valetudinarianism. Similarly with Amiel who sterilized himself by a fastidiousness that could never 'brutaliser son sujet'.

Literature itself, it may be urged, is only lessened by being made an idol, and only degraded by being exalted from human to divine. 'Ce qui fit le bonheur de la littérature sous Louis XIV, c'est qu'alors c'était une chose de peu d'importance'—'Les passions et les arts ne sont qu'une importance ridicule attachée à quelque petite chose'—these cynicisms of Stendhal have yet an element of truth often forgotten in Universities, studios, and salons. It is good to be a great writer: it remains more important to be an honest man.

More important for the man himself—yes. But not always for society. There have been writers whose lives were warped by excessive concentration on literature, yet of whom the world must say, as Hal of Falstaff, 'I could have better spar'd a better man.' Whether their infinite pains were really worth while for Pope or Flaubert or Tennyson, no one can know; but they were well worth while for us.

In any case there does not seem much practical danger of many authors rewriting their books seventeen times, or even seven. I suspect, on the contrary, that most authors do not revise enough, and that most books would be better for more pains.

In his interesting volume, *Modern Prose Style*, Professor Dobrée has said, 'The modern writer must not think of style'; and again, thirteen pages later, 'In a sense all good live prose is experimental—as all good poetry is—a desperate attempt to say what has never been said before in spite of having to use the same words to say it in. Any original writer is engaged in a continual struggle with words, to wrest out of them, to hammer into

them, meanings they never had before; if he did not
want to do this, he would not be an original writer.'
I hope he will forgive me if I do not find these two
precepts altogether easy to reconcile; nor either of them
altogether wise. I should have thought that any serious
writer would do well to think quite a lot about style; but
I doubt if all these 'desperate' efforts to hammer new
meanings into words are likely to do much service either
to the writer or to the language. In the end it is the
reader that may become 'desperate'. I distrust frantic
resolutions to be 'original'. I believe that a writer should
try, not to be different from others, but to be himself; not
to write 'originally', but as well as he possibly can. Real
originality is spontaneous. Aeschylus or Herodotus,
Shakespeare or Milton, even lesser writers like Beddoes or
Landor, could hardly have hidden theirs, even had they
tried. Caesar (not usually reckoned a timid character)
held that a writer should shun an unusual word as a
mariner a reef; he would hardly have been more favourable to unusual 'meanings'. His attitude towards language seems to me *too* conservative: perhaps it was a com-
pensation for an attitude towards politics the reverse of
conservative. But it is a tenable attitude; certainly I
doubt if one can reasonably dogmatize that 'all live prose'
must now do the opposite. Again, imagine Swift or
Voltaire taking off their coats to hammer new meanings
into words!

Those who chase originality (as is far too common
today) are more likely to find they have caught instead her
ugly sister, eccentricity—like Seneca and Lyly, Meredith
and Shaw. Progress may come from aiming, however
hopelessly, at perfection; I question if perfection has
often come in literature, from aiming at 'progress'.
Indeed, progress in literature has probably been as often
downwards as upwards.

My simple conclusion is that any writer with an

[284]

artistic conscience must share that passion of any honest craftsman which will not let him rest till a piece of work is as good as he can make it: but, even so, he should also remember the eternal wisdom of Greece, 'Nothing too much'; or of Israel, 'Be not righteous overmuch; why shouldst thou destroy thyself?'

Here are a great many words I have uttered about words—more than I had meant. The subject is indeed important, as I said at the beginning, not only to writers, but to all of us—both as readers and as ordinary human beings, who have to think in words, and to talk them, and to write them, at least in letters. It is important to us, too, as inheritors of our native tongue, which each of us, in his own minute degree, must help to leave better or worse for those that come after us. We may question, indeed, whether style has ever been much improved by books on style. The influence of creative writers, of national history, of social change, surely weighs far more. And no teaching can give talent; yet sometimes, perhaps, it may help to save talent from being wasted. A lot of writing is too confused and obscure; a lot is too wordy; a lot is too peevish or pompous or pretentious; a lot is too lifeless; a lot is too lazy. These are not hopeless faults to cure onself of, if only one can remember them. If you *can* remember to pursue clarity, brevity, and courtesy to readers; to be, if not gay, at least good-humoured; never to write a line without considering whether it is really true, whether you have not exaggerated your statement, or its evidence; to shun dead images, and cherish living ones; and to revise unremittingly—then, though you may not, even so, write well, you are likely at least to write less badly. For, obvious as such precepts are, nine-tenths of the books that are written seem to me to ignore one or more of them.

At least it is well that such things should be discussed. A civilized language cannot develop as the unself-

conscious child of circumstance, like the tongue of a
primitive people. And perhaps even primitive peoples
are less unselfconscious about it than we think. Even
Athenian fishwives had strong views on Attic Greek. In
any case, once education comes, it inevitably brings with
it rules and precepts; some for better, some for worse.
And these rules and precepts must constantly be open to
thought and questioning. Such has been my object. But
those who try to contribute to such questioning would be
foolish to hope too much. They must rest in the end, as
Pope said he was,

> Content, if hence th' unlearn'd their wants may view,
> The learn'd reflect on what before they knew.

What the world will be like a century hence, was never
so impossible to foresee. Like a gigantic snowball, larger
and larger, faster and faster, science hurtles with us all
into the unknown. Let us at least hope it is not towards a
world of swarming ant-heaps populated by highly
mechanized barbarians, a new Dark Age, with techno-
crats in place of theologians. But whatever the future,
no part of our traditional inheritance from the past seems
less likely to be superseded than human speech—together
with the memorable things that men have made with
words.

The English of that future, even if its bounds are ever
more widely set, will inevitably differ more and more
from ours.[1] That is part of the eternal change of things,
and can be accepted without too much regret. But what
that English of the hereafter is like, depends, as I have
said, in its minute degree on what each of us says each

---

[1] Broadcasting, for example, may perhaps tend to make style less
pompous by bringing it closer to ordinary talk; there remains the
danger that it might bring style *too* close to talk—that it might
vulgarize, as well as simplify. One can sometimes see this happening already.

day of our lives. One may hope that it will still be a language plain yet rich, simple yet subtle, graceful yet strong. Whether the effort to keep it so succeeds or fails, I trust that even those who disagree most strongly with all I have said, will yet agree that this effort needs, generation after generation, to be made.

day of our lives. One may hope that it will still be a language plain yet rich, simple yet subtle, graceful yet strong. Whether the effort to keep it so succeeds or fails, I trust that even those who disagree most strongly with all I have said, will yet agree that this effort needs, generation after generation, to be made.

INDEX